A Photographic Guide to

Shetland's Wild Flowers

A PHOTOGRAPHIC GUIDE TO

Shetland's Wild Flowers

David Malcolm

The Shetland Times Ltd.
Lerwick
2012

A Photographic Guide to Shetland's Wild Flowers

ISBN 978-1-904746-72-0

First edition published by The Shetland Times Ltd., 1990.
Second edition, 1992.
Third (revised and enlarged) edition, 2012.

A catalogue record for this book is available from the British Library.

Front cover (main picture): red campion at Easter Quarff.
Back cover – upper: English stonecrop in the Out Skerries.
Back cover – lower: sea aster on Isbister Holm.

Printed and published by
The Shetland Times Ltd.,
Gremista, Lerwick,
Shetland ZE1 0PX.

Dedication

I would like to dedicate the third edition of this book to my friend and mentor, Walter Scott, of Scalloway.

Walter became a member of the Botanical Society of the British Isles in 1955, and since 1961 has been the society's honorary recorder for the county of Shetland. In 1995 he was awarded an MBE for his services to botany in Shetland.

In the preparation of this edition, Walter has given freely and generously of his time and expertise. I am grateful to him for his assistance in the identifying of certain species, for accompanying me on numerous field trips to locate some of our more elusive and rare plants and for many hours spent reading through, checking and correcting the entire manuscript, and for his many other useful suggestions throughout the project.

In 1964 Walter found a hawkweed which was later identified as a new species. In 2006 it was published as *Hieracium scottii* (Scott's Hawkweed) by Peter Sell and Gina Murrell in their definitive account of British hawkweeds in volume 4 of their *Flora of Great Britain and Ireland*. I am delighted to include a photograph of *H. scottii* in this third edition.

Contents

Preface

The principal change in this third edition is the incorporation of 71 new species not included in the previous two editions. It is hoped this will greatly enhance the usefulness of the book, and to enable the reader to identify most of the flowering plants that they are likely to come across in Shetland.

In this edition, both the English and Latin names of plants follow those used in *Some aspects of the botany of the Shetland Islands* by Walter Scott. (See References and Further Reading.)

In the previous two editions, plants were classified as either 'native' or 'introduced'. In this volume, the term 'introduced' has been withdrawn and replaced by either 'alien' or 'casual'. (See Glossary of botanical terms for the meaning of those designations.)

Various friends have suggested that it would be interesting as well as helpful to know where the plants were photographed. The author is happy to oblige by adding this information to the captions.

Finally, this edition incorporates a section at the end of the book where the reader can list plants they have identified, and where locality and date can be recorded.

D. Malcolm

Acknowledgements

Walter Scott – see Dedication.

My good friend, Saro Saravanan – for hours spent transferring photos from camera to disc, arranging the pictures in sequence, and much more besides.

My daughter Mary – for typing all the captions.

My wife Priscilla – for assisting in the preparation of the manuscript.

I am grateful to the following friends for allowing me to use their photographs:

Tim Rich, National Museum of Wales – Plates 15, 16.
Andy Gear – Plates 29, 98, 109.
Jonathan Swale – Plates 74, 87.
Laurence A. Inkster – Plates 80, 149.
Shetland Museum and Archives – Plate 90.
Tony Mainland – Plate 112.

To Jenny Murray for bending over backwards to be helpful.

To all others who have offered helpful suggestions, advice and encouragement, I offer my sincere thanks.

Last, but by no means least, I wish to thank Jo and her colleague at The Shetland Times Bookshop for their 'by the way' comment that sparked this third edition into flame!

Introduction

This guide book is not an exhaustive photographic record of all Shetland's flowering plants but includes the majority of our more commonly occurring species with, in addition, a handful of unusual or special plants.

The most conspicuous feature of a plant to the layman is usually the colour of the flowers. With this in mind the plants in this guide have been grouped in sections based on the usual colour of their flowers. However, the colour of the flowers of a particular species may vary, e.g. heath milkwort (Plate 164) whose flowers are normally blue, but may be pink, lilac or even white.

Plants vary greatly in size according to soil type and degree of shelter available. Although a very approximate indication of the size of each species is included in the captions (see Abbreviations for details), this should not be relied upon too heavily, e.g. selfheal (Plate 169) may be a mere 2 cm high in exposed coastal grassland but over 20 cm in more favourable situations away from the sea.

The user of this guide may occasionally find that their specimen does not exactly match the photograph of the plant they believe they have found. It may be an untypical example of the species illustrated; more likely, however, they are dealing with a closely related plant not included in the illustrations. By consulting the following books, Scott & Palmer (1987), Scott (2011), along with a comprehensive and fully illustrated book on British plants,* they should be able to accurately establish the name of their plant. The descriptive notes have been deliberately kept simple and concentrate on the salient features only of the particular species shown in the accompanying photograph.

Shetland names are included in the captions where these have had a long and widespread usage throughout Shetland.

* See References and Further Reading for details of these and other books.

Abbreviations

1. The abbreviations given below precede the English name and give the reader a rough indication of the size of the plant illustrated.

(s) Small. Plants whose stems do not usually exceed 15 cm (6 inches), or in the case of trailing plants, do not spread more than 15 cm.

(m) Medium. Plants between 15 and 38 cm (6–15 inches) in height or spread.

(l) Large. Plants exceeding 38 cm (15 inches) in height or spread.

2. × indicates a hybrid (or cross) between two closely related species.

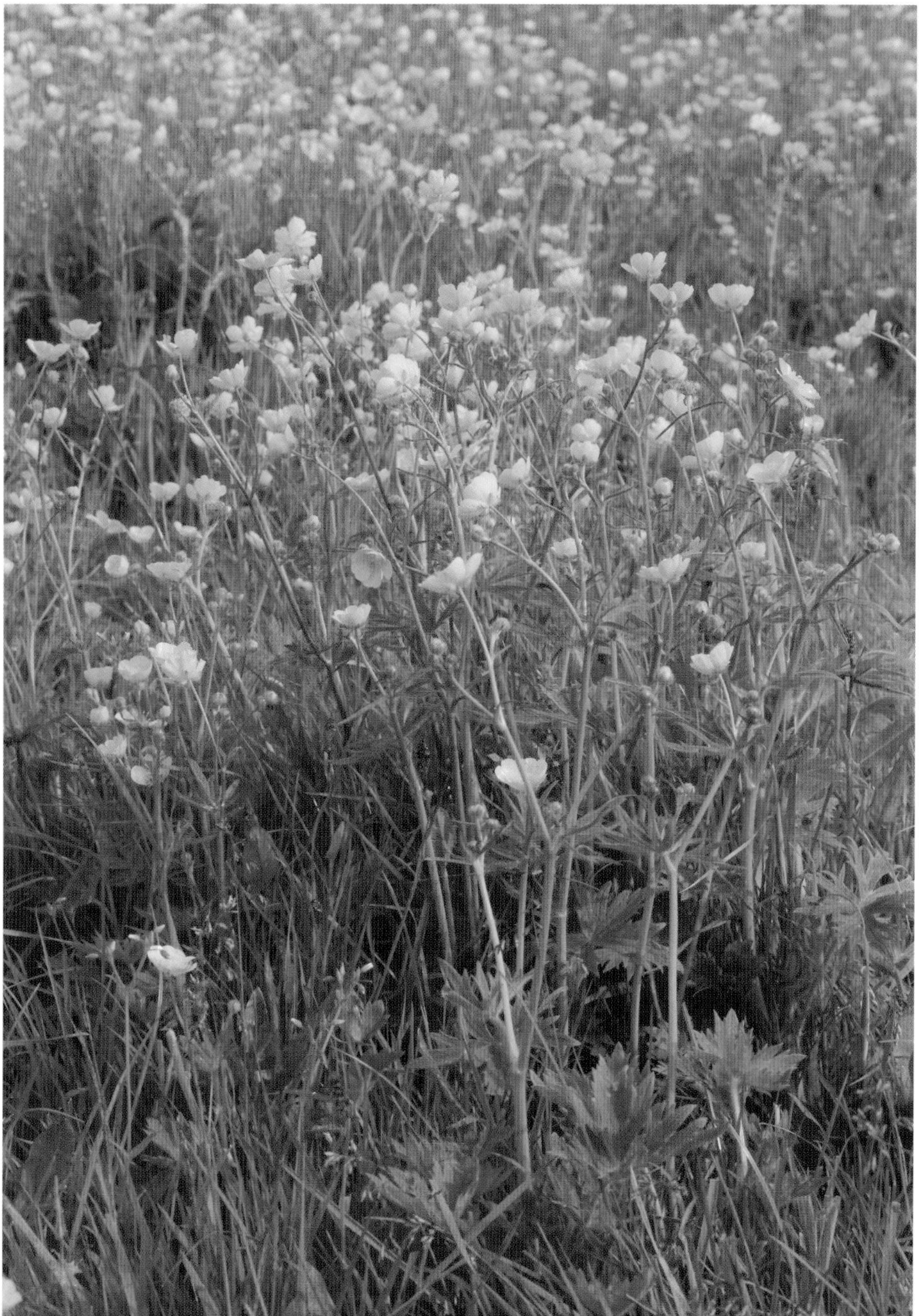

Plate 1 (m–l) **Meadow Buttercup** (*Ranunculus acris*) 'Craafit'
Flowers yellow, in forked terminal clusters, petals 5; sepals yellowish, erect; stems branched, hairy; basal leaves deeply palmately lobed, long-stalked, upper leaves deeply segmented, stalkless. Native. Pastures, streamsides, roadsides, coastal banks. Flowering May–September. Photograph: meadow, Tingwall.

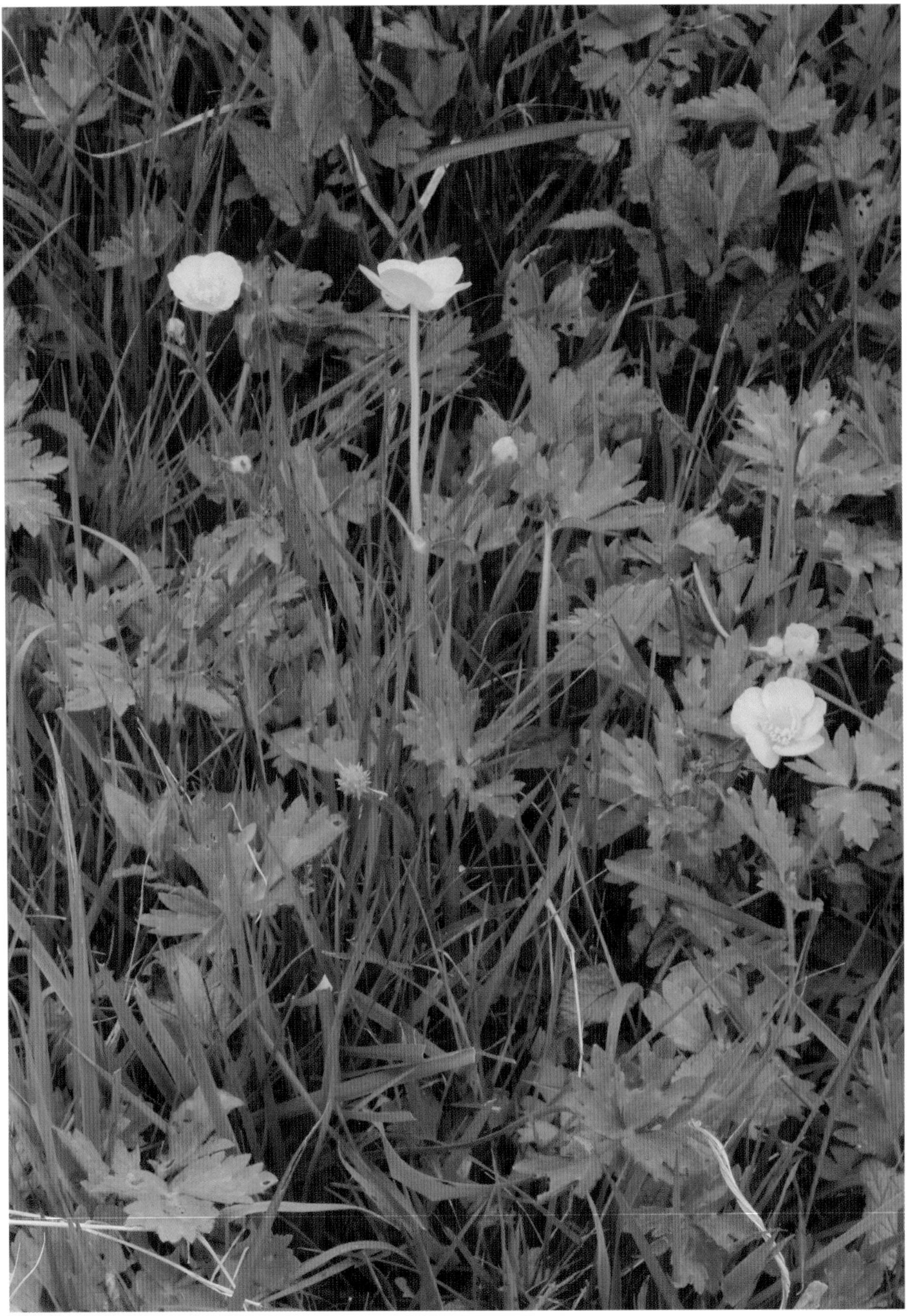

Plate 2 (s–l) **Creeping Buttercup** (*Ranunculus repens*)
Flowers yellow, petals 5 (up to 9); sepals erect; creeping plant with rooting runners; rosette-leaves and lower stem leaves divided into three leaflets, the central long-stalked, all leaflets further divided or lobed. Well-established alien. Damp cultivated ground, waste ground, beaches. Flowering late May-early September. Photograph: grassy banks, Easter Quarff.

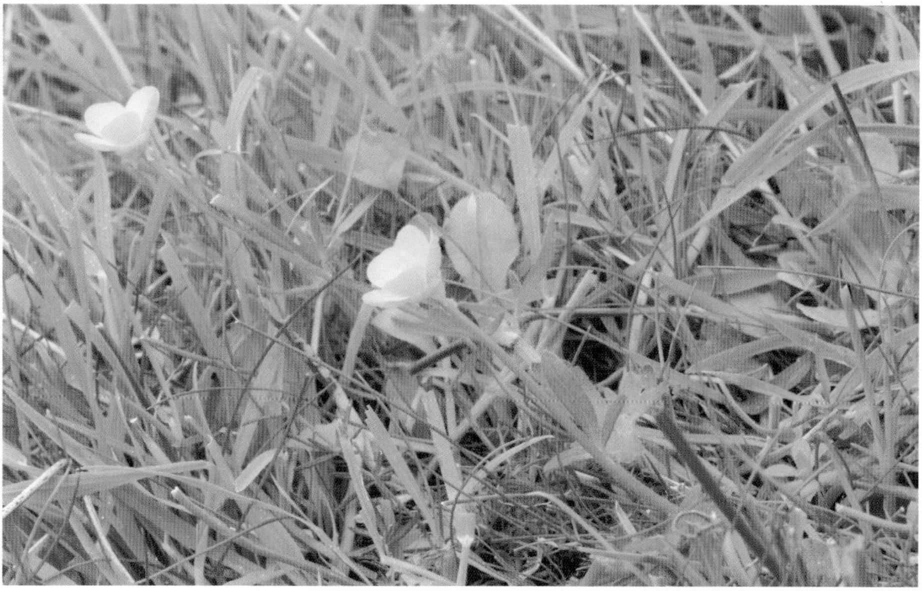

Plate 3 (s–m) **Bulbous Buttercup** (*Ranunculus bulbosus*)
Flowers yellow, petals 5; sepals yellow and turned downwards; stems may be hairy, especially below; the basal and lower stem leaves have three leaflets, the central long-stalked, all leaflets further divided or lobed. Native. Rare. Dry pastures, often near the coast. Flowering late May–early July. Photograph: sandy banks, St Ninian's Isle.

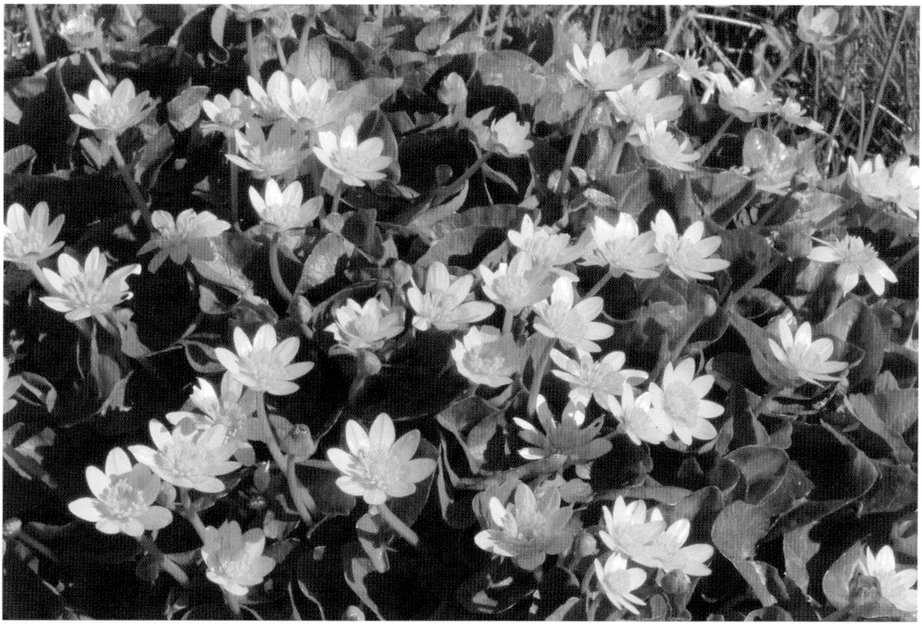

Plate 4 (s) **Lesser Celandine** (*Ranunculus ficaria*)
Flowers yellow, 2.0–3.0 cm wide, star-like, petals 8–12 opening only on bright days; stems spreading, succulent, hairless; leaves heart-shaped, long-stalked. Native. Streamsides, damp pastures. Flowing late March–June. Photograph: roadside verge, Asta, near Scalloway.

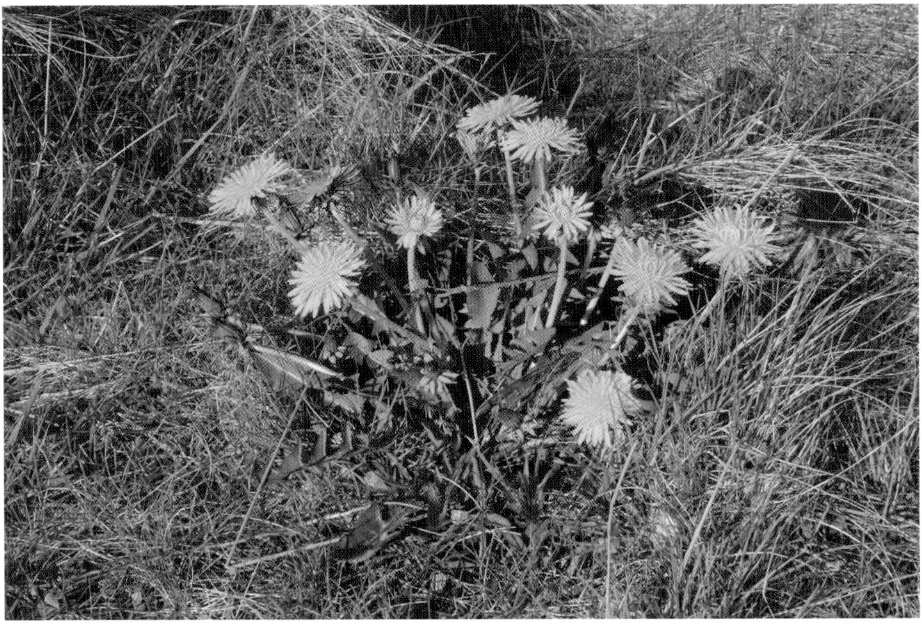

Plate 5 (s–m) **Dandelion** (*Taraxacum* sp.)
Flowerheads yellow, 3.0–3.5 cm wide, involucres in many species turning outwards and downwards; flower stalks leafless; leaves in a basal rosette, of many shapes but basically shallowly to deeply pinnately lobed, the lobes normally pointing backwards. Several native and numerous introduced species grow in Shetland. Flowering May–June. Photograph: roadside verge, East Voe of Scalloway.

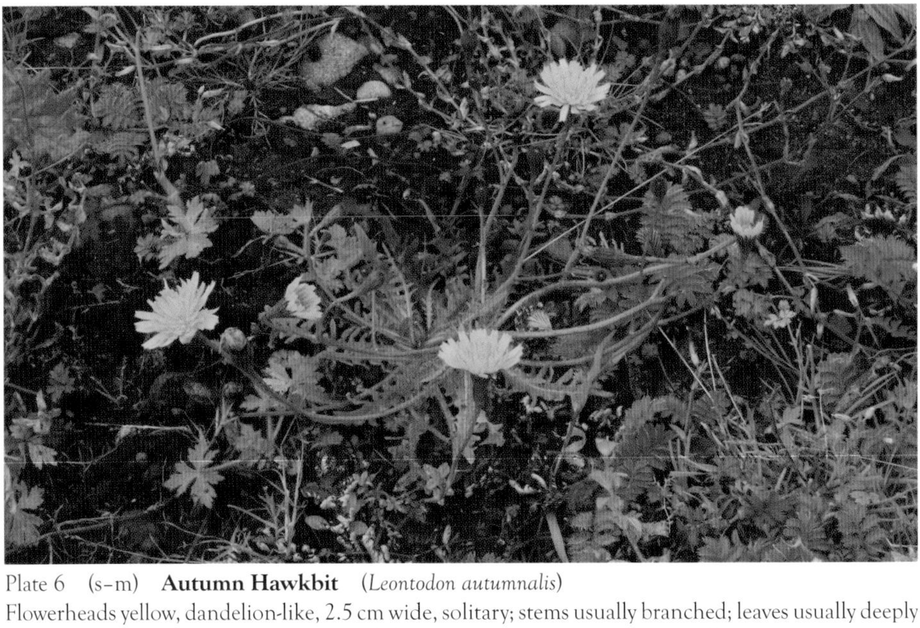

Plate 6 (s–m) **Autumn Hawkbit** (*Leontodon autumnalis*)
Flowerheads yellow, dandelion-like, 2.5 cm wide, solitary; stems usually branched; leaves usually deeply pinnately lobed, often hairless, terminal lobe long, narrow, pointed. Native. Pastures, meadows, etc; found in many habitats. Shetland's most common dandelion-like plant. Flowering July–October. Photograph: gravelly area by dwelling house, Scatness, Sumburgh.

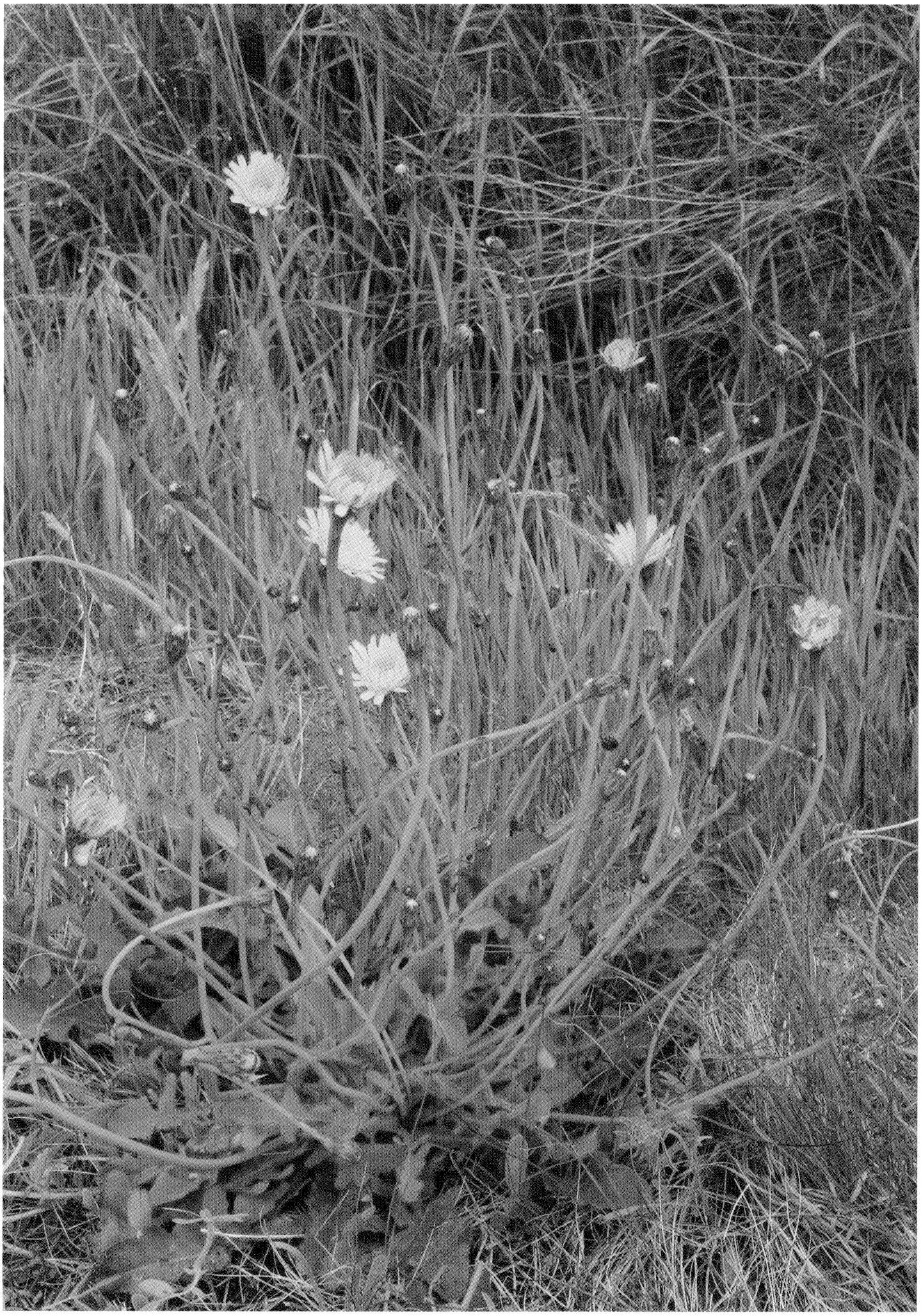

Plate 7 (s–l) **Cat's-ear** (*Hypochaeris radicata*)

Flowerheads bright yellow, dandelion-like, 2.0–4.0 cm wide, solitary on leafless stems bearing numerous small scale-like bracts; stems little branched; leaves in a basal rosette, oblong-lanceolate with wavy, toothed or lobed margins, roughly hairy. Well-established alien. Grassy roadsides, embankments, pastures, low grassy sea-banks. Flowering late May–early October. Photograph: roadside verge, East Voe of Scalloway.

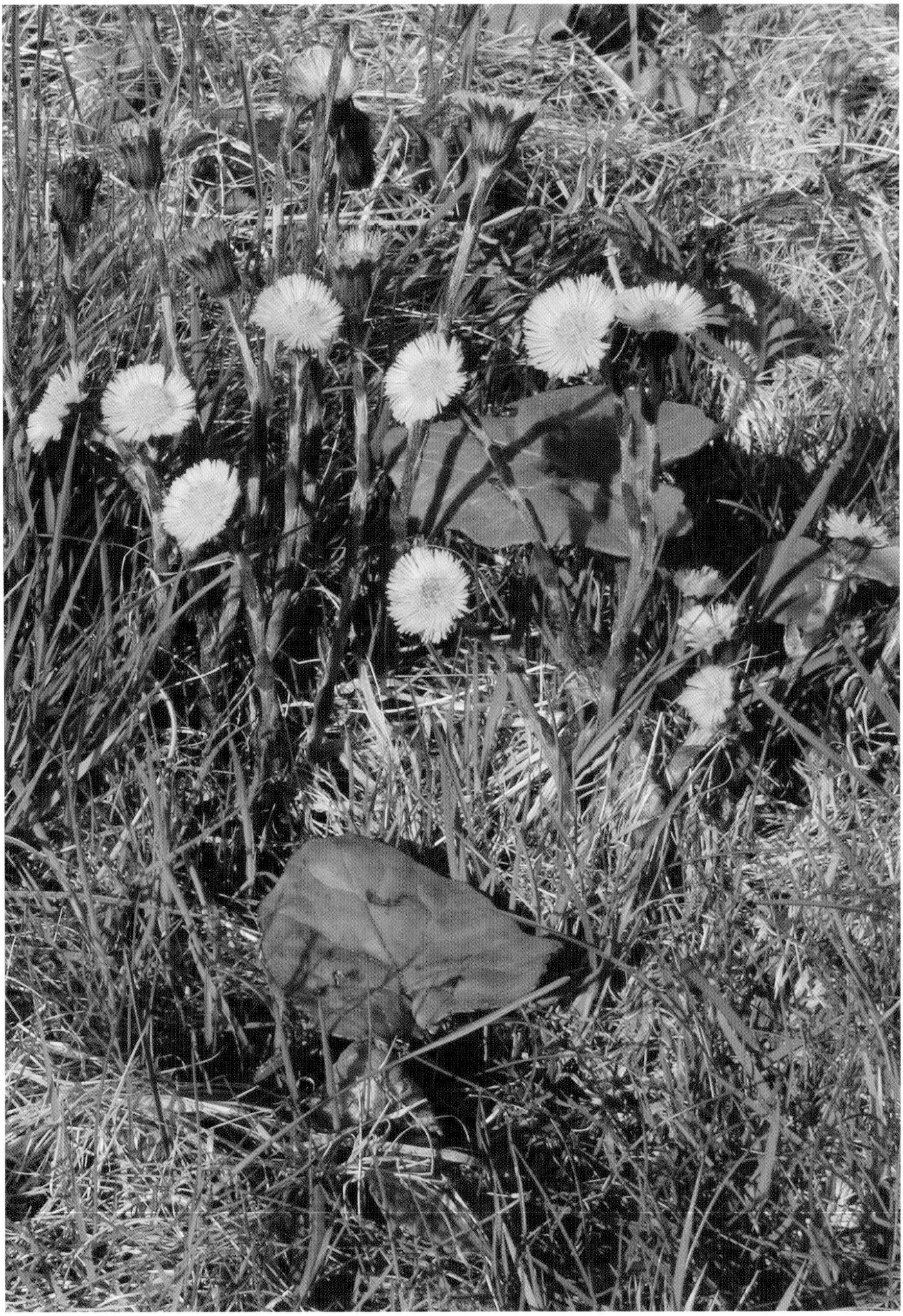

Plate 8 (s–m) **Colt's-foot** (*Tussilago farfara*)

Flowerheads yellow, with narrow rays, solitary on stems covered with purplish scales. Flowers open long before leaves appear. Creeping plant; leaves form a basal rosette. Well-established alien. Roadside verges, waste ground, by burns, around houses. Flowers late March–April. Photograph: roadside verge, East Voe of Scalloway.

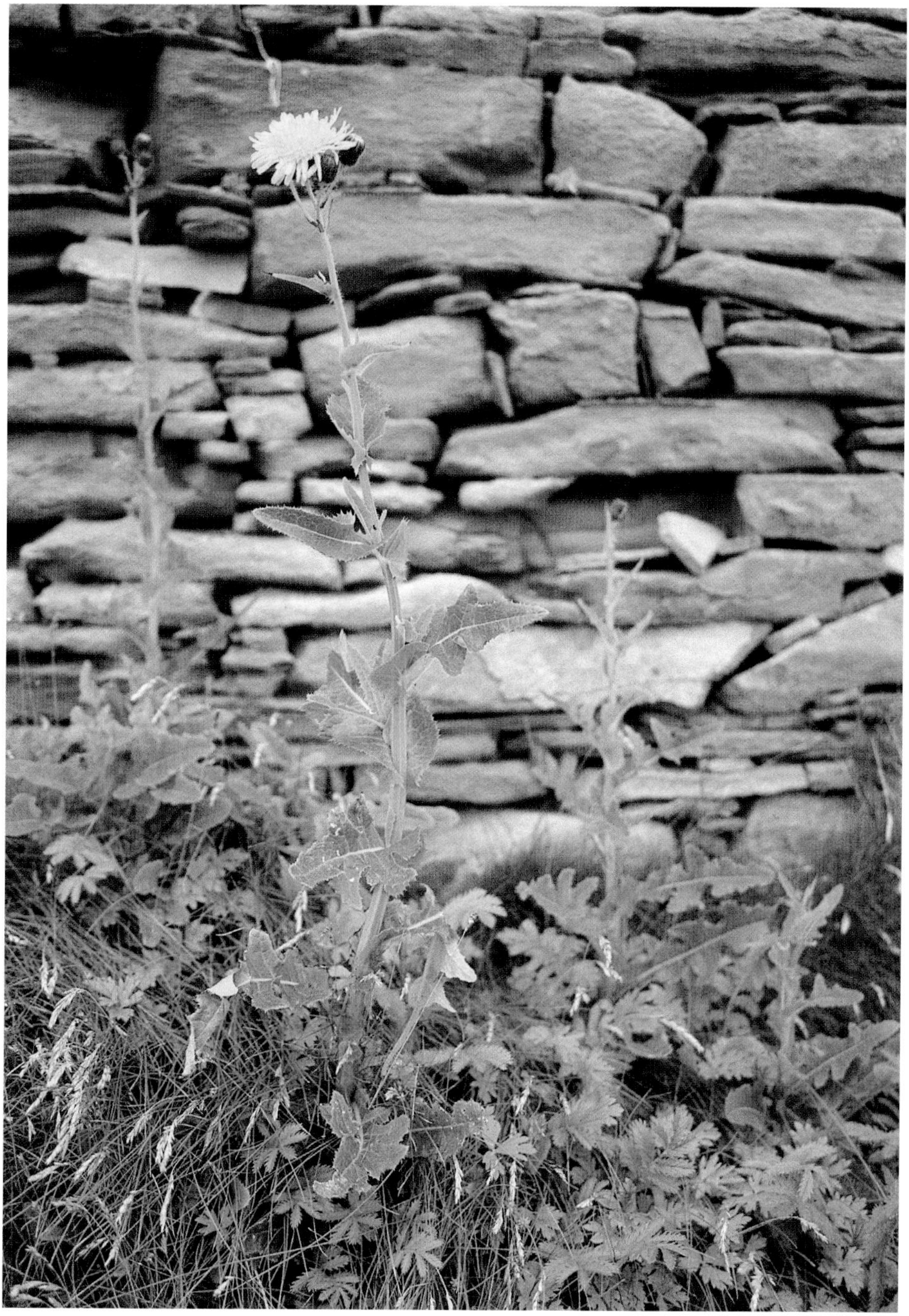

Plate 9 (l) **Perennial Sow-thistle** (*Sonchus arvensis*)
Flowerheads yellow, dandelion-like, 5.0 cm wide, involucre with many yellowish hairs; stems branched, lower part hairless; lower leaves pinnately lobed with rounded lobes clasping stem; upper stem leaves spear-shaped with prickly margins. Well-established alien. Arable land, foreshores, beaches. Flowering July–September. Photograph: by an old house, Levenwick.

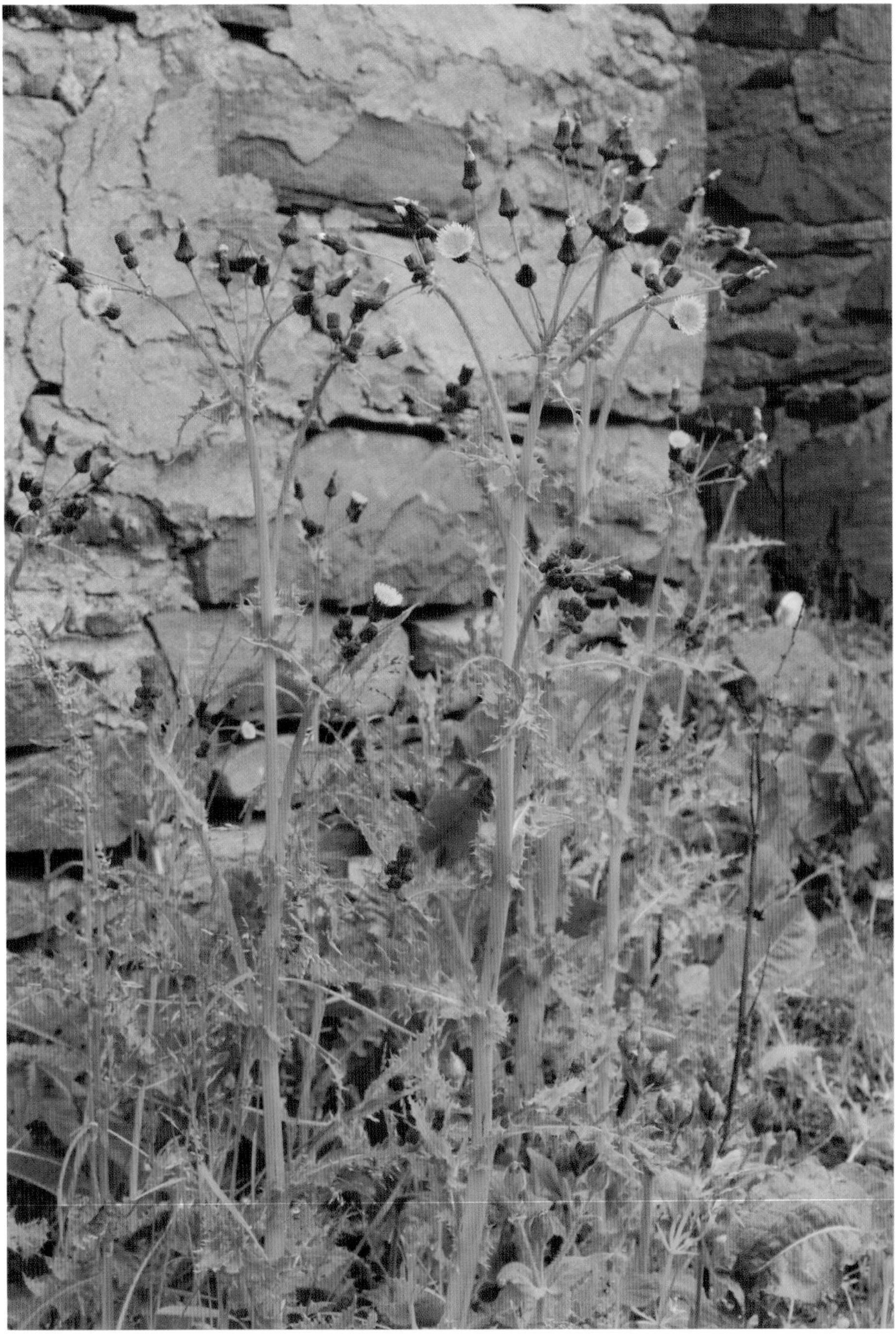

Plate 10 (l) **Prickly Sow-thistle** (*Sonchus asper*)
Flowerheads yellow, dandelion-like; leaves glossy, very spiny, clasping the stem with rounded lobes. Well-established alien. Cultivated ground, rubbish dumps, roadside verges. Flowering June–November.
Photograph: by ruins of crofthouse, Levenwick.

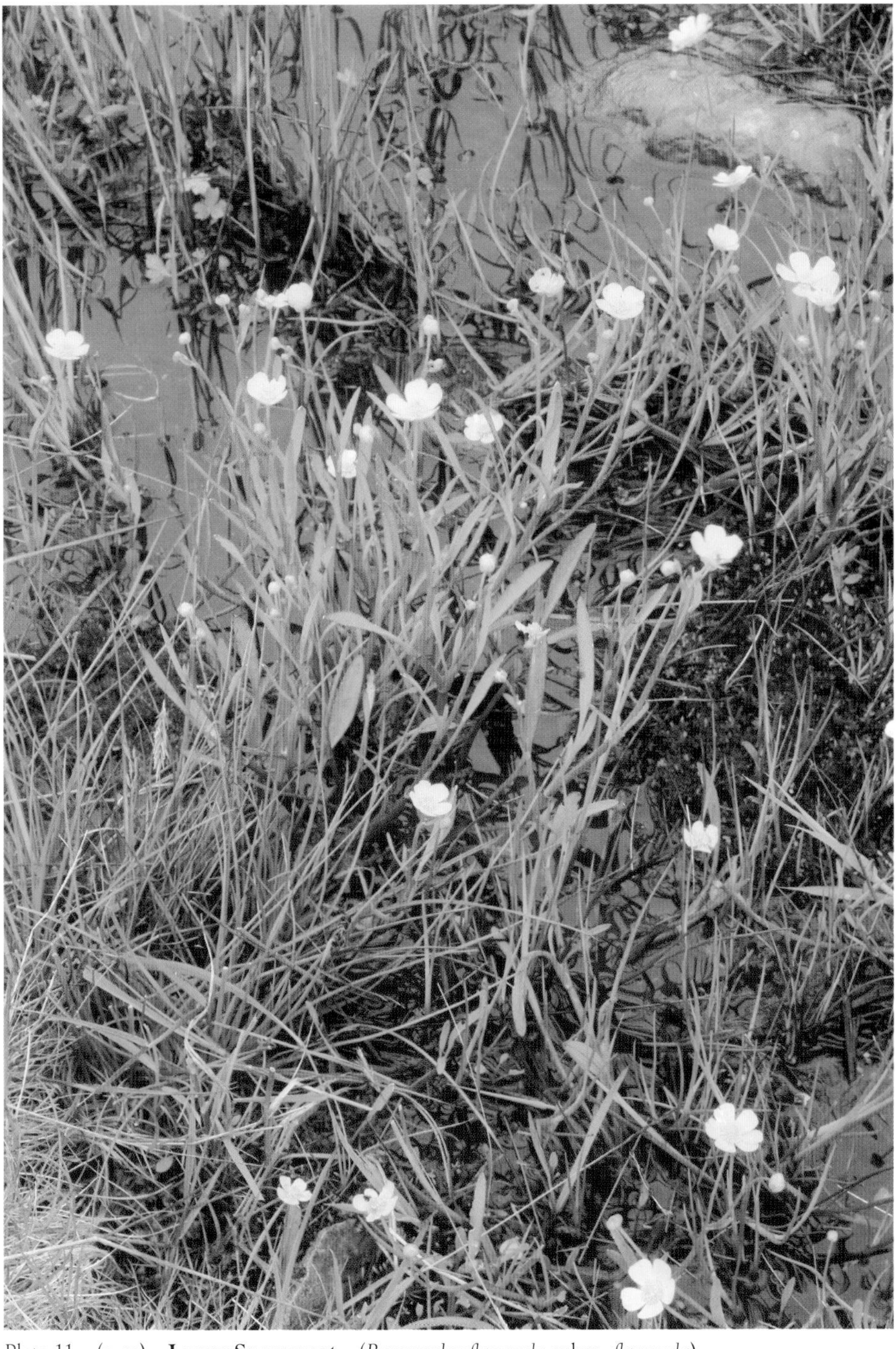

Plate 11 (s–m) **Lesser Spearwort** (*Ranunculus flammula* subsp. *flammula*)
Flowers yellow, petals 5; sepals yellowish; stems succulent, hairless; leaves elliptical to lanceolate, lower leaves stalked. Native. Streams, ditches, bogs, marshes. Flowering May–August. Photograph: ditch, Wester Quarff.

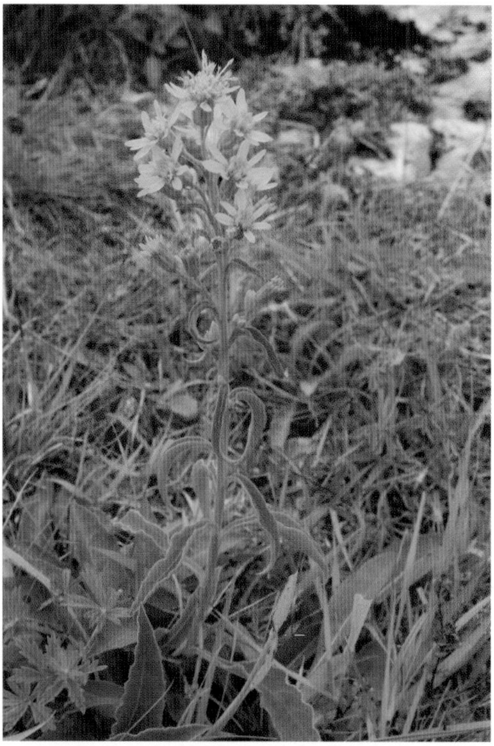

Plate 12 (s–m) **Goldenrod**
(*Solidago virgaurea*)
Flowerheads bright yellow, shortly rayed, 6–10 mm wide, in branched spikes; leaves oval or lanceolate, usually toothed. Native. Dry places: heathy pastures, rocky outcrops, heathery sides of burns. Flowering July–early September. Photograph: rocky grassland, Ponton, Clousta.

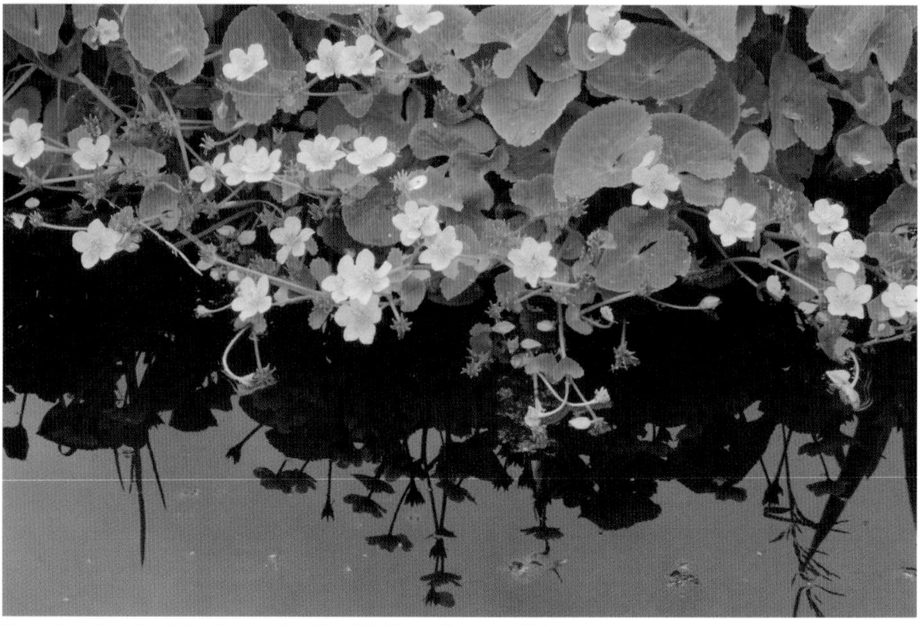

Plate 13 (m–l) **Marsh-marigold** (*Caltha palustris*) 'Blugga'
Flowers yellow, up to 5.0 cm wide, petals (actually coloured sepals) 5; stems smooth; leaves dark green, kidney-shaped, glossy. Native. Marshes, streams, ditches. Flowering late April–June. Photograph: burn running into Strand Loch, Tingwall.

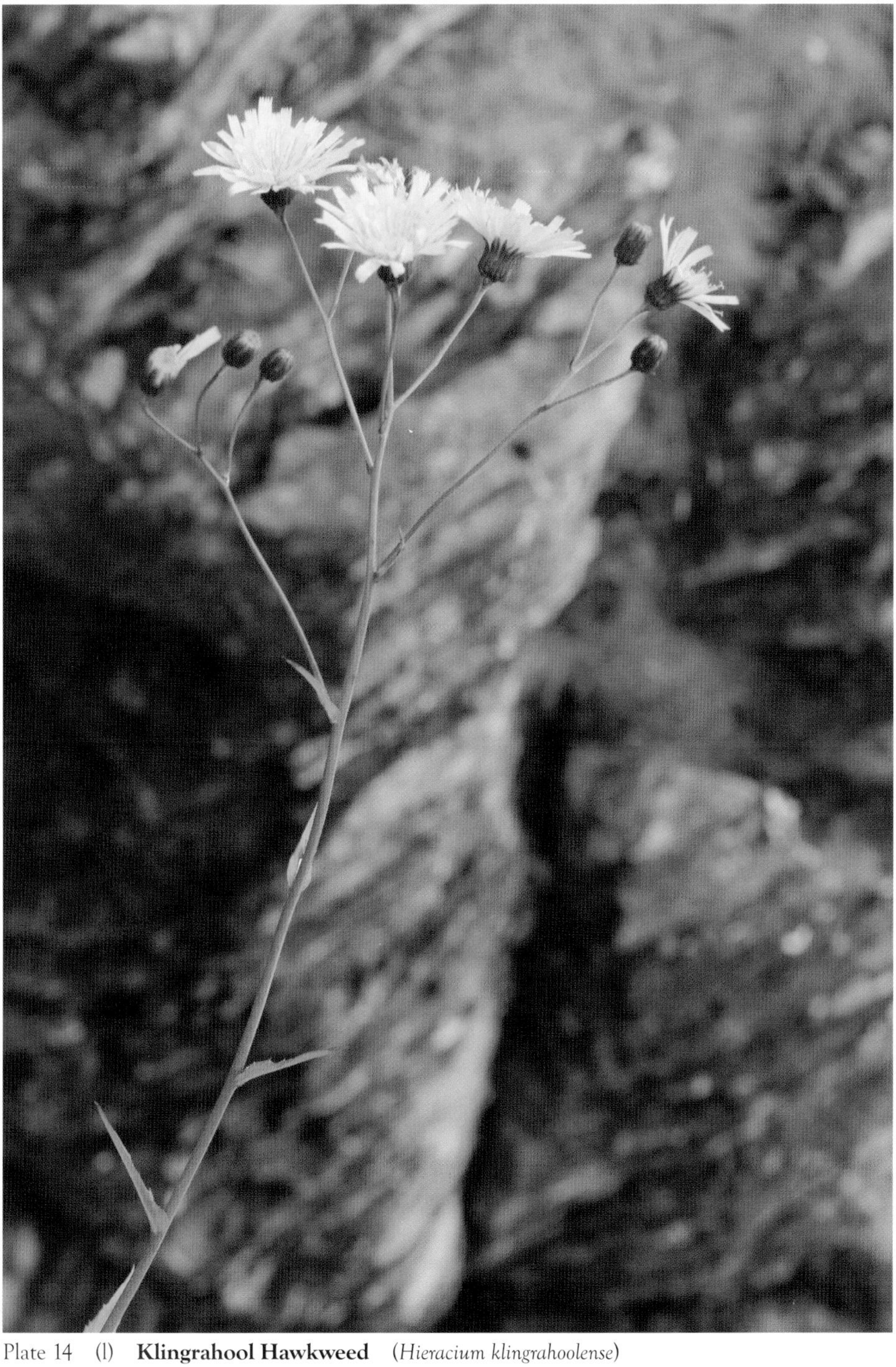

Plate 14 (l) **Klingrahool Hawkweed** (*Hieracium klingrahoolense*)
Flowers yellow, dandelion-like, 3.5 cm wide; stems very leafy; leaves narrow. Native, endemic. Found mainly in and around the Muckle Roe area on sea-banks and by streams. Flowering late July–early September. Photograph: Burn of Crookadale, South Nesting.

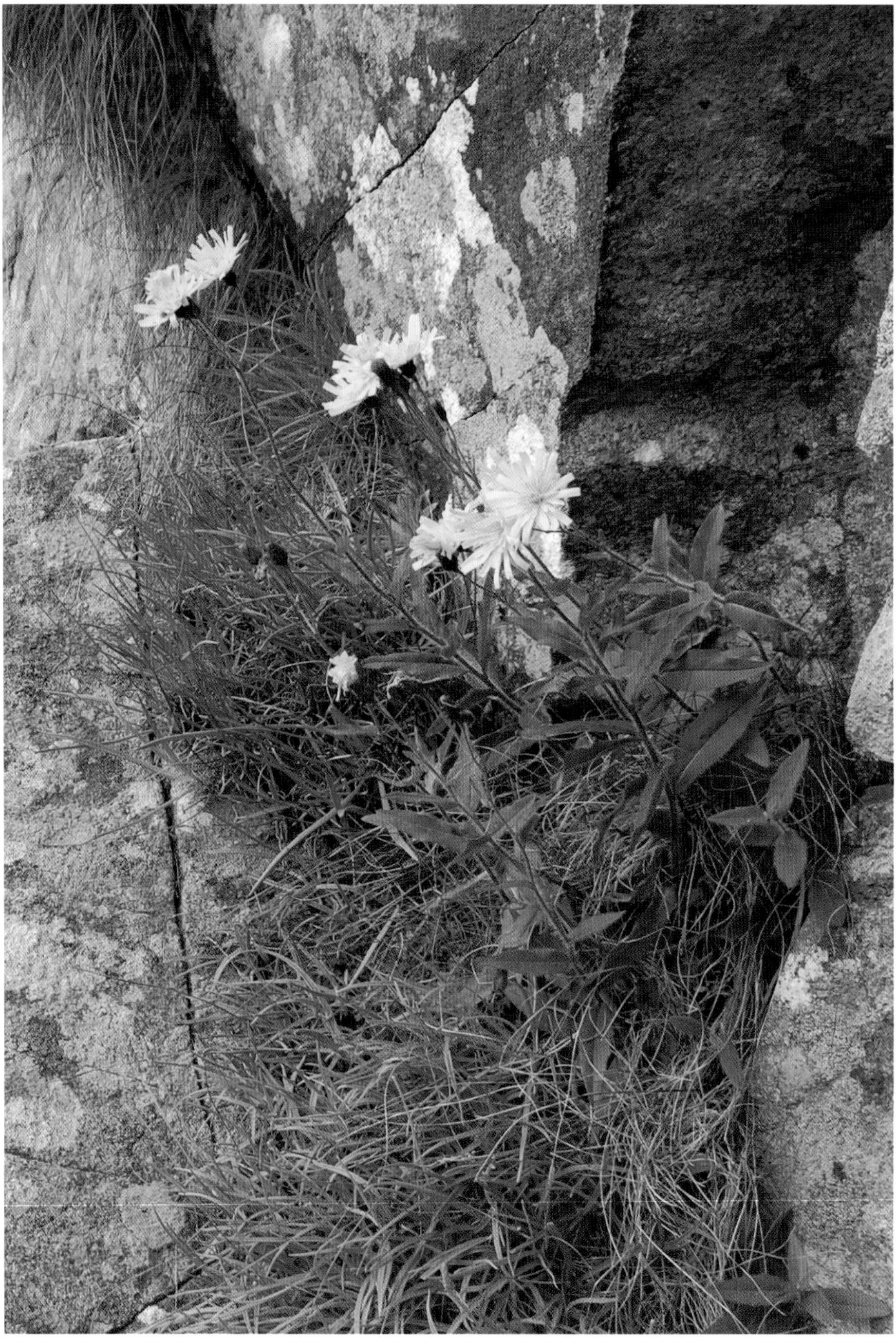

Plate 15 (l) **Mainland Hawkweed** (*Hieracium subtruncatum*)
Flowers yellow, dandelion-like, 4.0 cm wide; stems moderately leafy; leaves oval; plant often tinged purplish. Native, endemic. Rocky or grassy streamsides, ravines and crags. Flowering July–early August. Photograph: near Islesburgh, Northmavine.

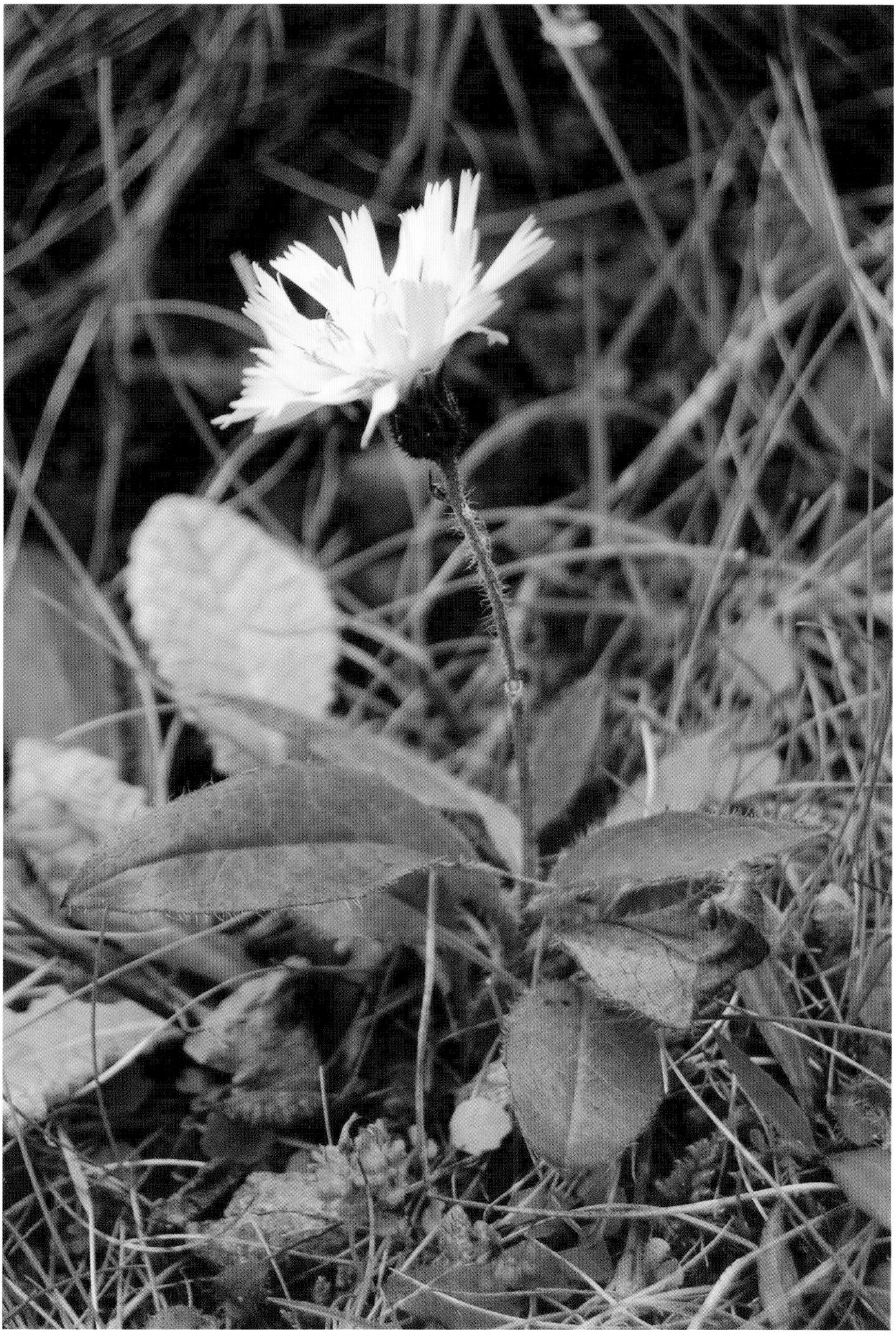

Plate 16 (m) **Scott's Hawkweed** (*Hieracium scottii*)
Flowers yellow, dandelion-like, 4.0 cm or more wide; stems few-leaved; leaves broadly oval. Native, endemic, very rare. Sea-banks and rocky pastures in West Mainland only. Flowering July–early August. Photograph: sea-bank, West Mainland.

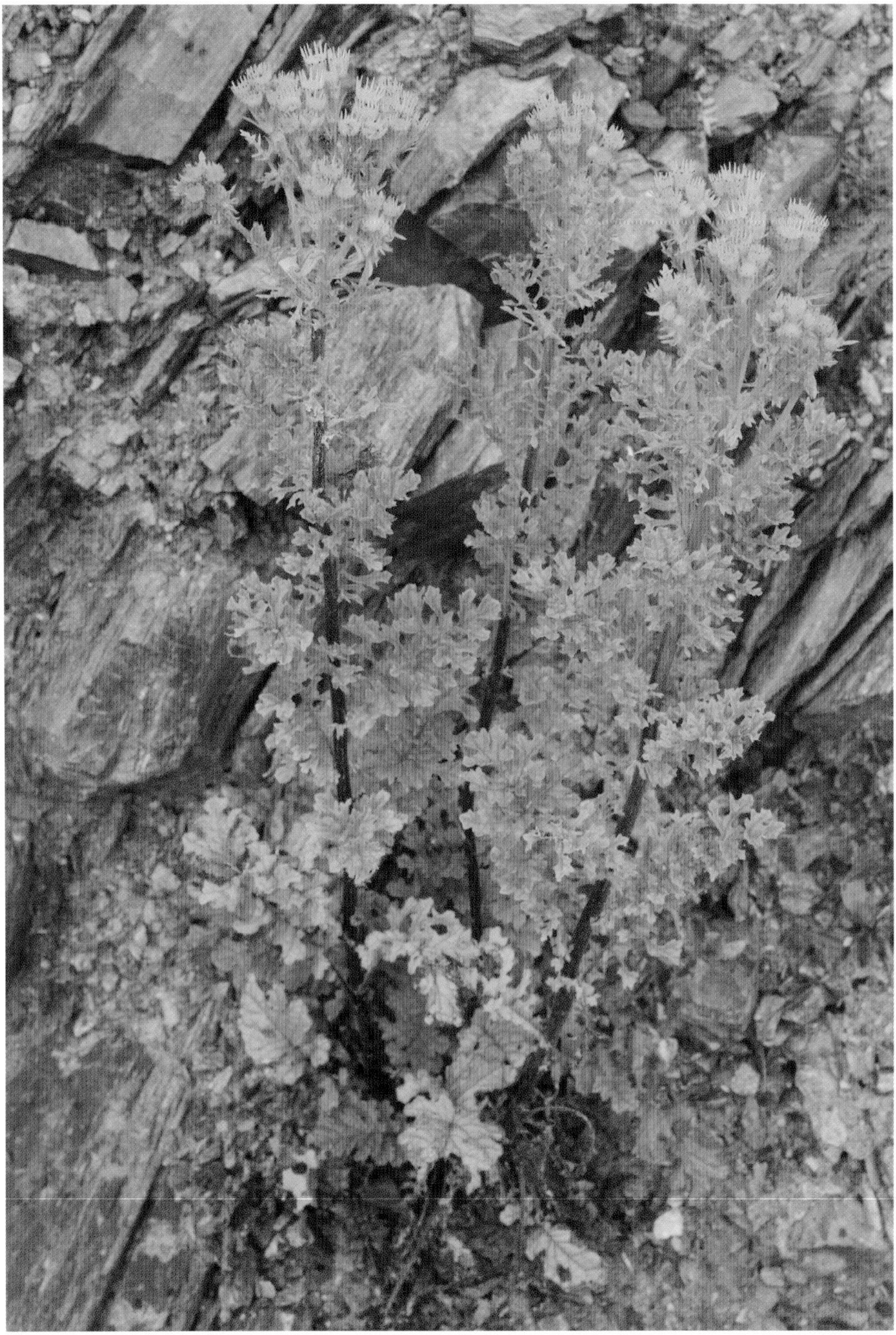

Plate 17 (m) **Common Ragwort** (*Senecio jacobaea*)
Flowerheads yellow, 15–25 mm wide, in dense branched clusters; leaves pinnately lobed, end lobe small, blunt. Well-established alien. Dry grassy places, waste ground, about quarries. Flowering late July–early October, Photograph: waste ground, Port Arthur, Scalloway.

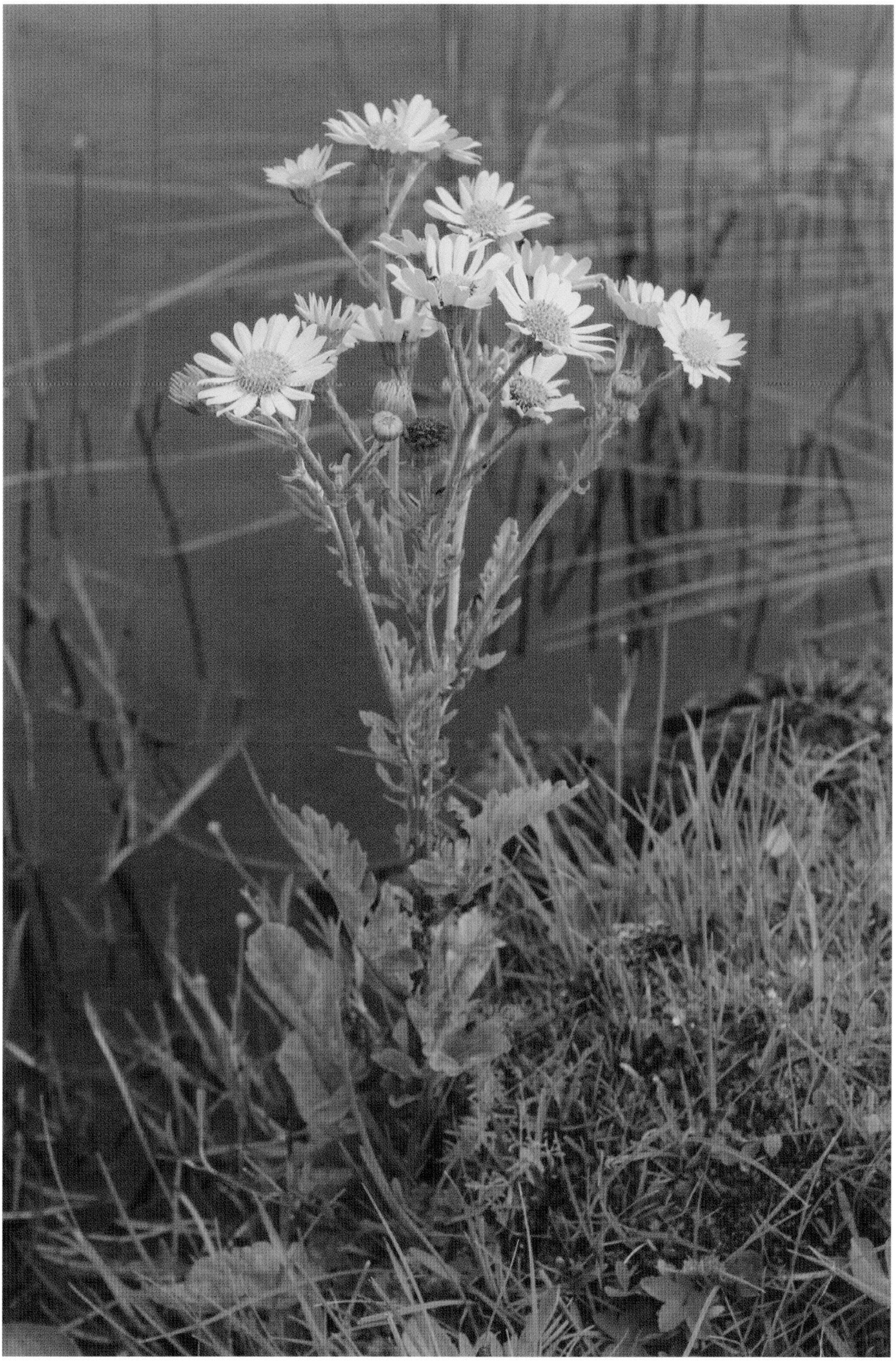

Plate 18 (m–l) **Marsh Ragwort** (*Senecio aquaticus*) 'Gowan'
Flowerheads yellow, large; leaves pinnately lobed, end lobe largest, blunt. Native. Pastures, streamsides, roadsides. Flowering late June–September. Photograph: Loch of Setter, Clousta.

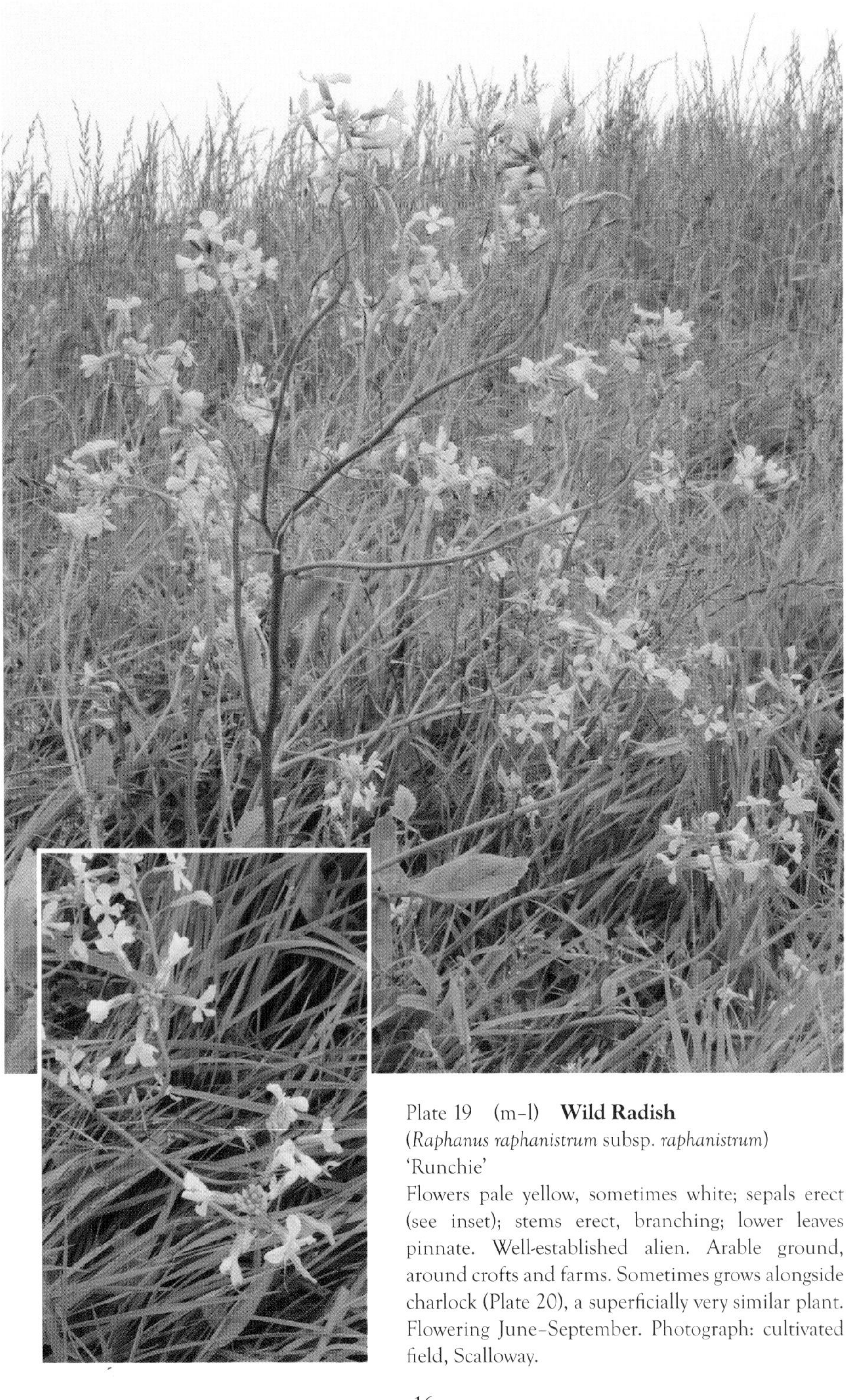

Plate 19 (m–l) **Wild Radish**
(*Raphanus raphanistrum* subsp. *raphanistrum*)
'Runchie'

Flowers pale yellow, sometimes white; sepals erect (see inset); stems erect, branching; lower leaves pinnate. Well-established alien. Arable ground, around crofts and farms. Sometimes grows alongside charlock (Plate 20), a superficially very similar plant. Flowering June–September. Photograph: cultivated field, Scalloway.

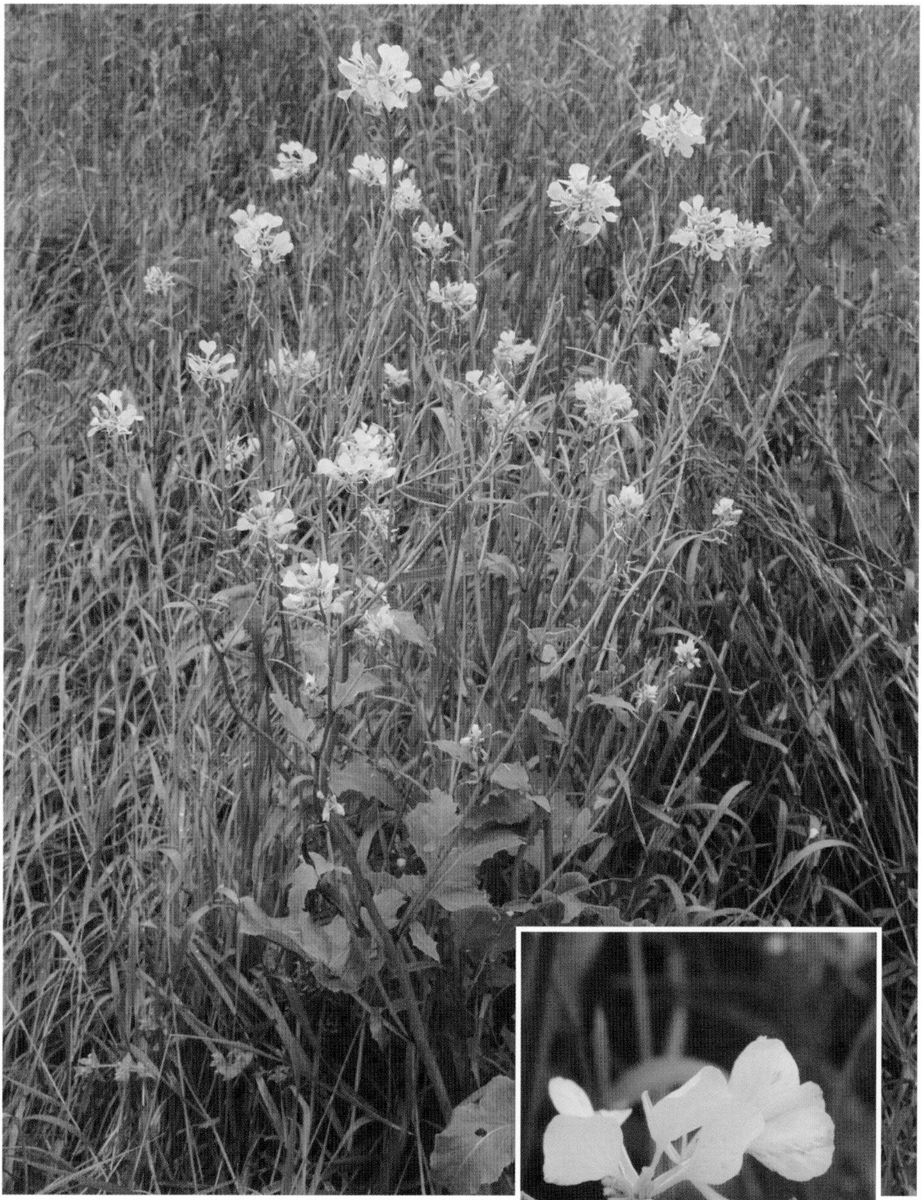

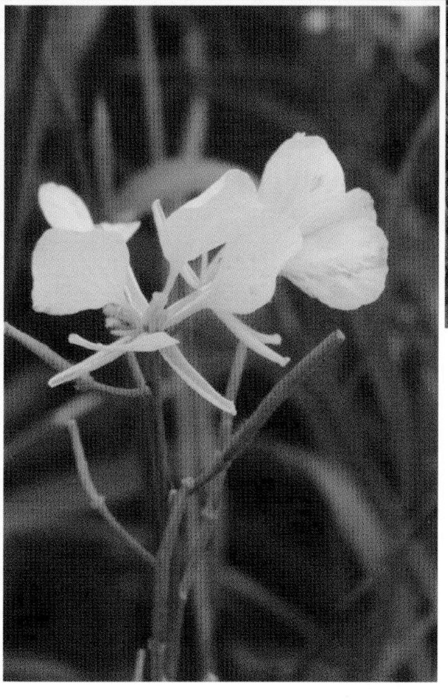

Plate 20 (m–l) **Charlock** (*Sinapis arvensis*)
'Runchie'
Flowers bright yellow, 15–20 mm wide; sepals spreading (see inset); lower leaves large, toothed, upper leaves narrower. Well-established alien. Arable ground, rubbish dumps, roadside verges. Sometimes grows alongside wild radish (Plate 19), a superficially very similar plant. Flowering June–November. Photograph: cultivated field, Scalloway.

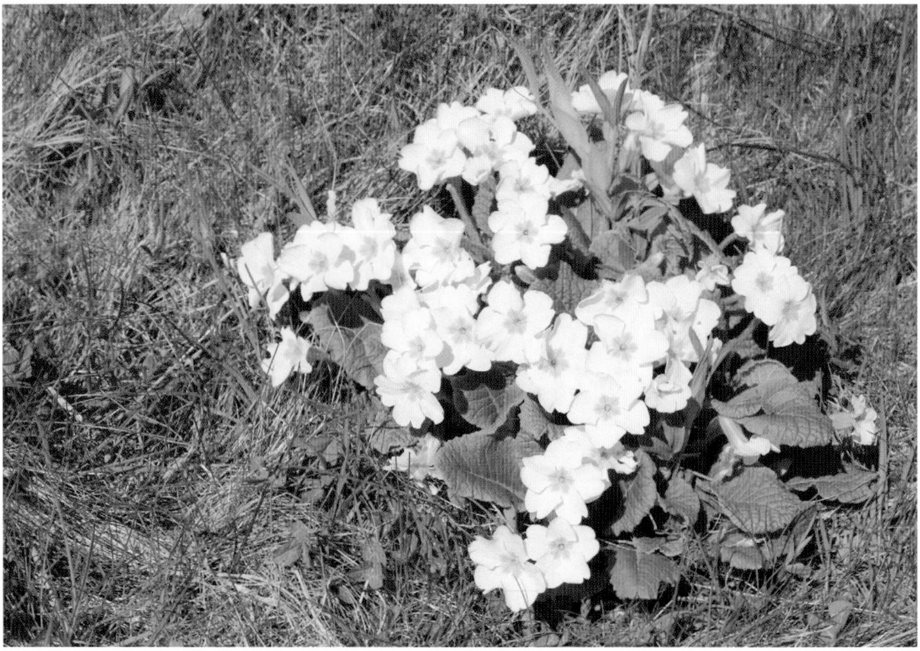

Plate 21 (s–m) **Primrose** (*Primula vulgaris*) 'Meyflooer'
Flowers pale yellow, on long, hairy stalks, petals 5, notched; leaves oval, wrinkled. Native. Grassy cliffs, banks, pastures, roadsides, streamsides. Flowering chiefly April–June. Photograph: rocky outcrop in dry pasture, Fladdabister.

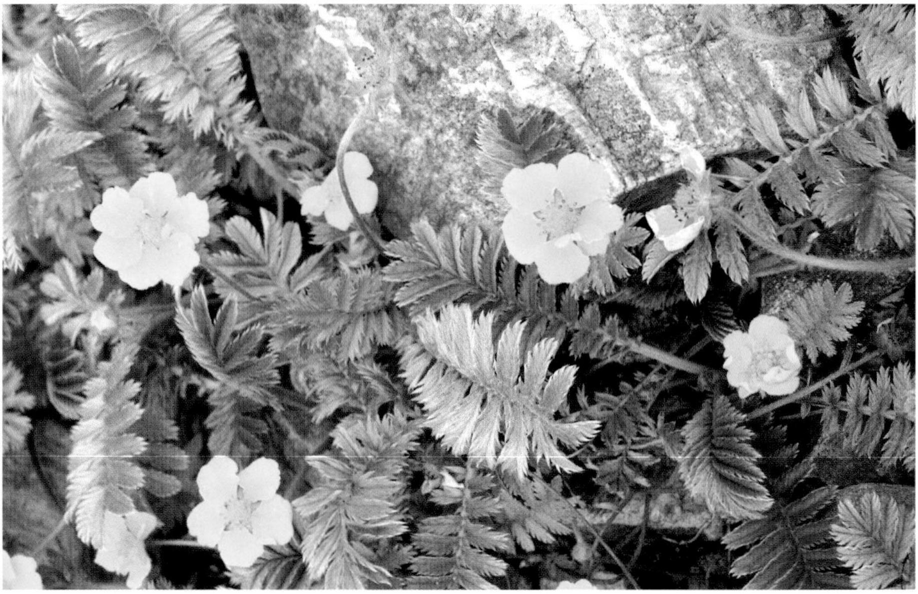

Plate 22 (m–l) **Silverweed** (*Potentilla anserina*)
Flowers yellow, 2.0 cm wide, petals 5; stems downy; leaves pinnate, leaflets toothed. A native plant of shingly and sandy beaches and coastal grassland easily recognised by its silvery leaves and red runners. Flowering late May–August. Photograph: shingly beach, Easter Quarff.

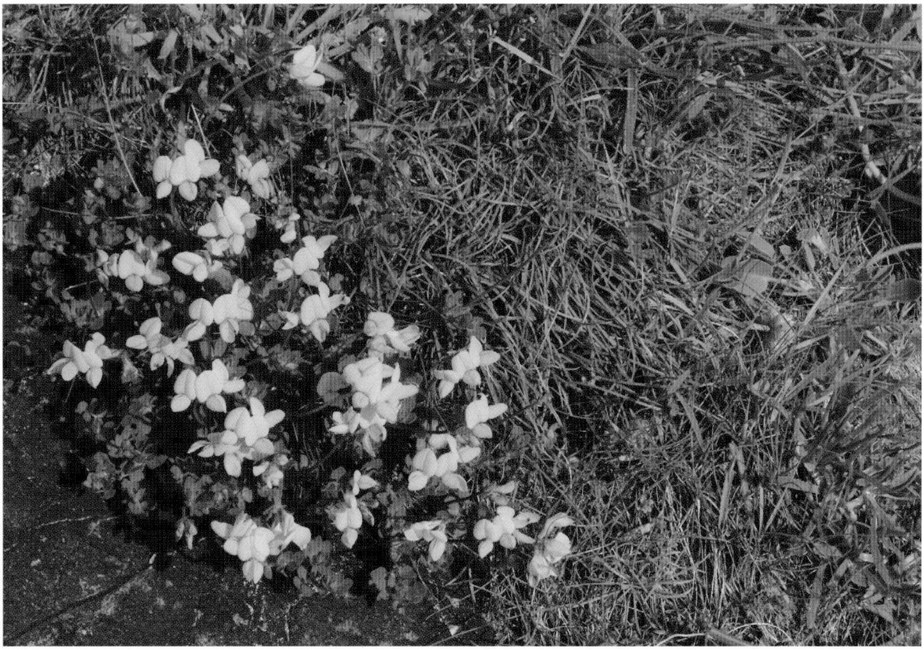

Plate 23 (s–m) **Common Bird's-foot-trefoil** (*Lotus corniculatus*) 'Kattikloo'
Flowers yellow, often tinged red, in clusters, petals 5, the lower two fused to form the keel; stems straggling; leaves divided into 5 leaflets. Native and alien. Dry grassy places. Flowering late May–August. Photograph: grassy coastal banks, St Ninian's Bay.

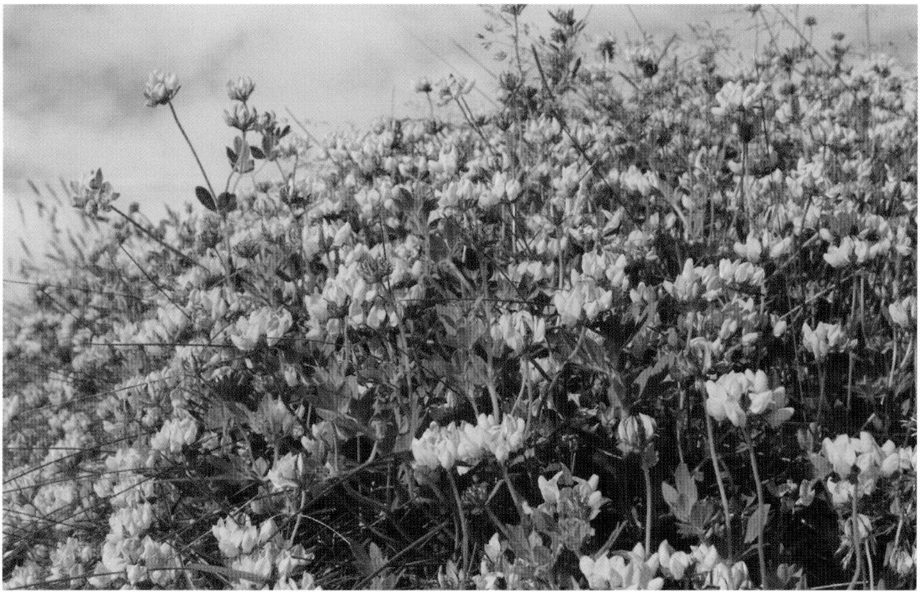

Plate 24 (m) **Greater Bird's-foot-trefoil** (*Lotus pedunculatus*)
Flowers yellow, 5–12 in each head; stems hairy; leaves divided into 5 leaflets. Well-established alien. Streambanks, roadsides and marshy ground. Flowering late May–August. Photograph: roadside, East Burrafirth.

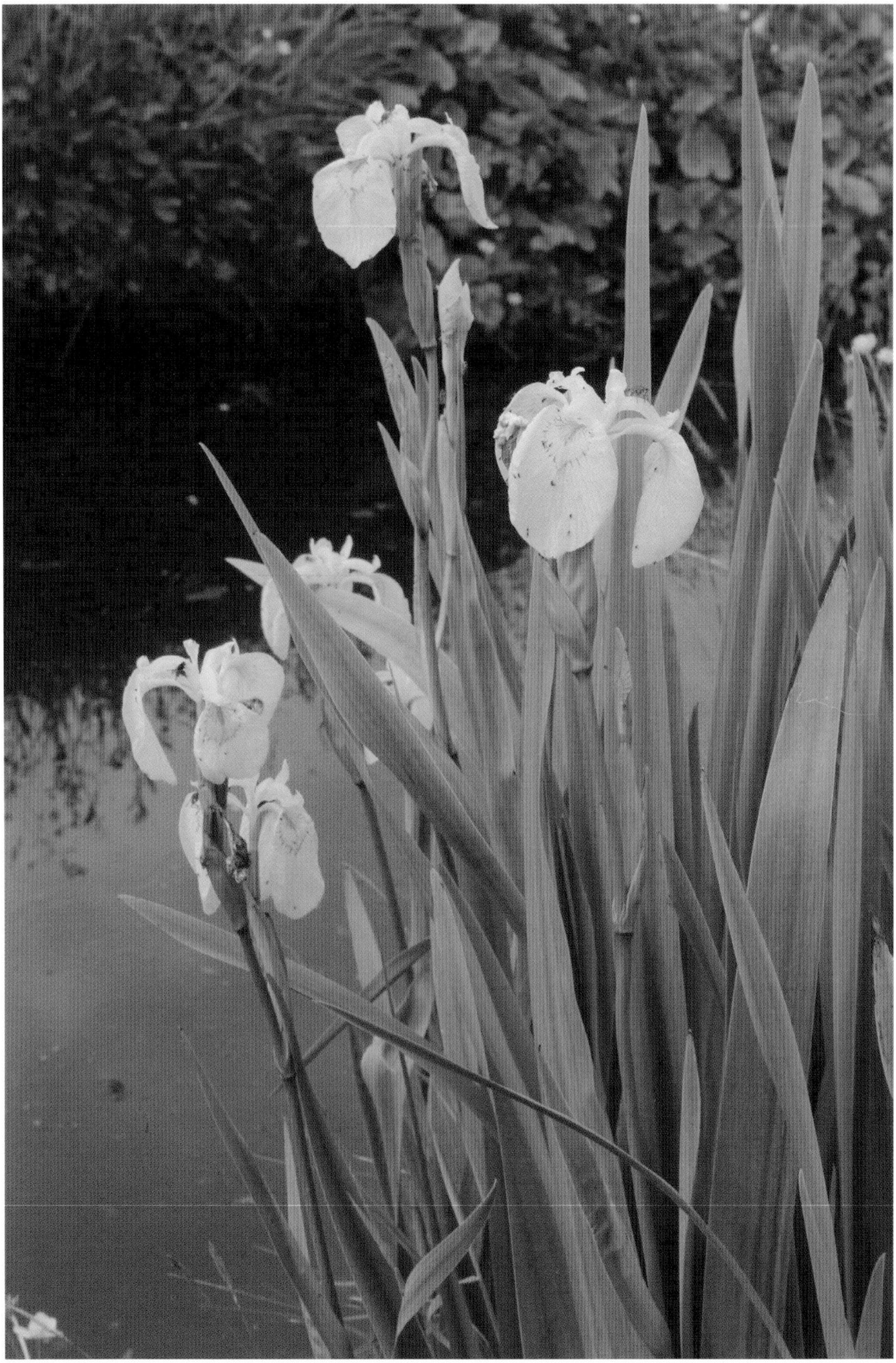

Plate 25 (l) **Yellow Iris** (*Iris pseudacorus*) 'Seggi-flooer'
Flowers yellow, showy; leaves stout, sword-like. Native. Streams, marshes, margins of lochs. Flowering July–early August. Photograph: burn running into Strand Loch, Tingwall.

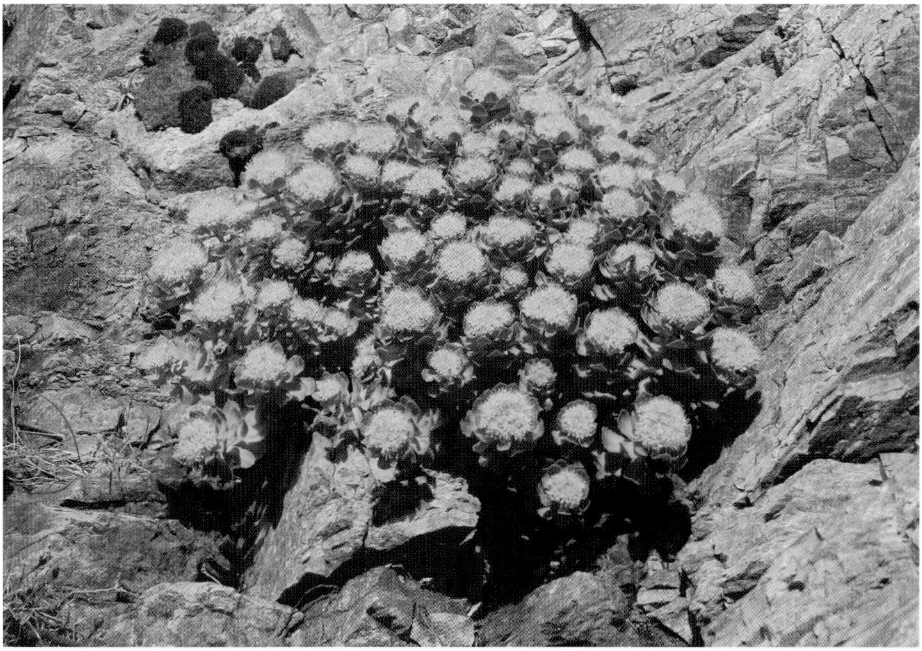

Plate 26 (m) **Roseroot** (*Sedum rosea*)
Flowers greenish-yellow, in dense clusters; leaves thick, succulent. Native. Found chiefly on sea-cliff faces and ledges. Flowering May–July. Photograph: sea-cliffs, Hillswick.

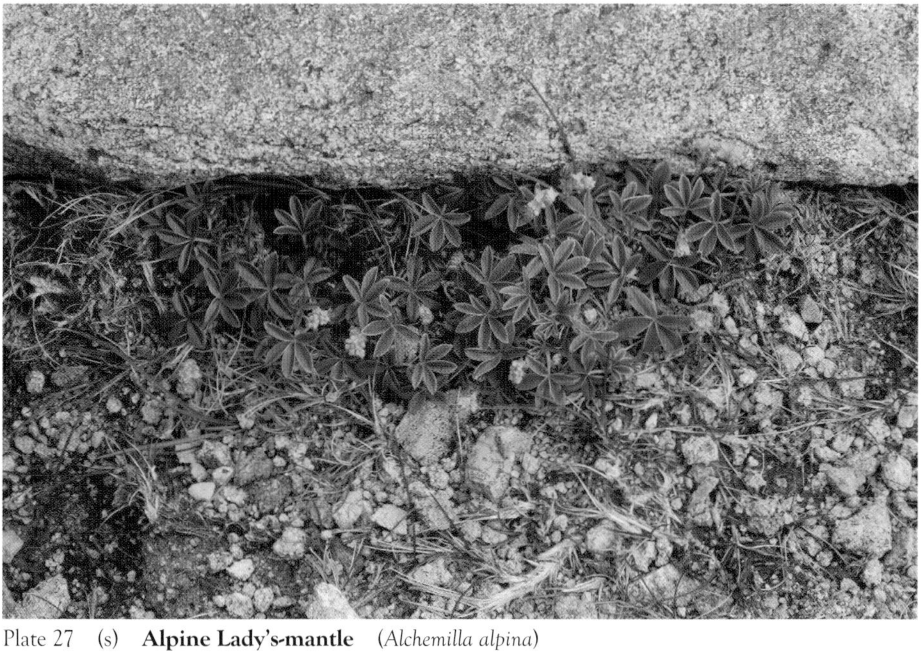

Plate 27 (s) **Alpine Lady's-mantle** (*Alchemilla alpina*)
Flowers pale green, tiny, in tight clusters; stems hairy; leaves palmately lobed, cut to base, green above, silvery below. Native. Granite gravel on Ronas Hill, its only Shetland station. Flowering June–August. Photograph: eastern slopes of Ronas Hill.

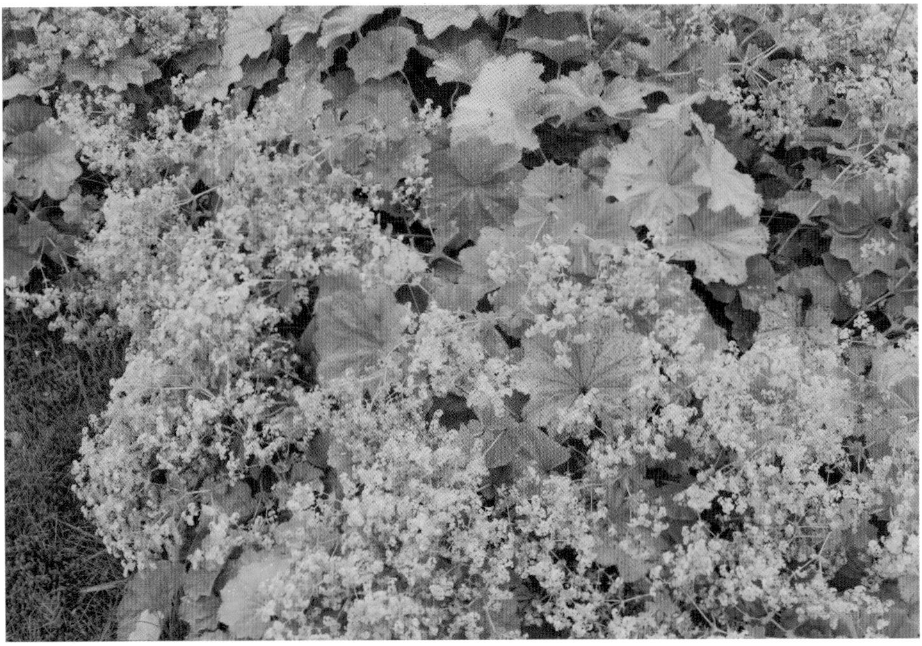

Plate 28 (l) **Soft Lady's-mantle** (*Alchemilla mollis*)
Flowers lime green, small, numerous, in diffuse clusters; leaves rounded and palmately lobed. Casual. A garden outcast and prolific seeder which is not uncommonly seen by roadsides. Flowering June–August. Photograph: roadside verge near Scalloway.

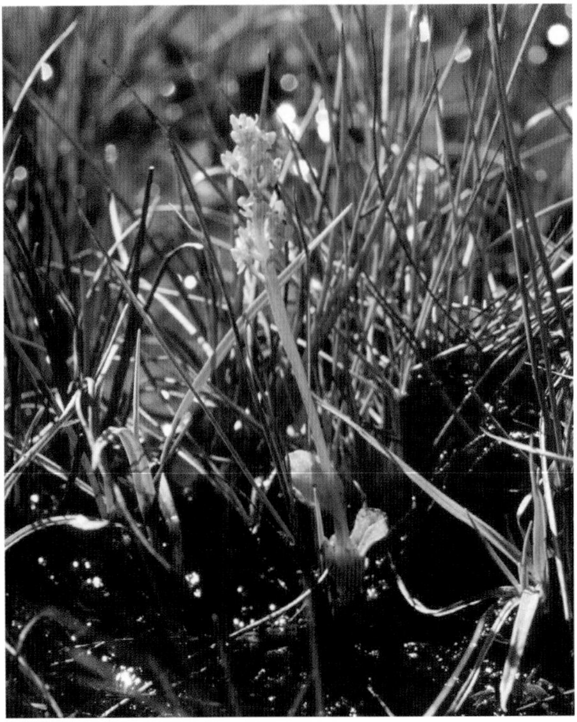

Plate 29 (s) **Bog Orchid**
(*Hammarbya paludosa*)
Flowers yellow-green; leaves 2–3, pale green and near the base, narrowly oval and with a fringe of tiny bulbils. Native. Very rare. Wet sphagnous places. Flowering July–August. Photograph: by Loch of Colvister, Yell.

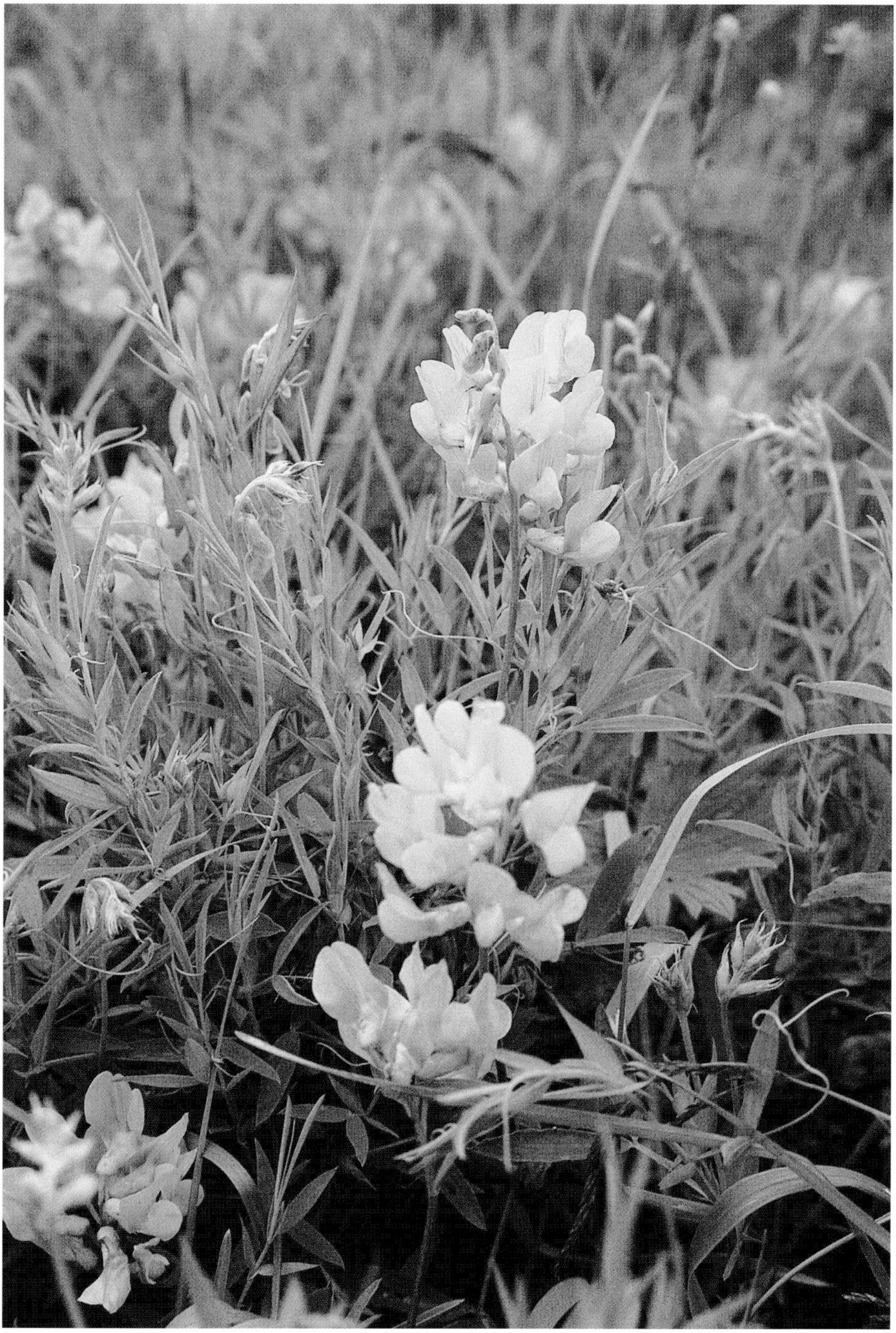

Plate 30 (m–l) **Meadow Vetchling** (*Lathyrus pratensis*)
Flowers yellow, in clustered spikes, petals 5, the lower two fused to form the keel; stems angled; leaves pinnate with a terminal tendril. Native. Rough grassy places, grassy sea-banks. Flowering late June–September. Photograph: roadside verge, Tingwall.

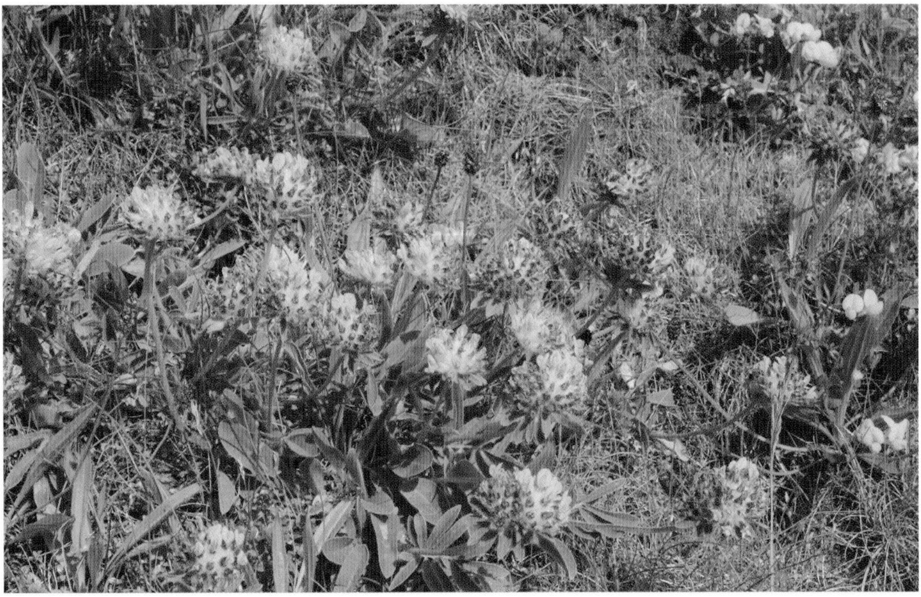

Plate 31 (s–m) **Kidney Vetch** (*Anthyllis vulneraria*)
Flowers bright yellow, occasionally cream or lemon, rarely tinged with red, clustered in a rounded flowerhead; base of flower surrounded by a woolly calyx; flowerhead encircled by a leafy involucre; stems bearing silky hairs; leaves pinnate. Native and alien. Grassy sea-cliffs, sea-banks, pastures, roadside verges. Flowering late May–early July. Photograph: grassy coastal banks, St Ninian's Bay.

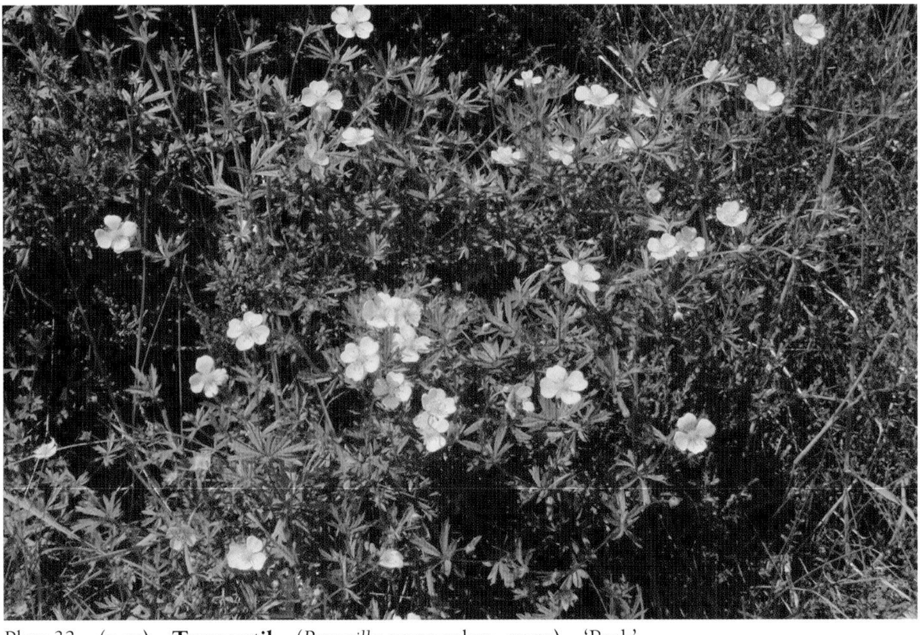

Plate 32 (s–m) **Tormentil** (*Potentilla erecta* subsp. *erecta*) 'Bark'
Flowers yellow, 6–10 mm wide, petals 4, notched; stems slender, straggly, finely hairy, leaves divided into three toothed leaflets, stipules conspicuously leaf-like. Native. Heathland, moorland, waysides, etc. Flowering May–September. Photograph: grassy bank by roadside, Green Head, Lerwick.

Plate 33 (s–m) **Lady's Bedstraw** (*Galium verum*)
Flowers yellow, tiny, in dense clusters, fragrant, petals 4; stems angled. Native. Dry grassland, rocky streamsides. Flowering July–August. Photograph: dry, rocky grassland, Catfirth, South Nesting.

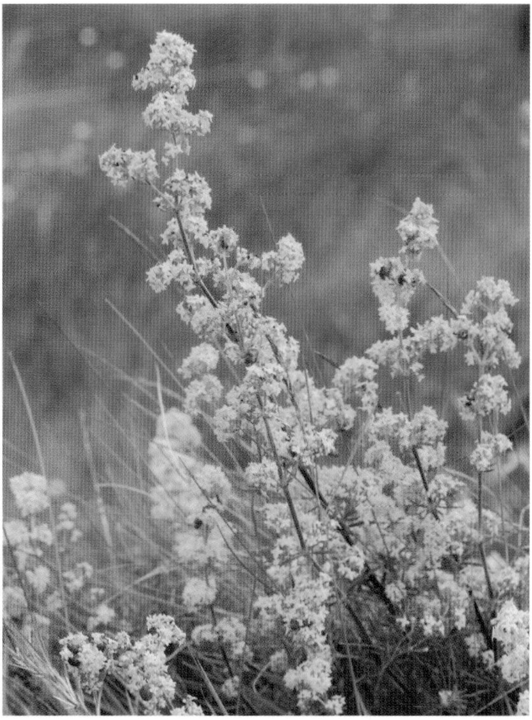

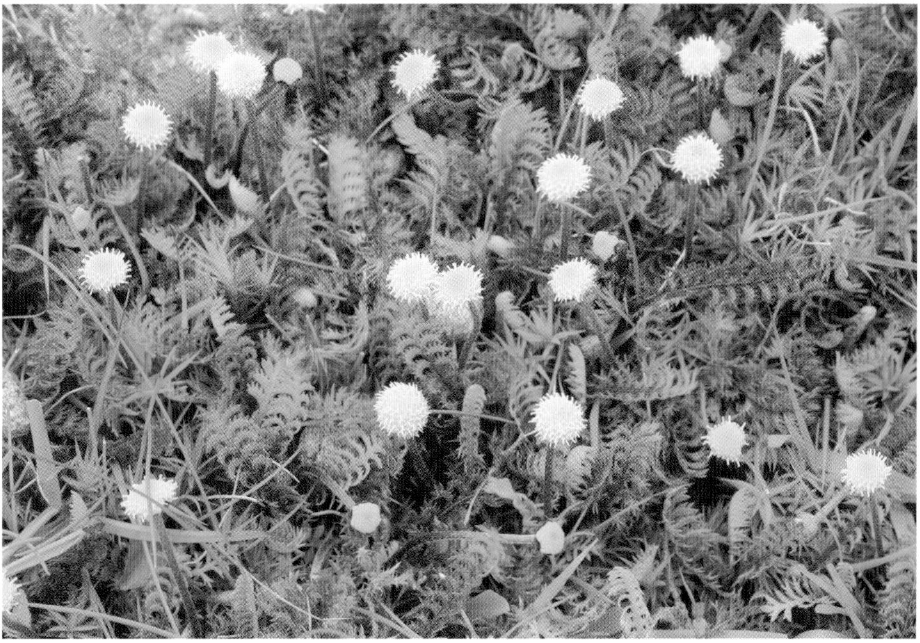

Plate 34 (s) **Leptinella** (*Cotula squalida*)
Flowerheads button-like, rayless, very pale lemon, solitary on long stalks. Well-established alien. Turfy or stony roadside verges, and extending into adjacent natural vegetation. Flowering June–August. Photograph: by the roadside above Dales Voe, North Mainland.

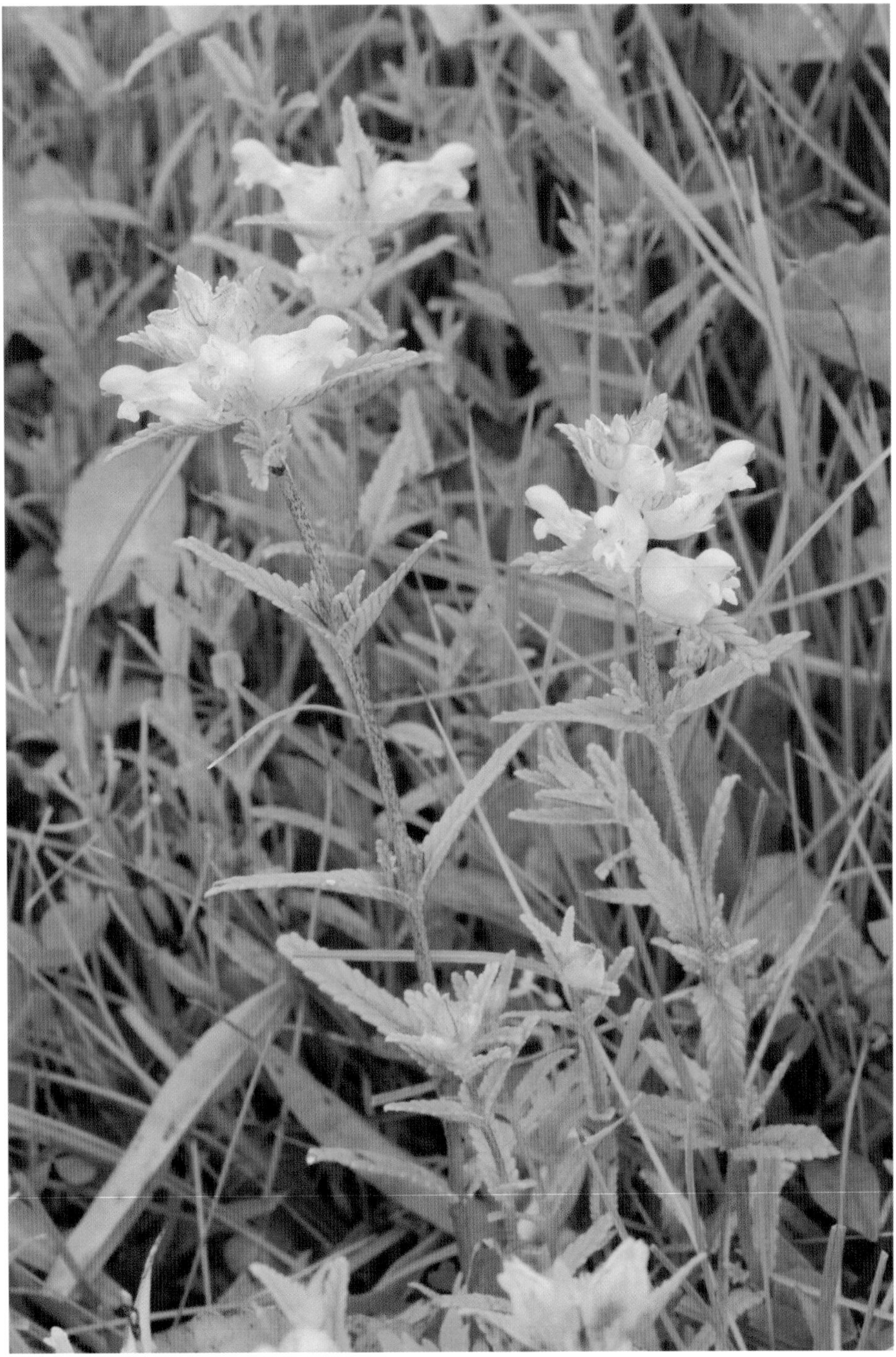

Plate 35 (s–m) **Yellow-rattle** (*Rhinanthus minor*) 'Dog's Pennies'
Flowers yellow, 2-lipped with upper tinged indigo; stems smooth, square; leaves opposite, unstalked, toothed. Native. Grassland. Flowering late June–August. Photograph: meadow, Burland, Trondra.

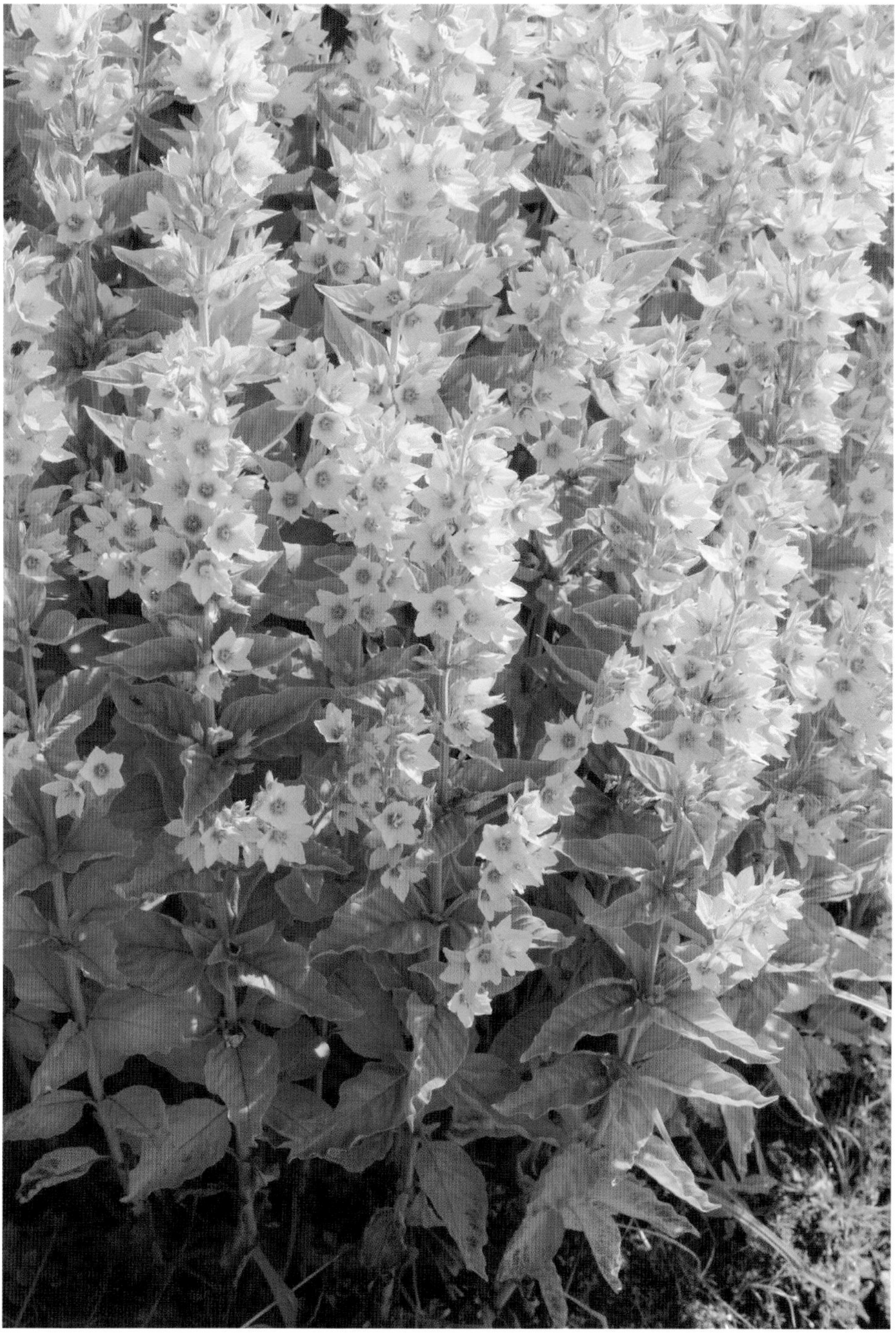

Plate 36 (m–l) **Dotted Loosestrife** (*Lysimachia punctata*)
Flowers yellow, up to 3.5 cm wide, in branched clusters; leaves short-stalked, hairy margins. Casual. Garden plant, seen near houses where it has been planted or thrown out. Flowering August-September. Photograph: roadside, Trondra.

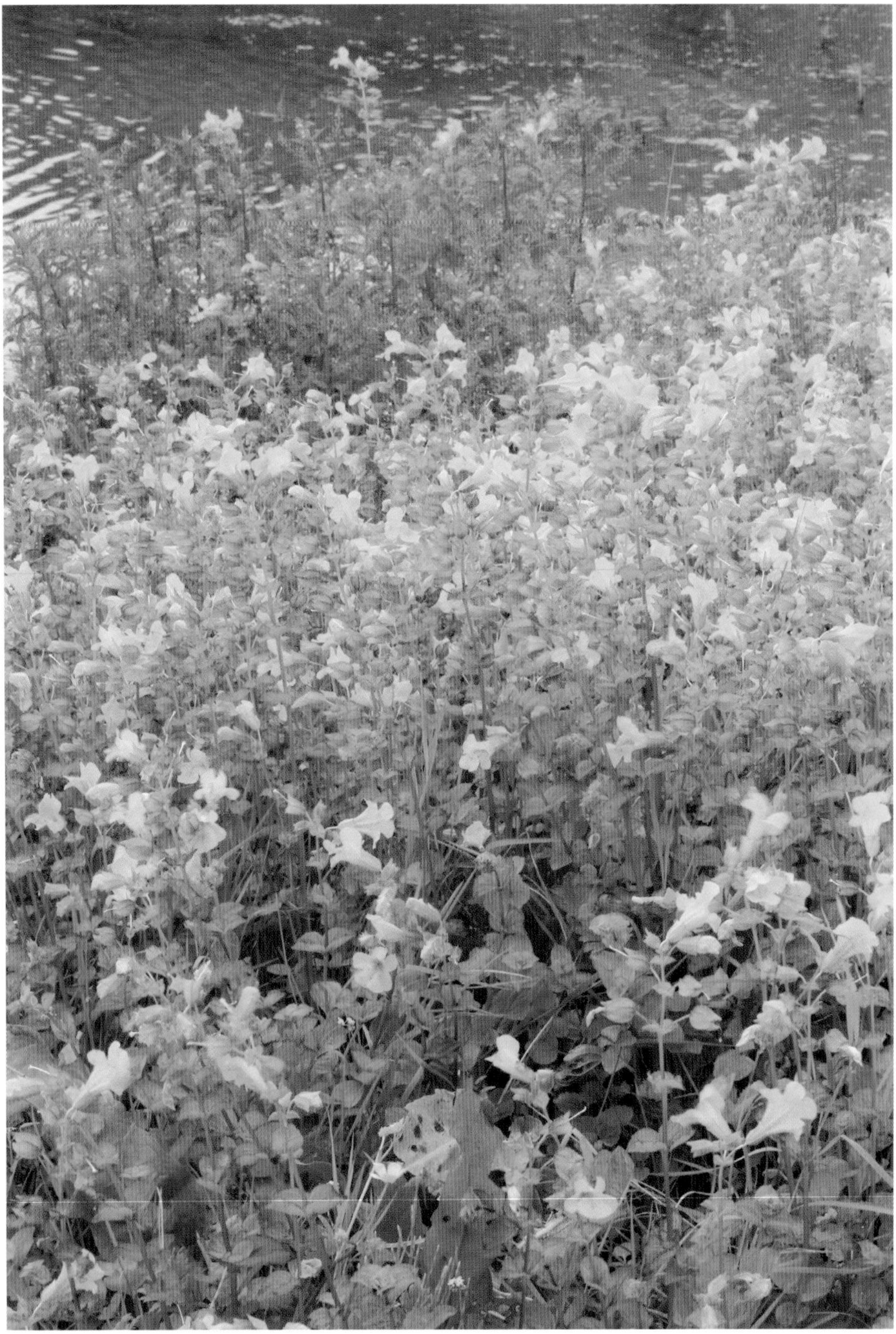

Plate 37 (m–l) **Monkeyflower** (*Mimulus guttatus*)
Flowers yellow, 2-lipped, the lower lip bearing red spots; stems succulent, hairless; flower-stalks hairy; leaves rounded, opposite, toothed. Well-established alien. Streamsides, ditches. Flowering July-September. Photograph: pond behind the Bay of Quendale.

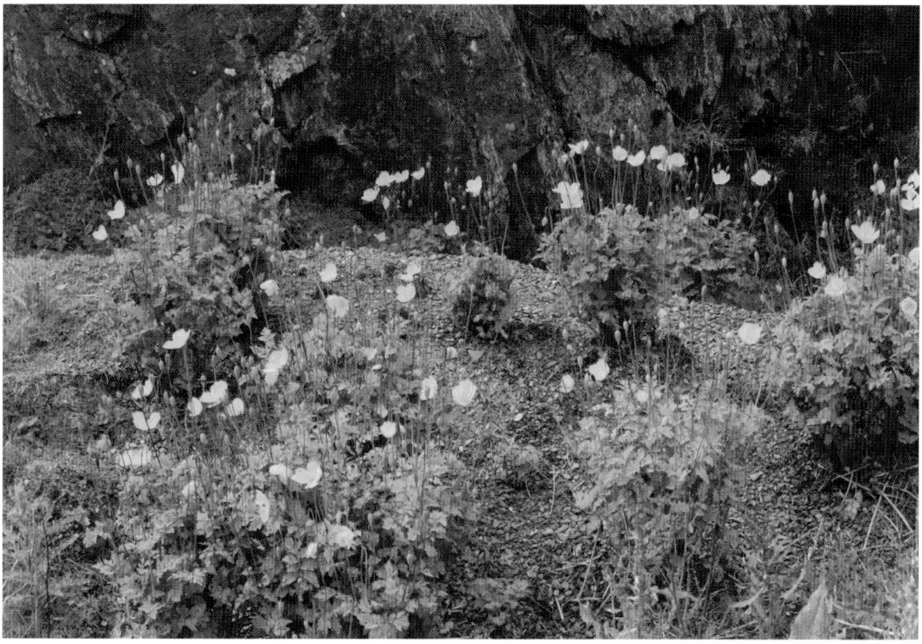

Plate 38 (m) **Welsh Poppy** (*Meconopsis cambrica*)
Flowers yellow, usually more than 5.0 cm wide, carried on erect, slender stalks; stems slightly hairy; root leaves long-stalked and deeply lobed, stem leaves short-stalked. Well-established alien. Near gardens, old quarries. Flowering June–August. Photograph: disused quarry, Girlsta.

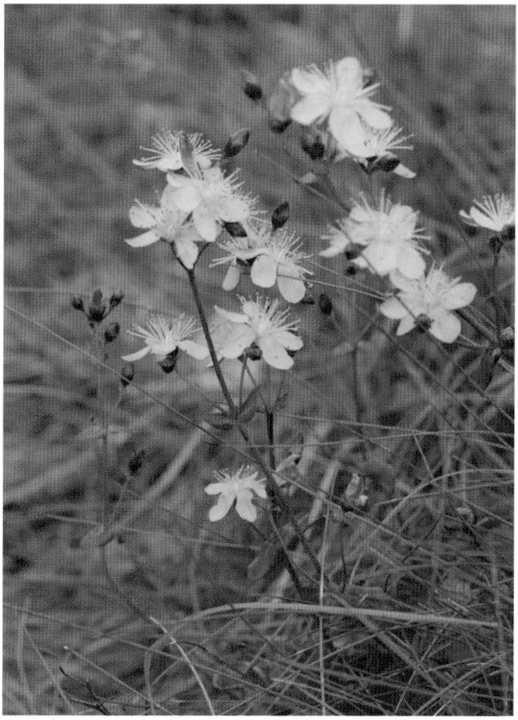

Plate 39 (s–m)
Slender St John's-wort
(*Hypericum pulchrum*)
Flowers rich yellow, petals 5, reddish below with blackish dots on margins; stems hairless; leaves untoothed, tinged red. Native. Steep-sided streambanks, stony places, rocky-heathery burnsides, rocky or stony heaths. Flowering late June–early September. Photograph: dry, rocky grassland, Catfirth, South Nesting.

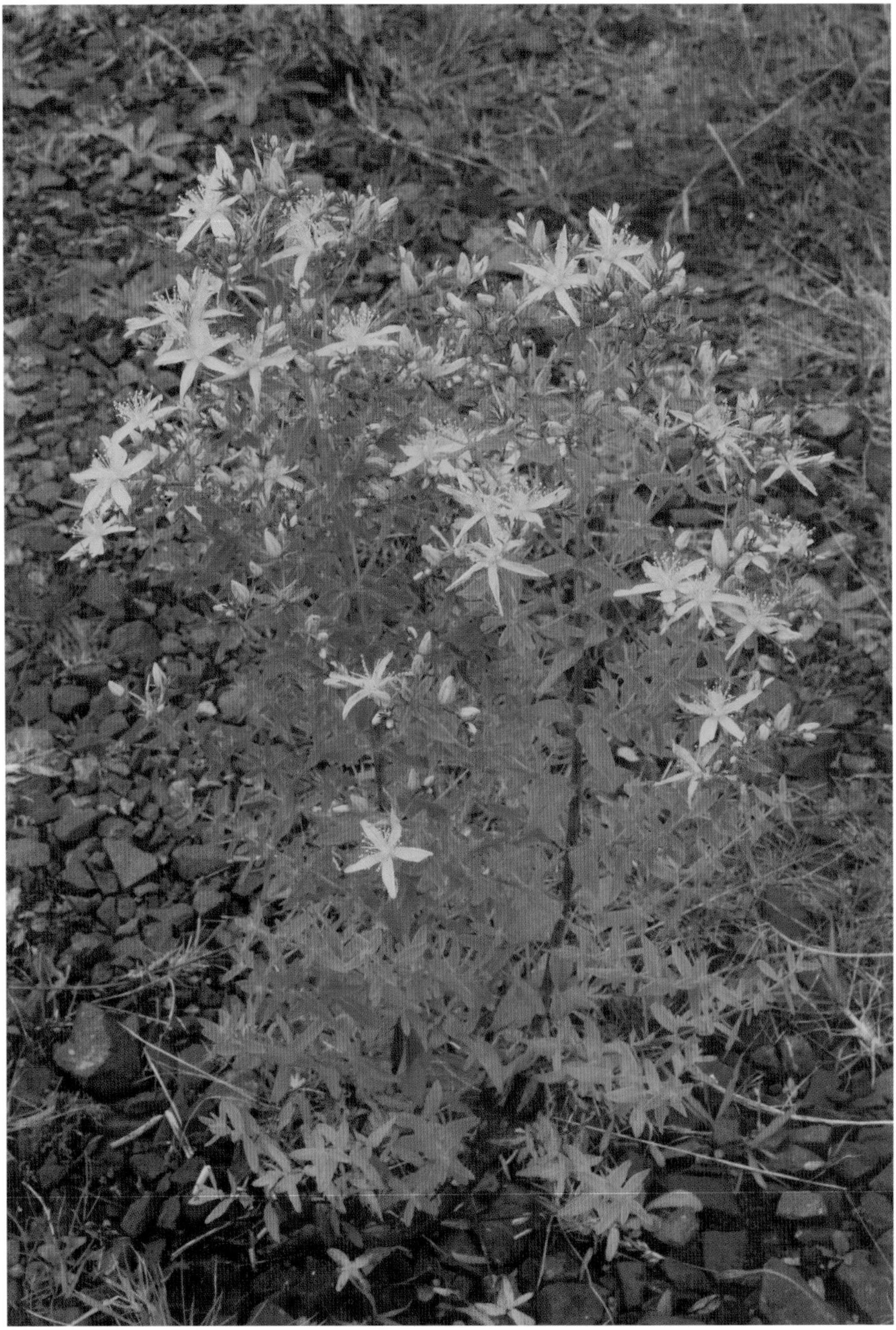

Plate 40 (m) **Perforate St John's-wort** (*Hypericum perforatum*)
Flowers orange-yellow, petals 5, black-dotted, especially on margins; stems with two raised lines along their length. A rare casual. Roadside verges. Flowering July–September. Photograph: roadside, Channerwick.

Plate 41 (s) **Bog Asphodel**
(*Narthecium ossifragum*)
Flowers yellowish-orange, star-like, in narrow spikes, anthers red, petals 6; stems erect; leaves narrow, clasping stem. A clove-scented native of wet heaths and moors. Flowering July–August. Photograph: wet heathy grassland, Trondra.

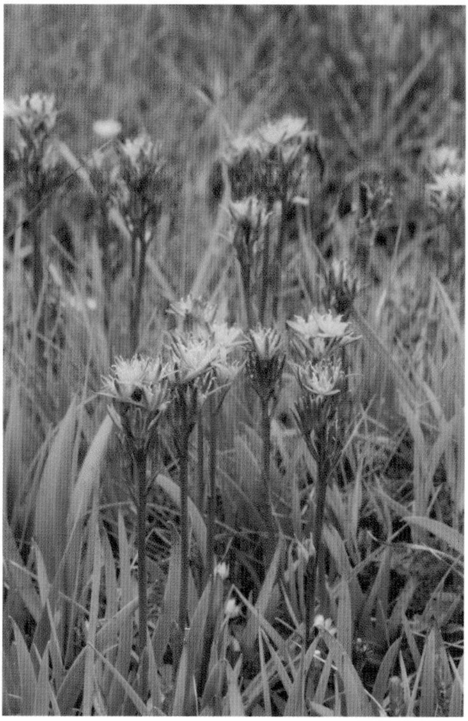

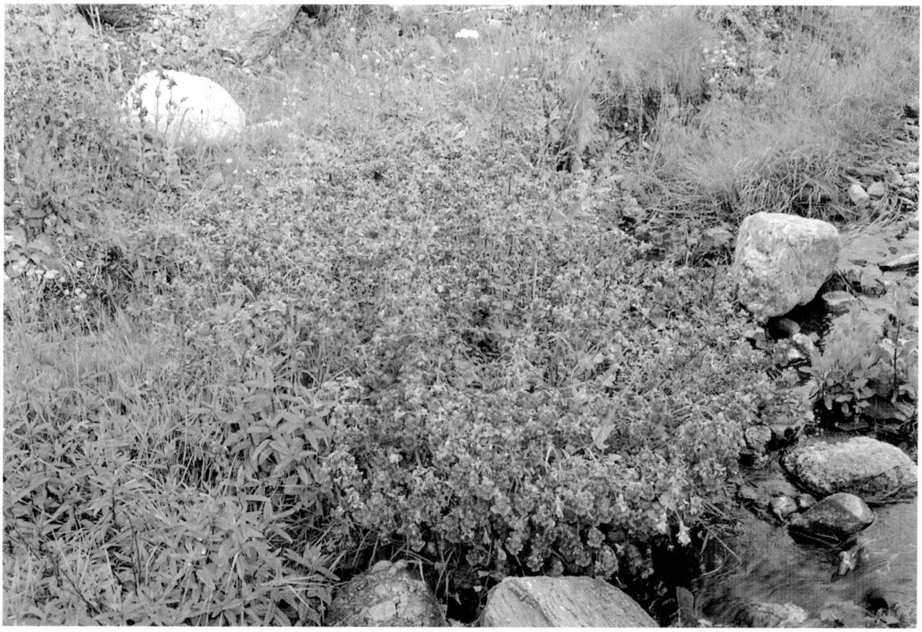

Plate 42 (m–l) **Coppery Monkeyflower** (*Mimulus × burnetii*)
Flowers orange-yellow, 2-lipped, calyx often petal-like, giving a double-flowered appearance; stems smooth; leaves rounded, opposite, toothed. Well-established alien. Ditches, streamsides. Flowering late June–August. Photograph: streamside, Easter Quarff.

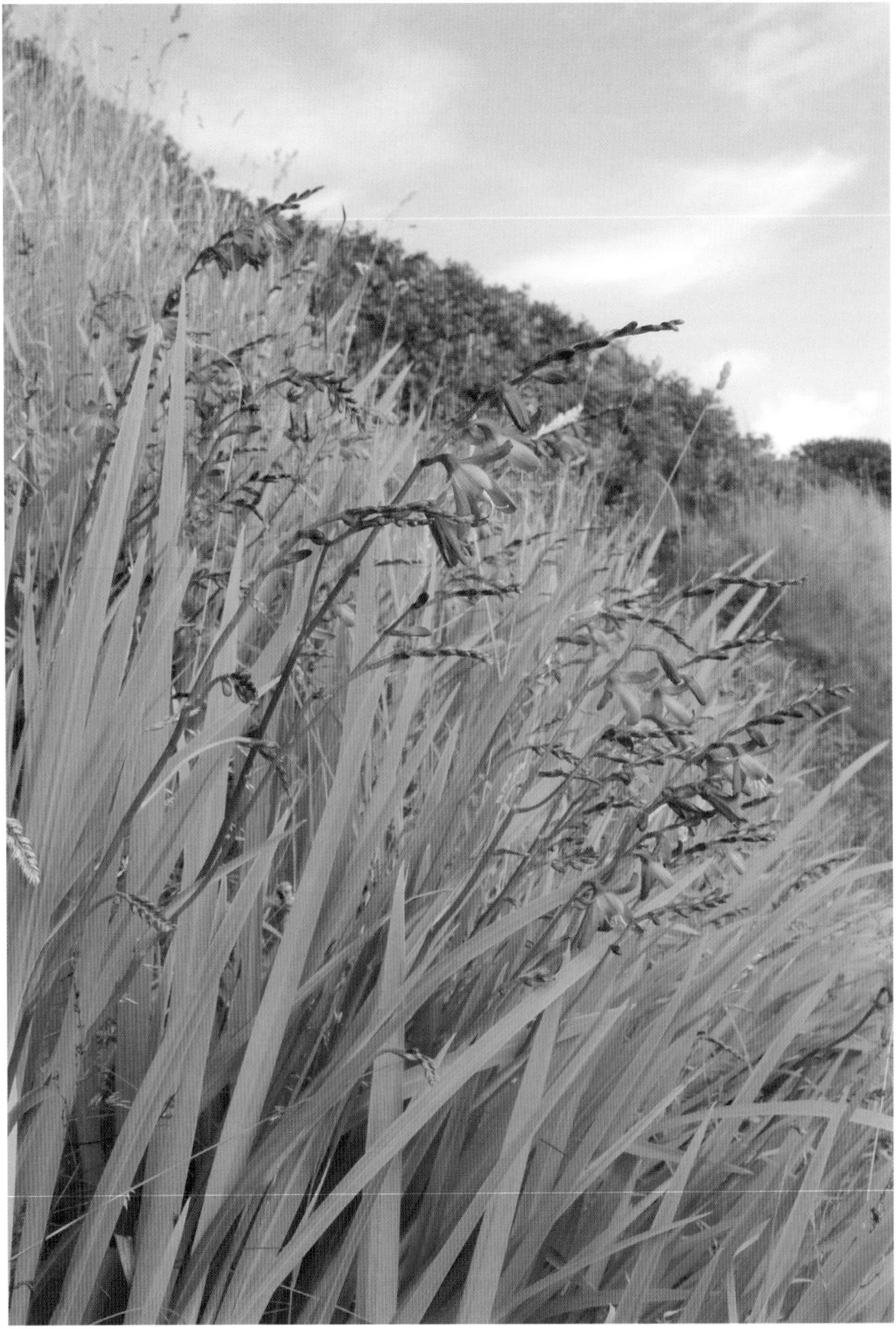

Plate 43 (m–l) **Montbretia** (*Crocosmia × crocosmiiflora*)
Flowers orange, on one-sided spikes; leaves sword-like. Well-established alien. Garden outcast or escape. About houses, streamsides, roadsides. Flowering late August–early November. Photograph: grassy bank, Westshore, Scalloway.

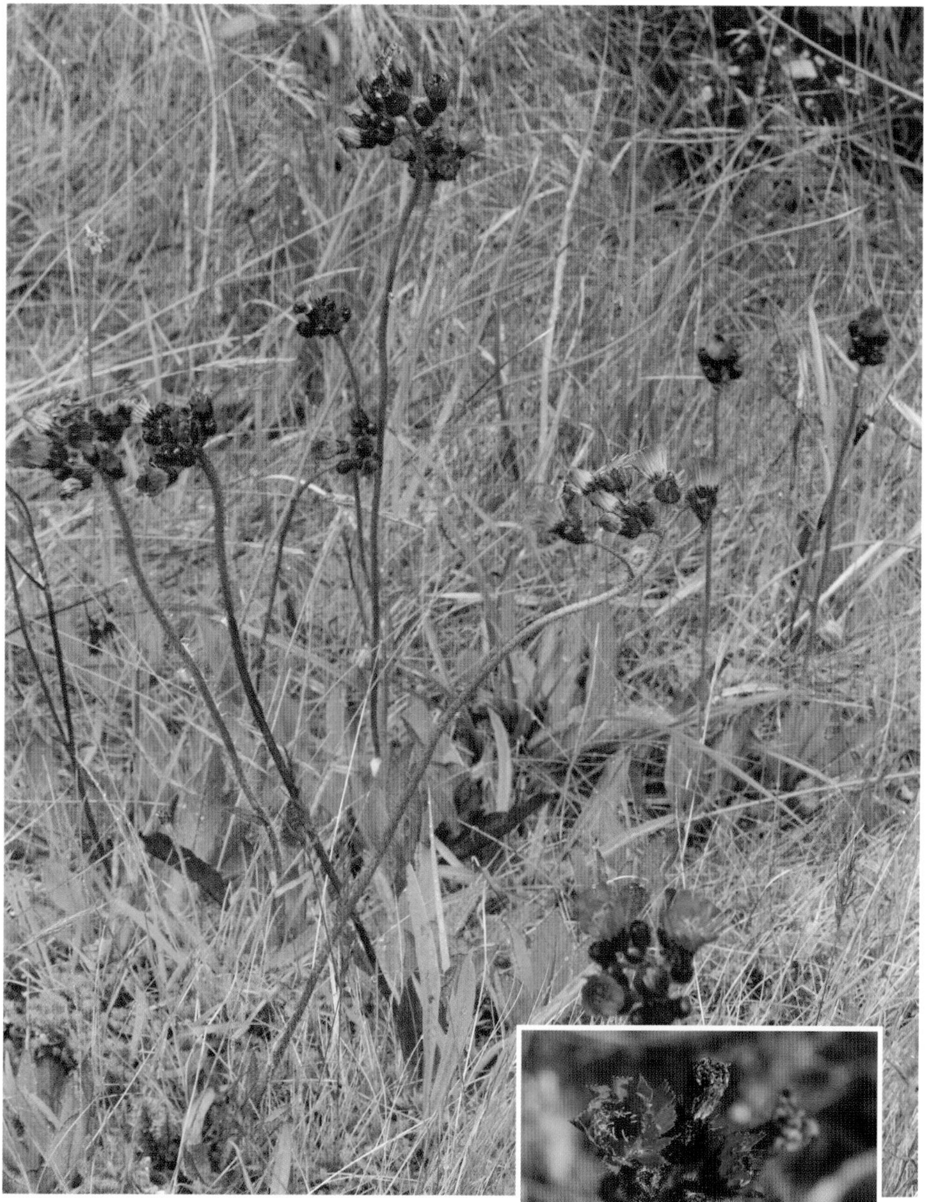

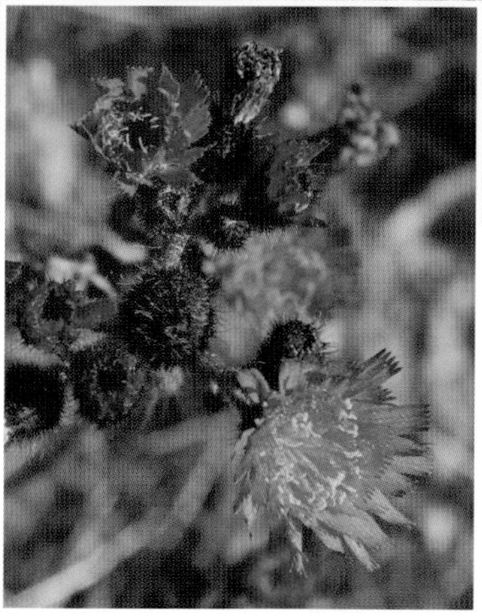

Plate 44 (m–l) **Fox-and-cubs**
(*Pilosella aurantiaca*)
Flowerheads reddish-orange; stems long, slender, hairy, and like the calyx, has the appearance of having been spattered with soot; leaves lanceolate, hairy, mostly from the base. Well-established alien. A garden escape or outcast, on grassy banks or roadside verges. Flowering August–September. Photograph: roadside verge near Easter Quarff.

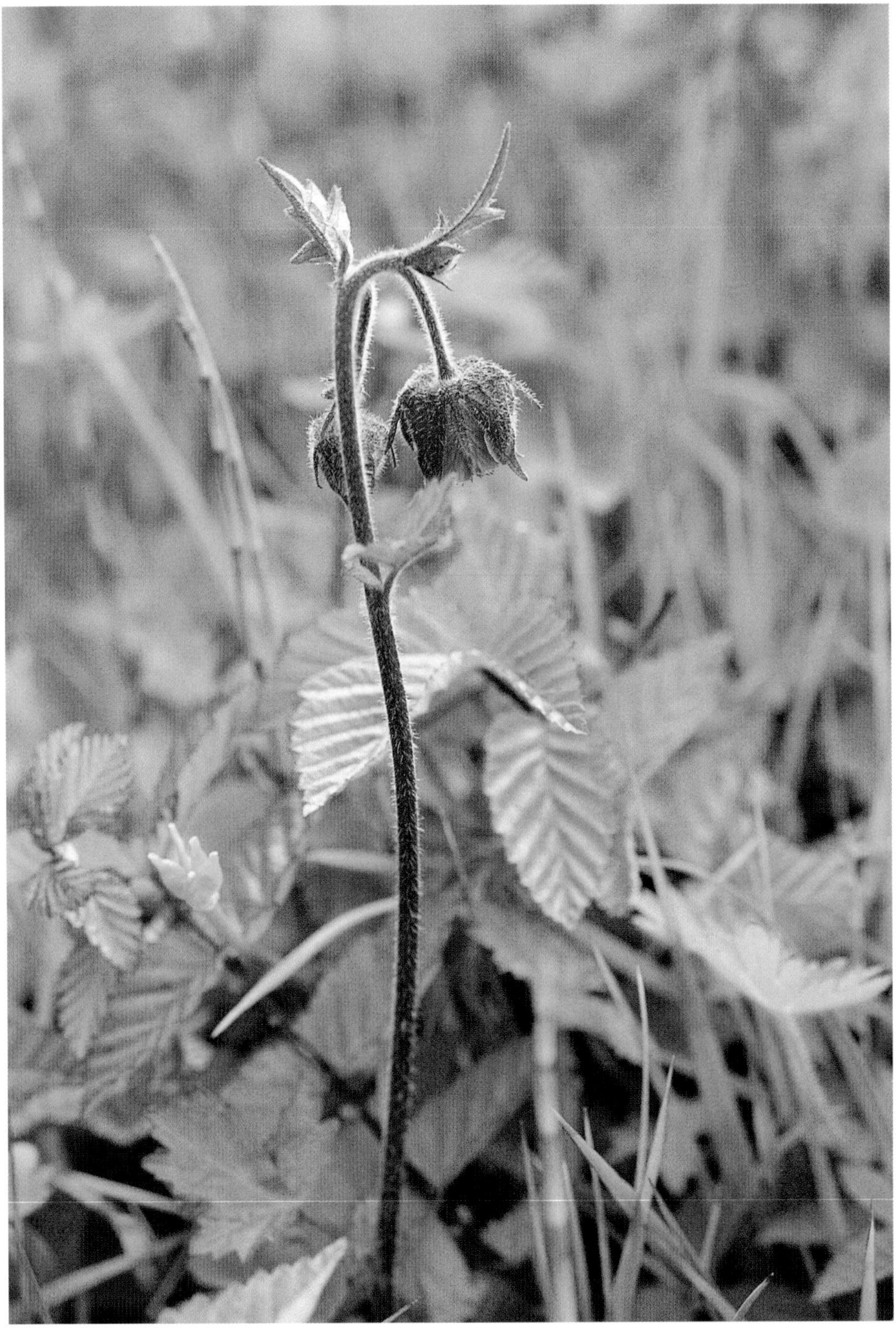

Plate 45 (m) **Water Avens** (*Geum rivale*)
Flowers peach-red, cup-shaped, nodding, petals 5; sepals large, purple; stems downy; lowest leaves pinnate, end lobe large, leaflets, toothed, downy. Native. Wet places on rich ground. Flowering late May–August. Photograph: wet pasture, Whiteness.

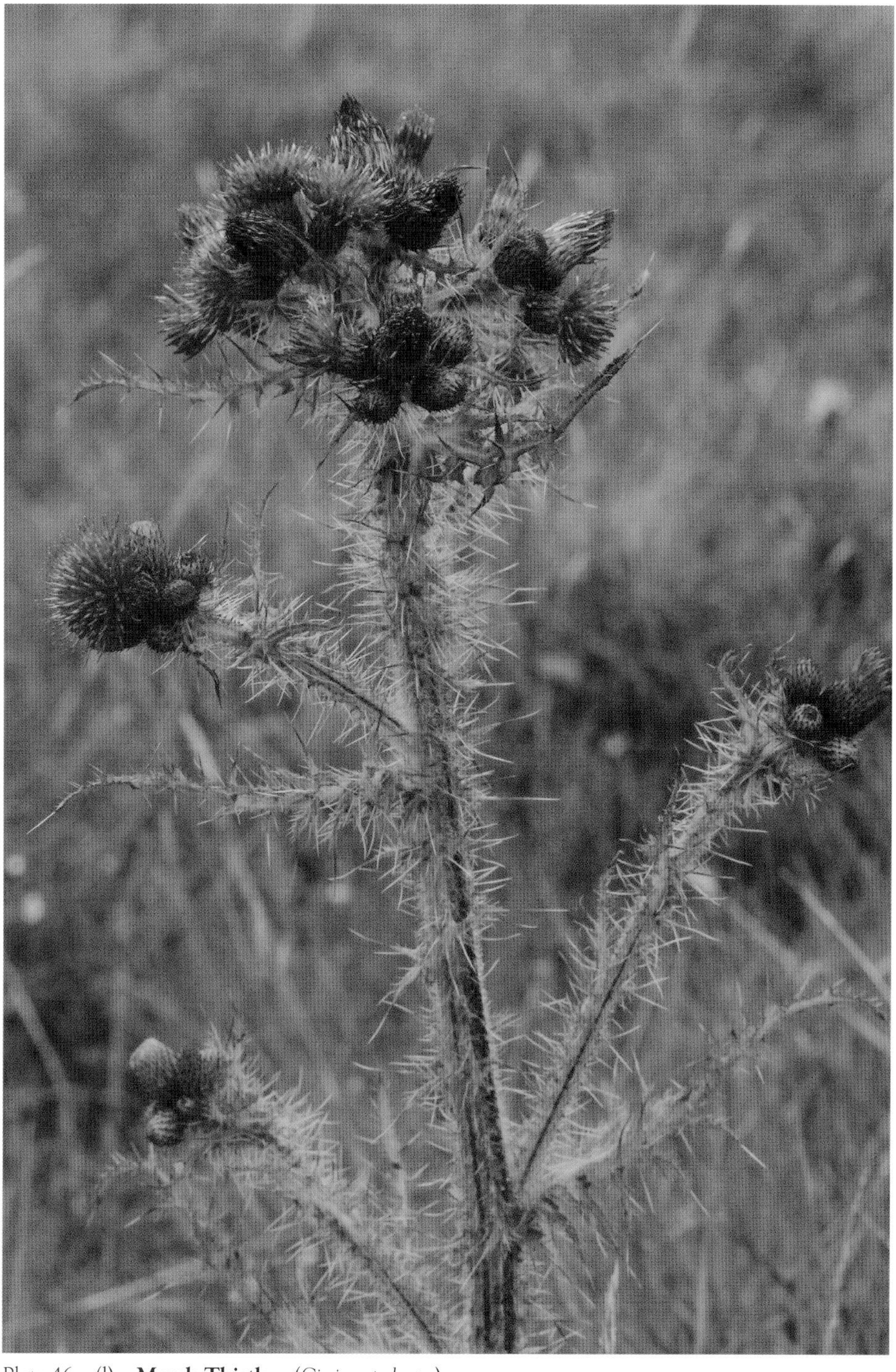

Plate 46 (l) **Marsh Thistle** (*Cirsium palustre*)
Flowerheads reddish-purple; leaves sharply spiny. Native. Rough marshy meadows, coastal slopes, roadsides, etc. Flowering late June–August. Photograph: coastal grassland, Tresta, Fetlar.

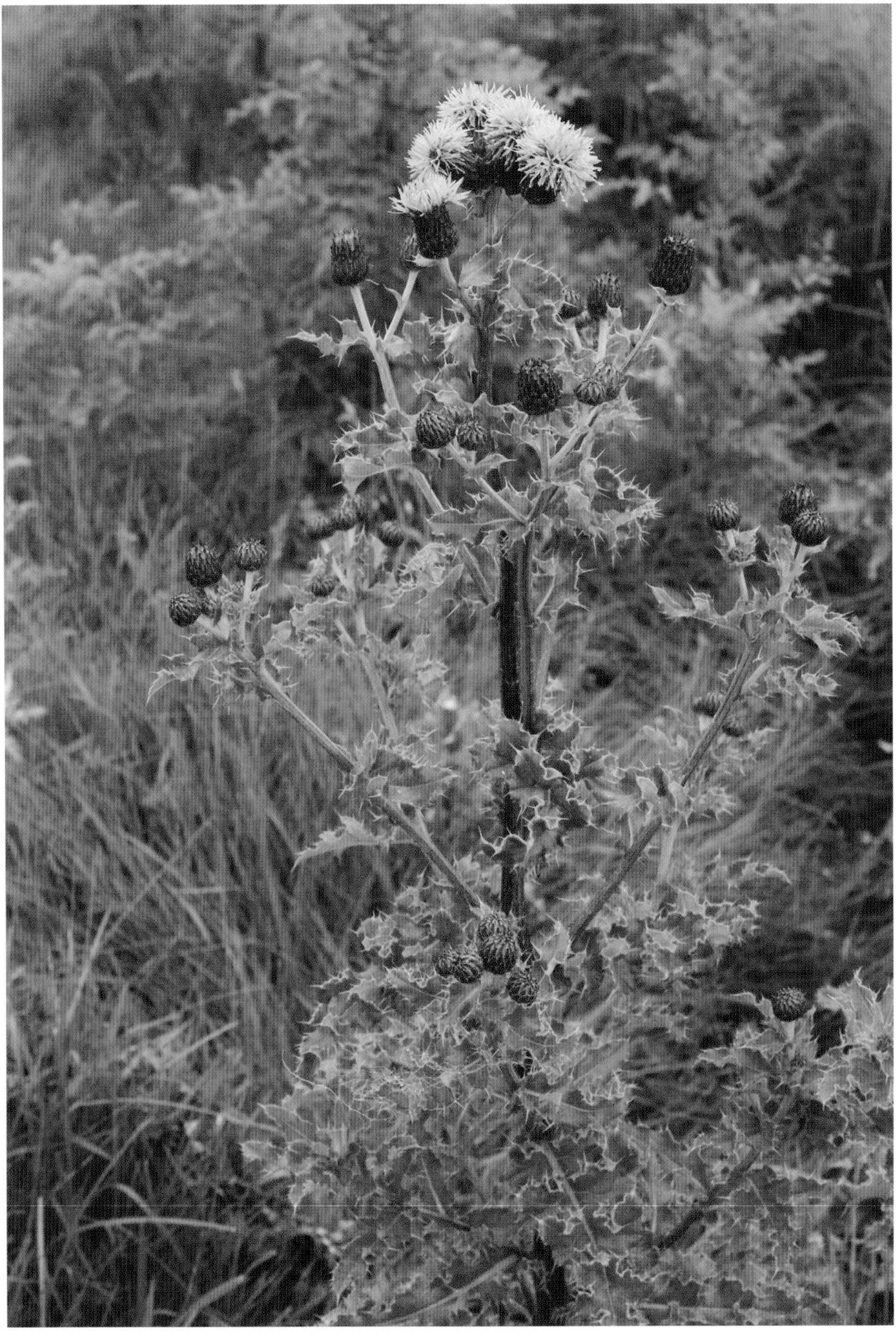

Plate 47 (l) **Creeping Thistle** (*Cirsium arvense*)
Flowerheads lilac, fragrant; stems spineless; leaves usually sharply spined. Well-established alien if not native. Waste ground, roadsides, sandy soils. Flowering late June–September. Photograph: roadside verge, Scalloway.

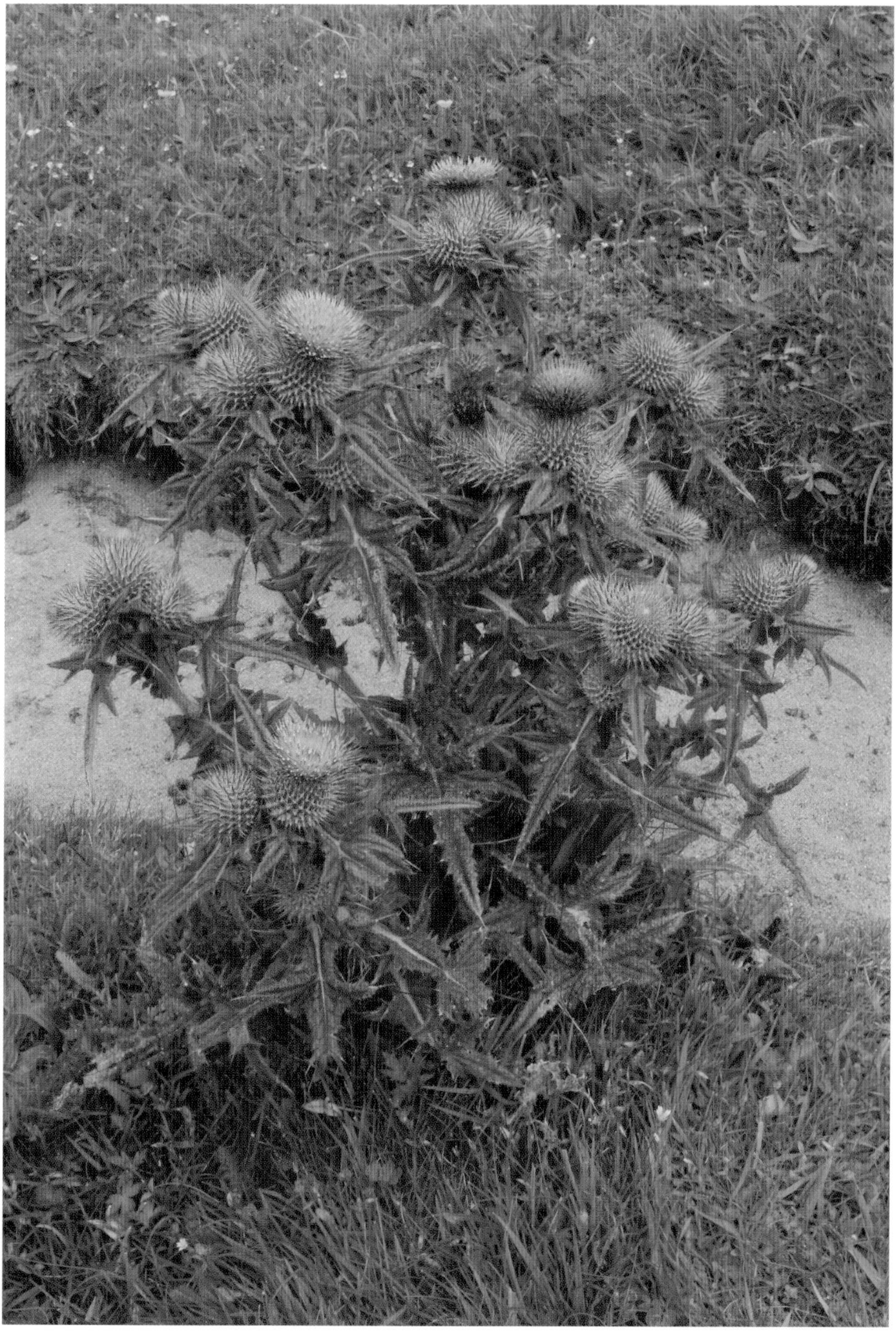

Plate 48 (l) **Spear Thistle** (*Cirsium vulgare*)
Flowerheads pinkish, large; stems cottony, sharply spiny; leaves deeply pinnately lobed, spiny. Native. Dry pastures, also occasionally on dry roadside verges, upper parts of beaches. Flowering late July-October. Photograph: grassland, Tresta, Fetlar.

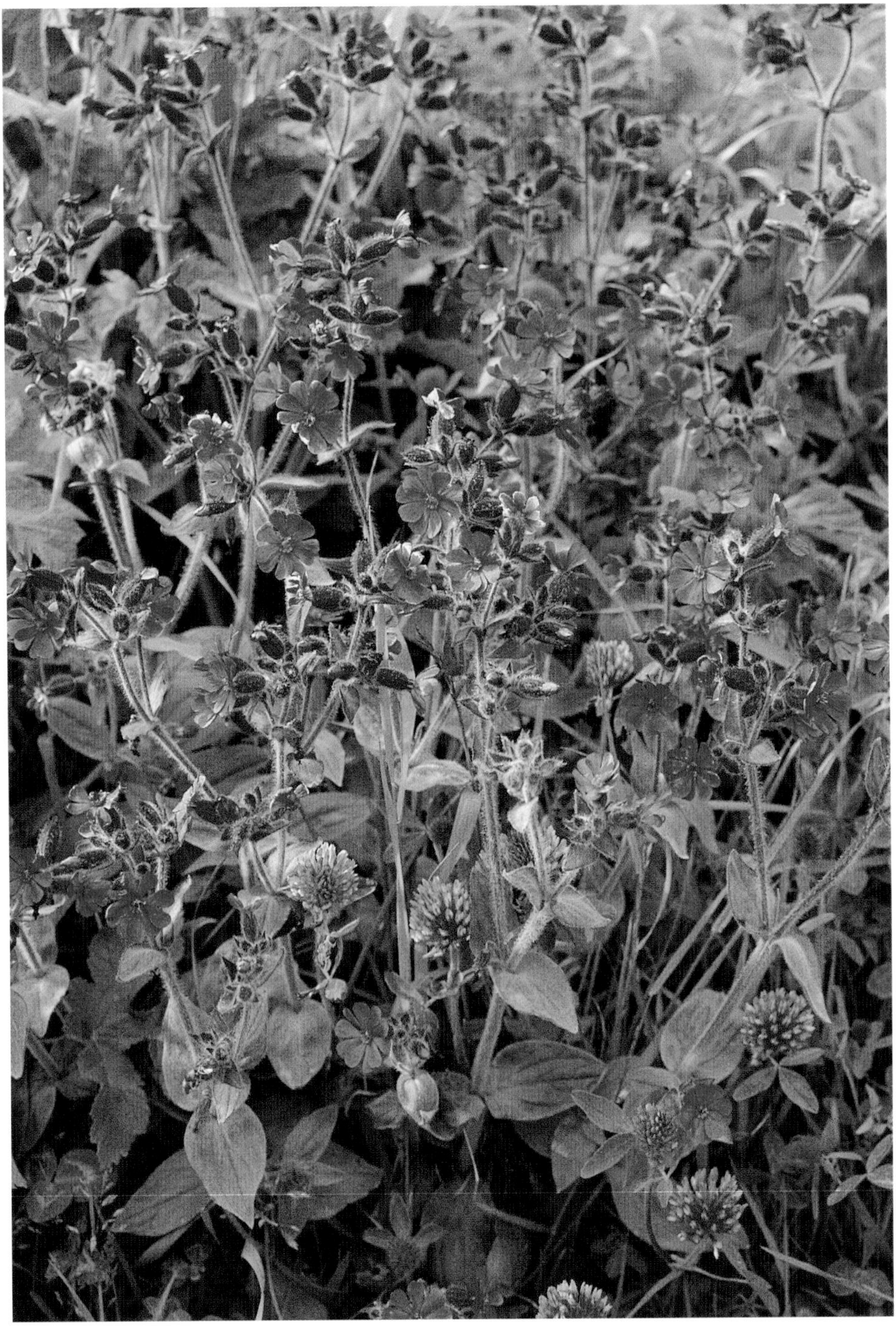

Plate 49 (m–l) **Red Campion** (*Silene dioica*) 'Sweet William'
Flowers pinkish-magenta, petals 5, deeply cleft; sepal tube enlarged, 5-toothed, hairy; stems erect, hairy; leaves oval, pointed. Native. Grassy sea-cliffs, coastal banks, roadsides, old quarries. Flowering May–September. Photograph: grassy bank, Easter Quarff.

Plate 50 (m) **Marsh Cinquefoil**
(*Potentilla palustris*)
Flowers reddish-maroon, star-shaped, petals 5, narrow, shorter than the sepals; leaves pinnate, leaflets oval, toothed. Native. Marshes, ditches, streamsides. Flowering late June–August. Photograph: bog, Burland, Trondra.

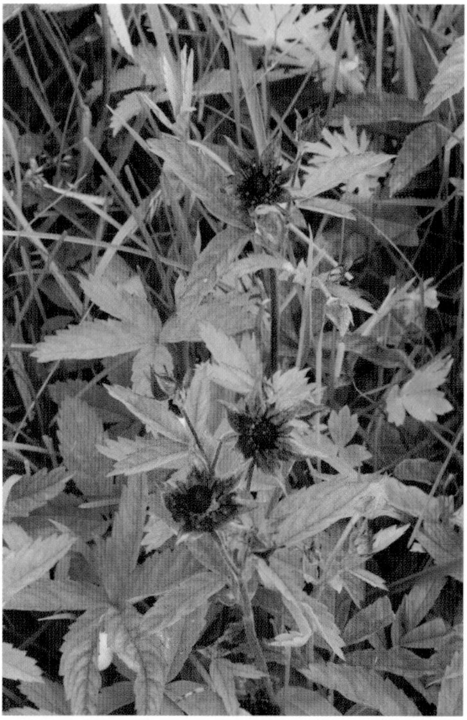

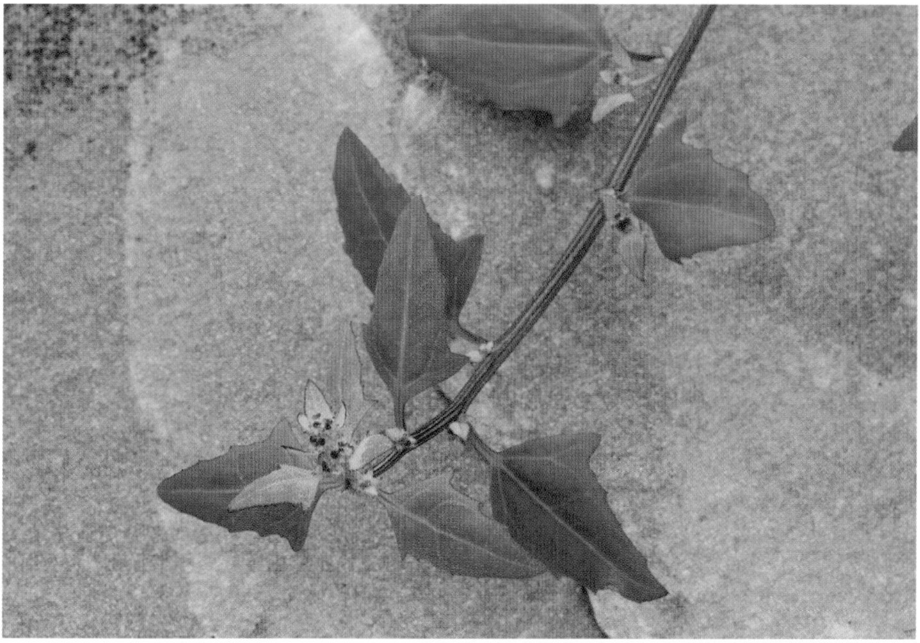

Plate 51 (s) **Orache** (*Atriplex prostrata* group)
Flowers often reddish, inconspicuous; seeds enclosed by 2 triangular bracts; stems striped red and green; leaves fleshy. Native. Shingly beaches and coastal rocks. Flowering August–September. Photograph: stony beach, Boddam.

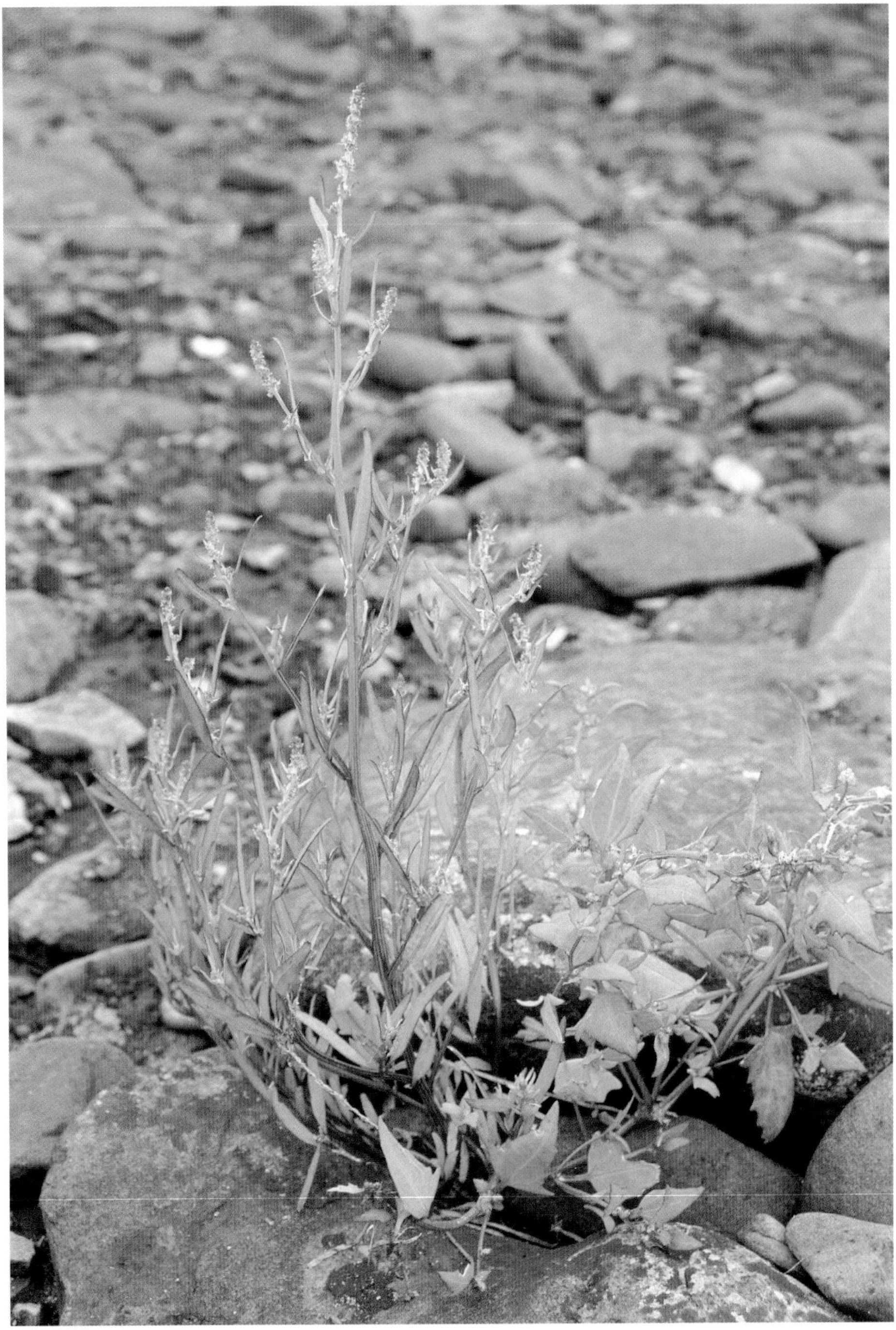

Plate 52 (m–l) **Grass-leaved Orache** (*Atriplex littoralis*)
Flowers inconspicuous; stems stout, much branched; leaves linear-oblong, the lower short-stalked, the upper unstalked. Native. Very rare, confined to South Mainland. Flowering late August–early September. Photograph: stony beach, Boddam.

Plate 53 (s) **Red Bartsia**
(*Odontites vernus* subsp. *litoralis*)
Flowers purplish-pink, 2-lipped, lower lip 3-lobed, in leafy one-sided spikes; stems often purplish tinged; leaves lanceolate, toothed, unstalked, opposite. Native. Pastures near the sea. Flowering July–early September. Photograph: near Sumburgh Hotel.

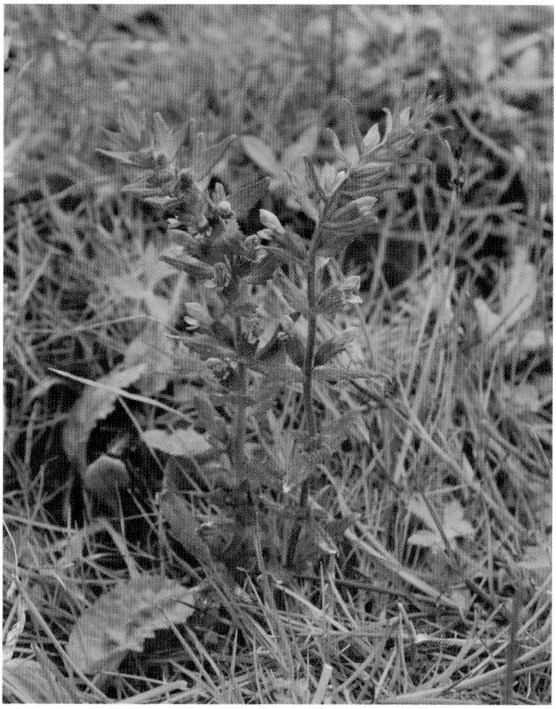

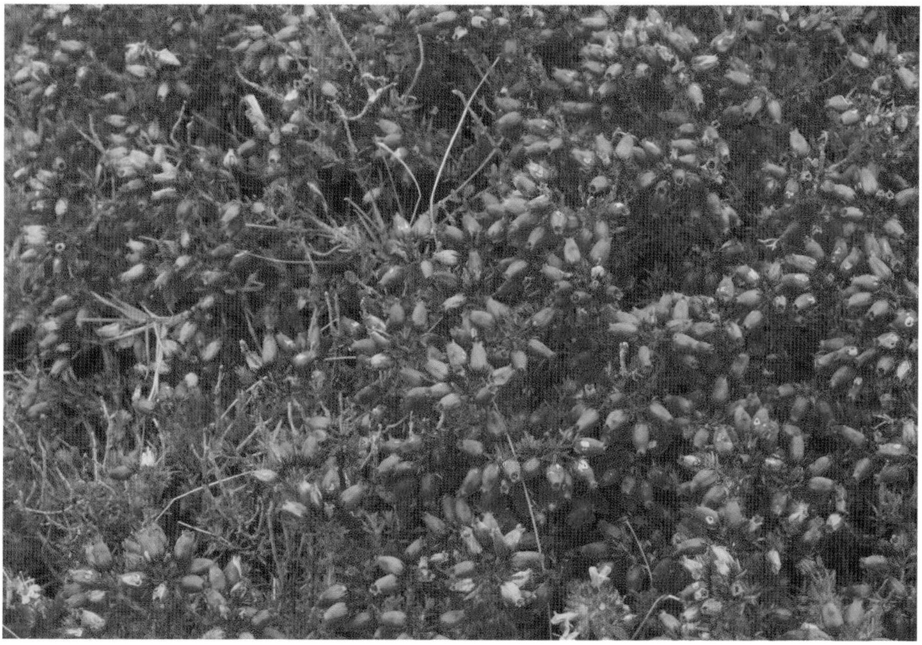

Plate 54 (s–m) **Bell Heather** (*Erica cinerea*)
Flowers reddish-purple, globular, in clusters on woody branching stems; leaves in whorls of 3 along the stem, dark green. Native. Dry heaths and moors, rocks. Flowering July–August. Photograph: moorland near Scalloway.

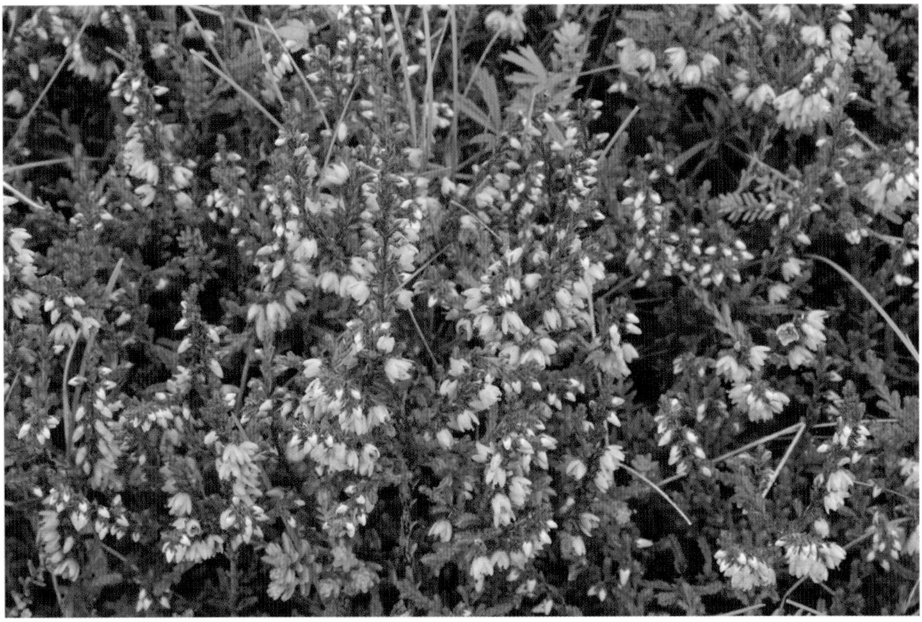

Plate 55 (s–l) **Heather** (*Calluna vulgaris*)
Flowers in spikes, petals (actually coloured sepals) 4, pale purple; stems branching, woody; leaves small, opposite, feather-like. Native. Dry or wet moors and heaths. Flowering July–August. Photograph: heather moorland near Scalloway.

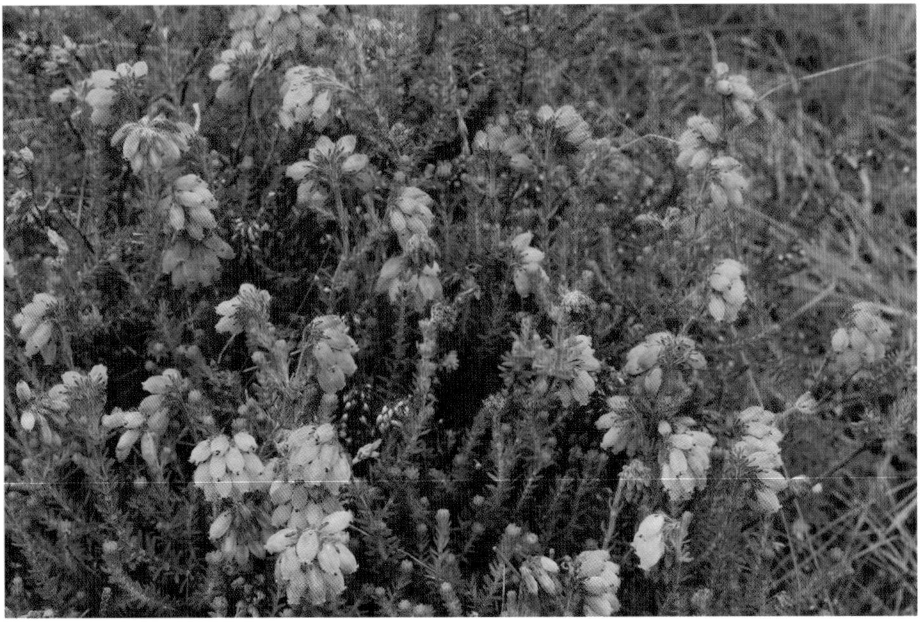

Plate 56 (s–m) **Cross-leaved Heath** (*Erica tetralix*)
Flowers rose-pink, paler beneath, globular, clustered; stems slender, branching; leaves narrow, pointed, greyish-green, in whorls of 4 along the stem. Native. Wet moors and heaths. Flowering July–September. Photograph: side of peaty ditch, Trondra.

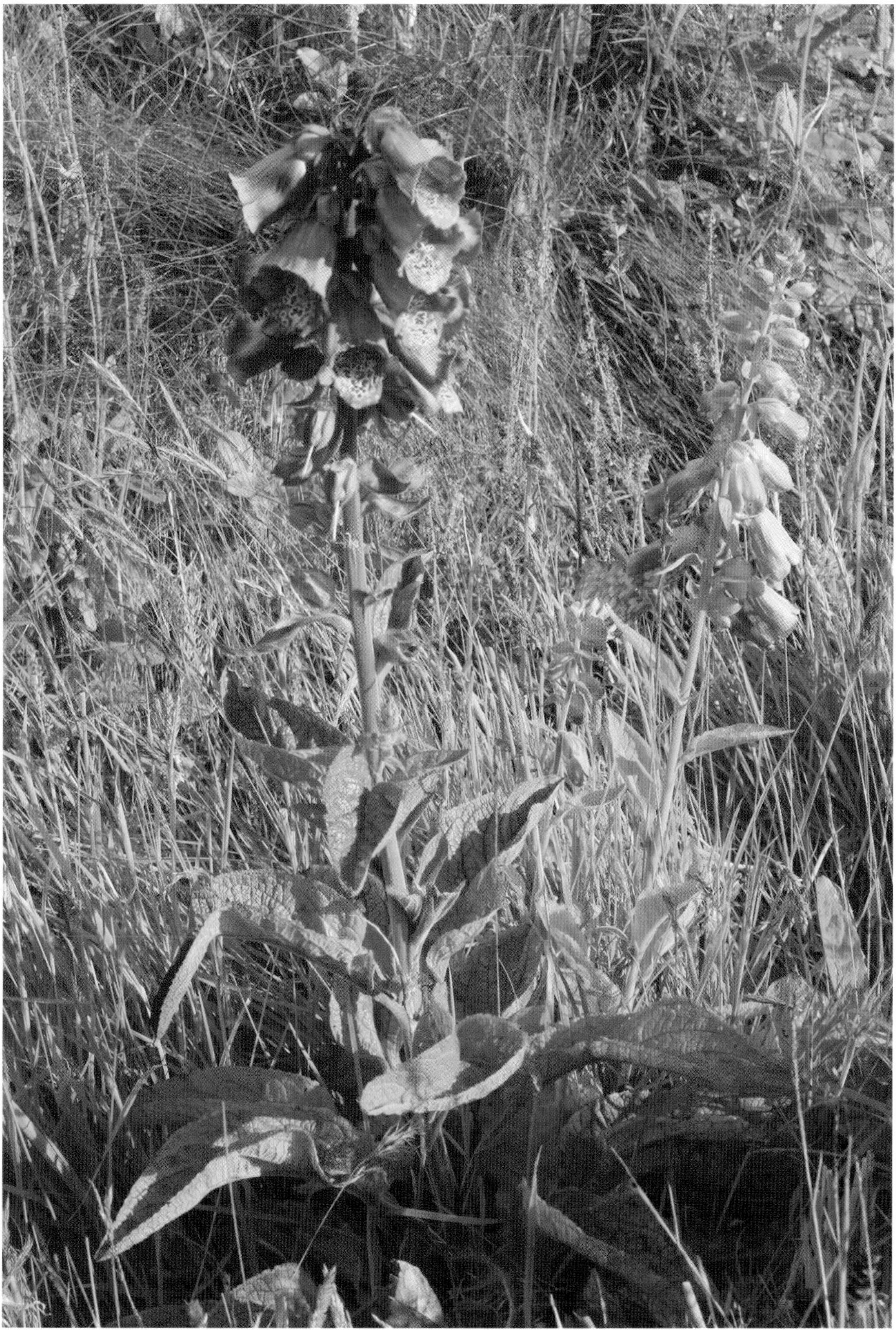

Plate 57 (l) **Foxglove** (*Digitalis purpurea*)
Flowers pinkish-purple, tubular, 2-lipped, in long tapering spikes. Casual. Escape or outcast, near houses, waste ground, roadside verges, old quarries. Flowering July–August. Photograph: roadside verge, Trondra.

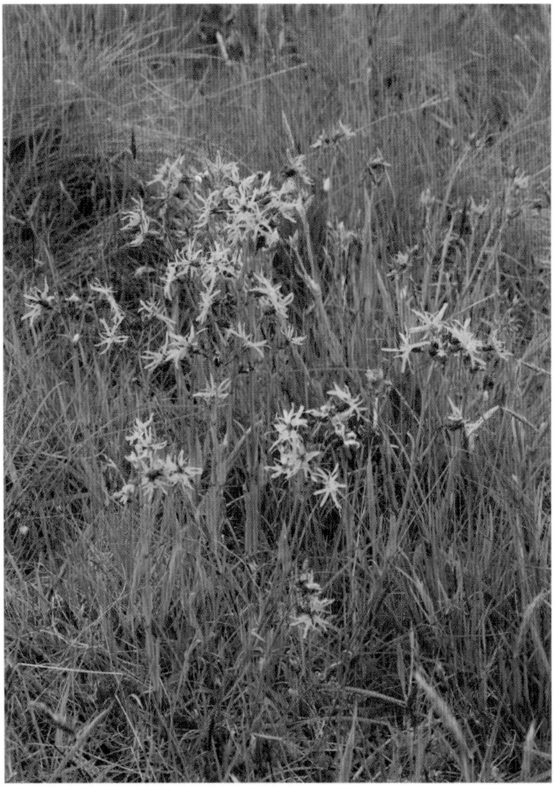

Plate 58 (m) **Ragged-Robin** (*Lychnis flos-cuculi*)
Flowers pink in forked clusters, petals 5, each divided into 4 narrow lobes; calyx 5-toothed, maroon, striped. Stems slender, slightly hairy; leaves lanceolate, paired. Native. Damp pastures, marshes. Flowering June–August. Photograph: damp grassy area, Burland, Trondra.

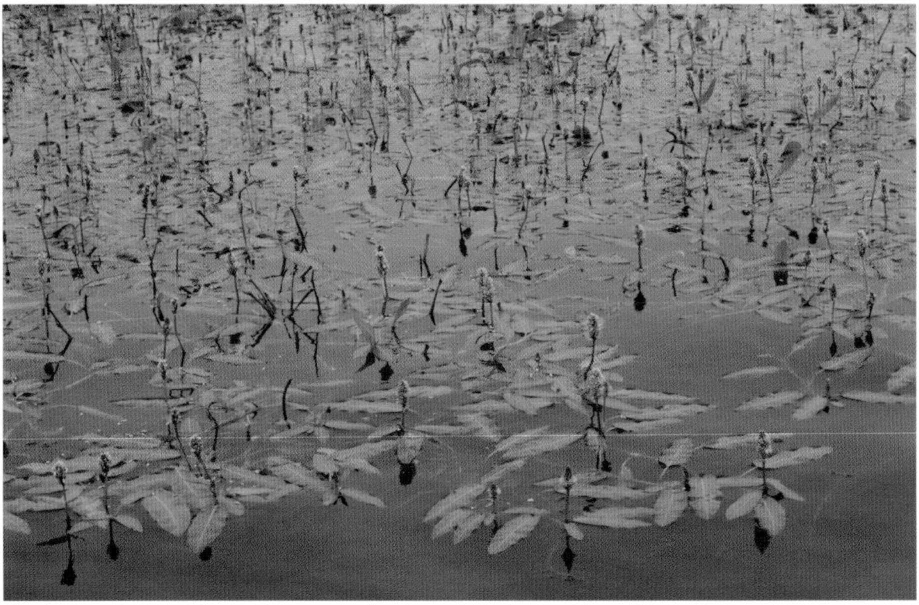

Plate 59 (s–m) **Amphibious Bistort** (*Persicaria amphibia*)
It is the aquatic form which is shown in this photograph. Flowers pink, in dense spikes. Native. Lochs, streams, ditches. Flowering July–August. Photograph: Loch of Gards, Scatness.

Plate 60 (s) **Redshank**
(*Persicaria maculosa*)
Flowers pink or white, in densely crowded spikes; stems branched, reddish. Leaves lanceolate, often black-blotched. Well-established alien. Arable ground, beaches, margins of lochs. Flowering July–early October. Photograph: cultivated field, Quendale.

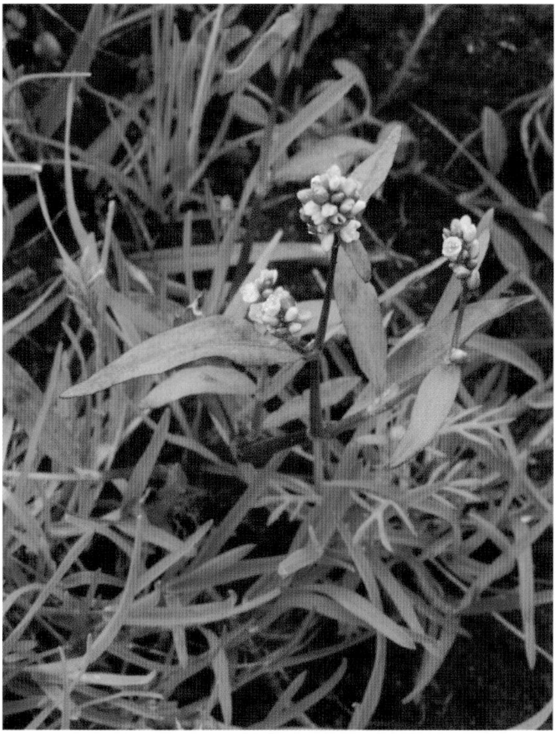

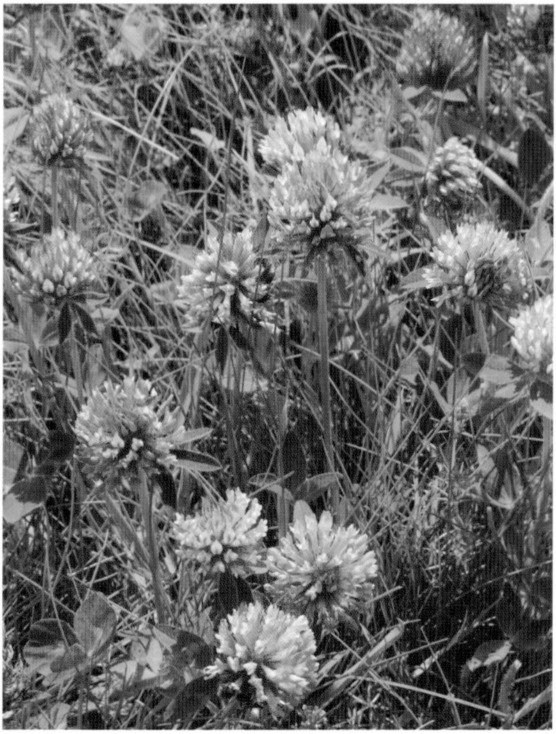

Plate 61 (m) **Red Clover**
(*Trifolium pratense*)
Flowers pinkish-purple, in globular clusters; stems hairy; all leaves trifoliate, the lower on long stalks, the two just below the flowerhead almost stalkless. Native and alien. Dry pastures, grassy sea-cliffs, roadsides verges. Flowering late May–August. Photograph: coastal grassland, Meal, Hamnavoe.

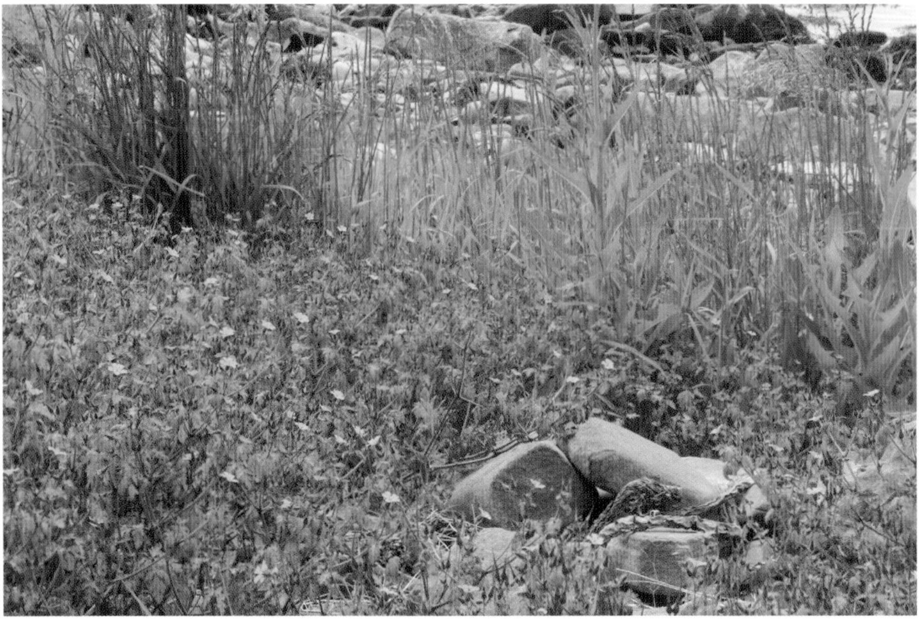

Plate 62 (m–l) **Herb-Robert** (*Geranium robertianum*)
Flowers pink, 15 mm wide, in pairs, petals 5; calyx red, hairy, stems hairy; leaves deeply palmately lobed, fern-like, greenish-red. A probable native. Confined to a shingly beach at Boddam. Flowering late May–September. Photograph: shingly beach, Boddam.

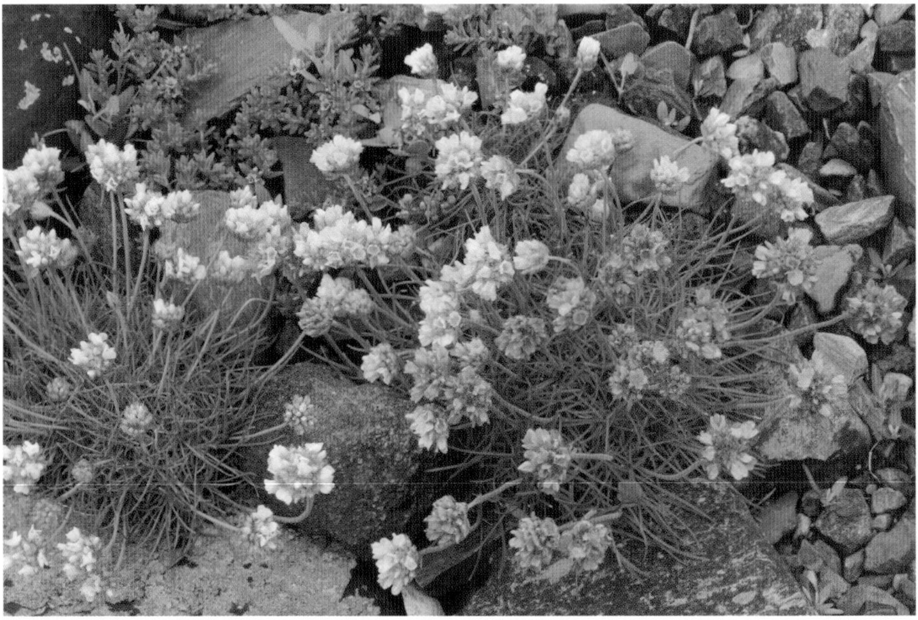

Plate 63 (s–m) **Thrift** (*Armeria maritima* subsp. *maritima*) 'Banksflooer'
Flowers rose-pink, closely packed in a rounded flowerhead; involucre brown, papery; base of plant cushion-like, leaves very narrow. Native. Grassy coastal banks, cliff-tops, rocks, beaches, stony ground. Flowering late May–July. Photograph: stony beach, East Voe of Scalloway.

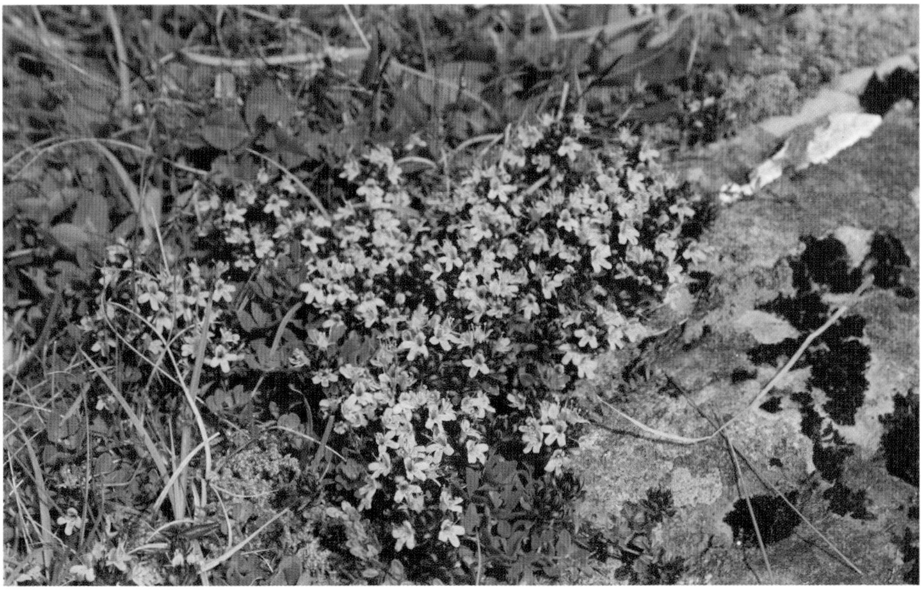

Plate 64 (s) **Wild Thyme** (*Thymus polytrichus*) 'Taegirse'
Flowers pinkish-purple, in clusters, 2-lipped; stems four-angled, hairy on two opposite sides; leaves tiny, oval, opposite, fringed with hairs. A slightly woody, aromatic native of dry, grassy banks, pastures, stony heaths, granite and serpentine gravel. Flowering June–September. Photograph: grassy coastal cliffs, St Ninian's Bay.

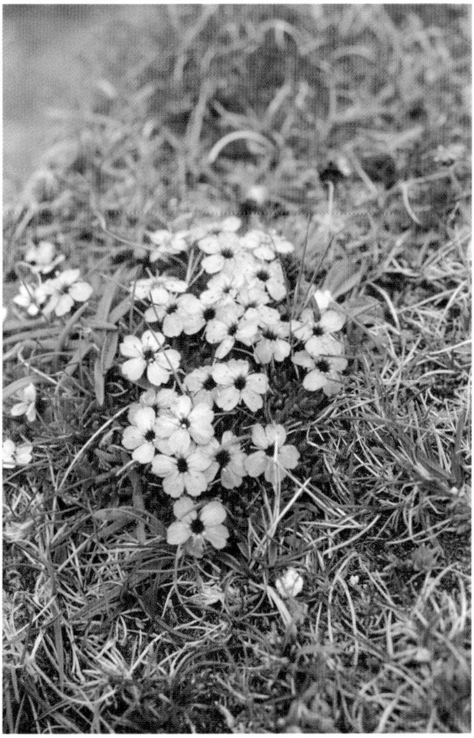

Plate 65 (s) **Moss Campion** (*Silene acaulis*)
Flowers pink, almost stalkless on rounded moss-like cushions, petals 5, notched. Native. Rocky slopes near the sea, cliff-tops, stony ground. Flowering late April–June. Photograph: coastal grassland with rocky outcrops, West Burra.

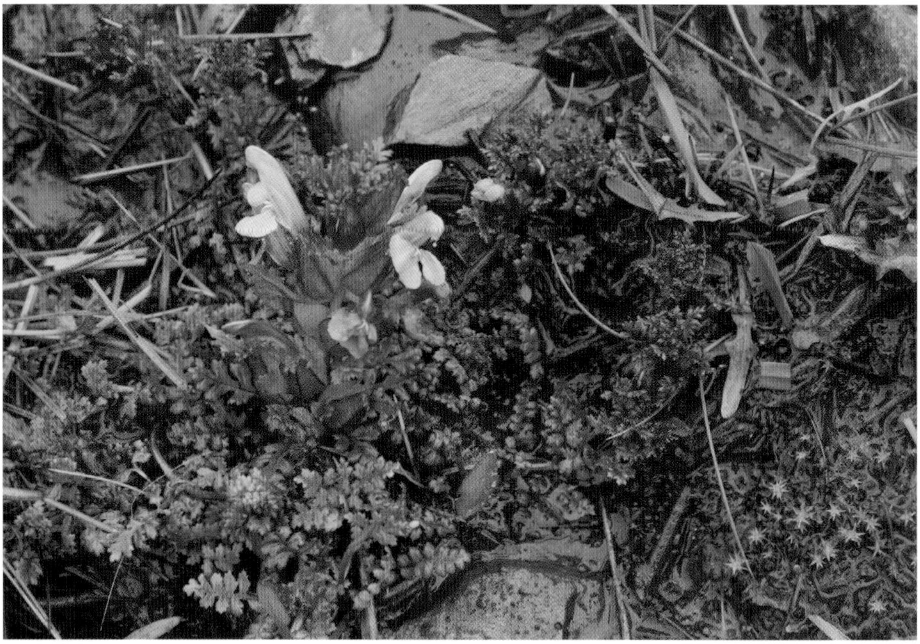

Plate 66 (s) **Lousewort** (*Pedicularis sylvatica* subsp. *sylvatica*) 'Sookies'
Flowers bright pink, 2-lipped; stems numerous, unbranched. Native. Wet pastures, damp heaths. Flowering late May–August. Photograph: ditch, Wester Quarff.

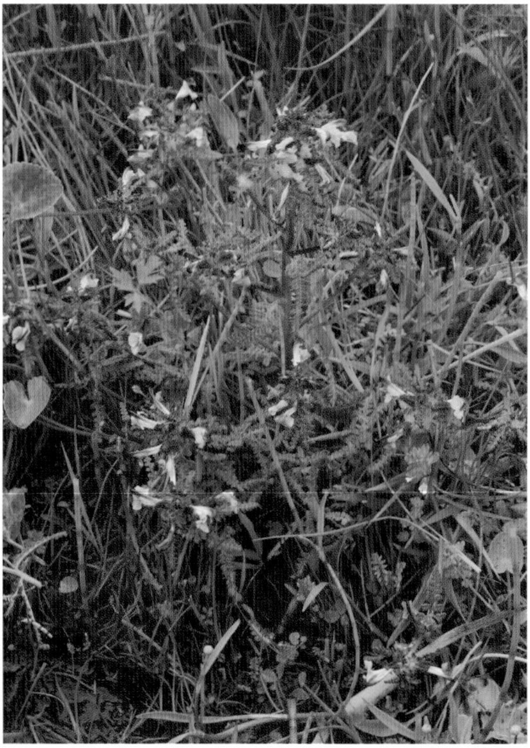

Plate 67 (m) **Marsh Lousewort** (*Pedicularis palustris*)
Flowers pinkish-purple, 2-lipped; stems much-branched; leaves pinnate. Native. Marshes. Flowering June–August. Photograph: marsh, Burland, Trondra.

Plate 68 (m) **Northern Knotgrass**
(*Polygonum boreale*)
Flowers small, pinkish-white, in leaf-axils. Well-established alien. Cultivated ground, beaches. Flowering June–September. Photograph: cultivated field, Scalloway.

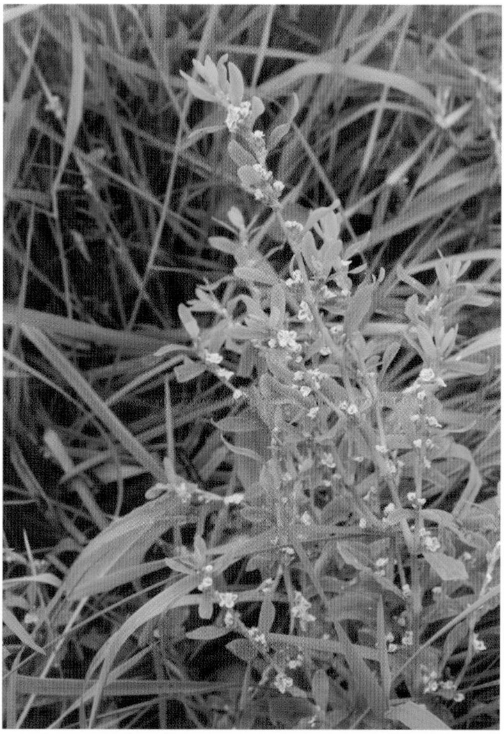

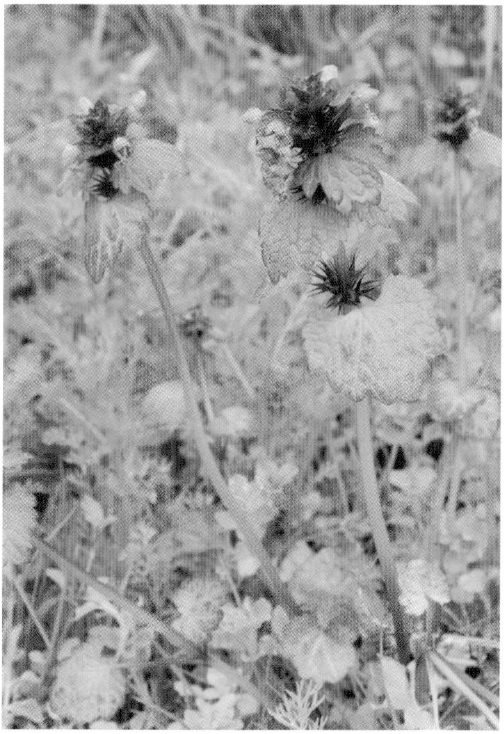

Plate 69 (s–m) **Red Dead-nettle**
(*Lamium purpureum*)
Flowers pinkish-purple, 2-lipped; stems square; leaves heart-shaped, opposite, all stalked. Well-established alien. Cultivated and waste ground. Flowering May–September. Photograph: waste ground, Scalloway.

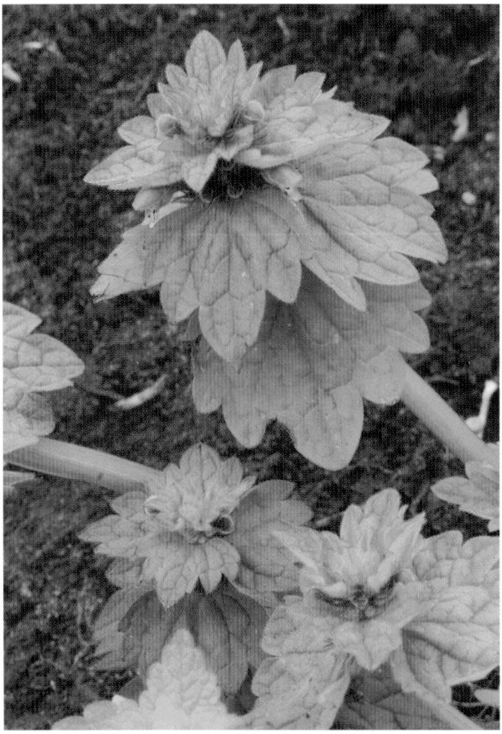

Plate 70 (s–m)
Northern Dead-nettle
(*Lamium confertum*)
Flowers pinkish-purple, in whorls, calyx with appressed hairs, teeth longer than corolla tube; leaves triangular. Well-established alien. Cultivated ground, waste ground. Flowering late May–early October. Photograph: cultivated field, Quendale.

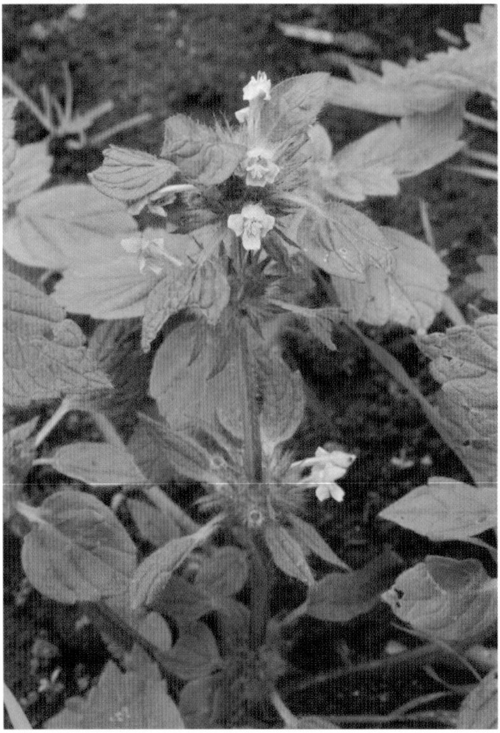

Plate 71 (m) **Common Hemp-nettle**
(*Galeopsis tetrahit*)
Flowers pinkish-purple, sometimes white, in whorls at base of upper leaves, 2-lipped with lower lip very obviously 3-lobed; stems square, roughly hairy, swollen at leaf junctions; leaves broadly lanceolate, toothed, stalked. Well-established alien. Arable land, waste ground. Flowering July–September. Photograph: cultivated field, Quendale.

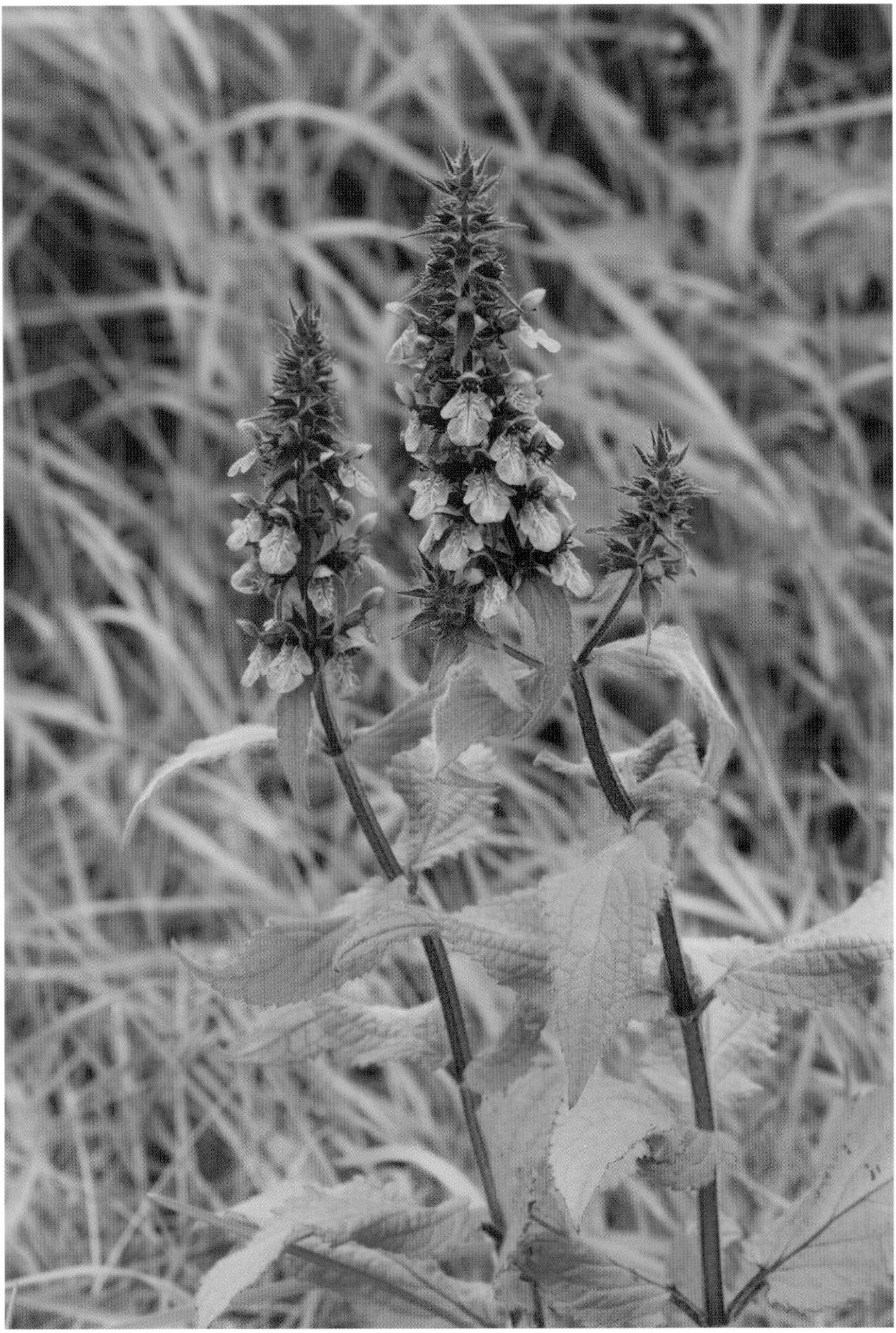

Plate 72 (m–l) **Hybrid Woundwort** (*Stachys × ambigua*)
Flowers pinkish-red, 2-lipped; stems square; leaves, stalked, opposite, oblong-lanceolate, pointed. Well-established alien. Cultivated land, roadside verges, waste ground. Flowering July–September. Photograph: roadside verge, Berry Farm, Scalloway.

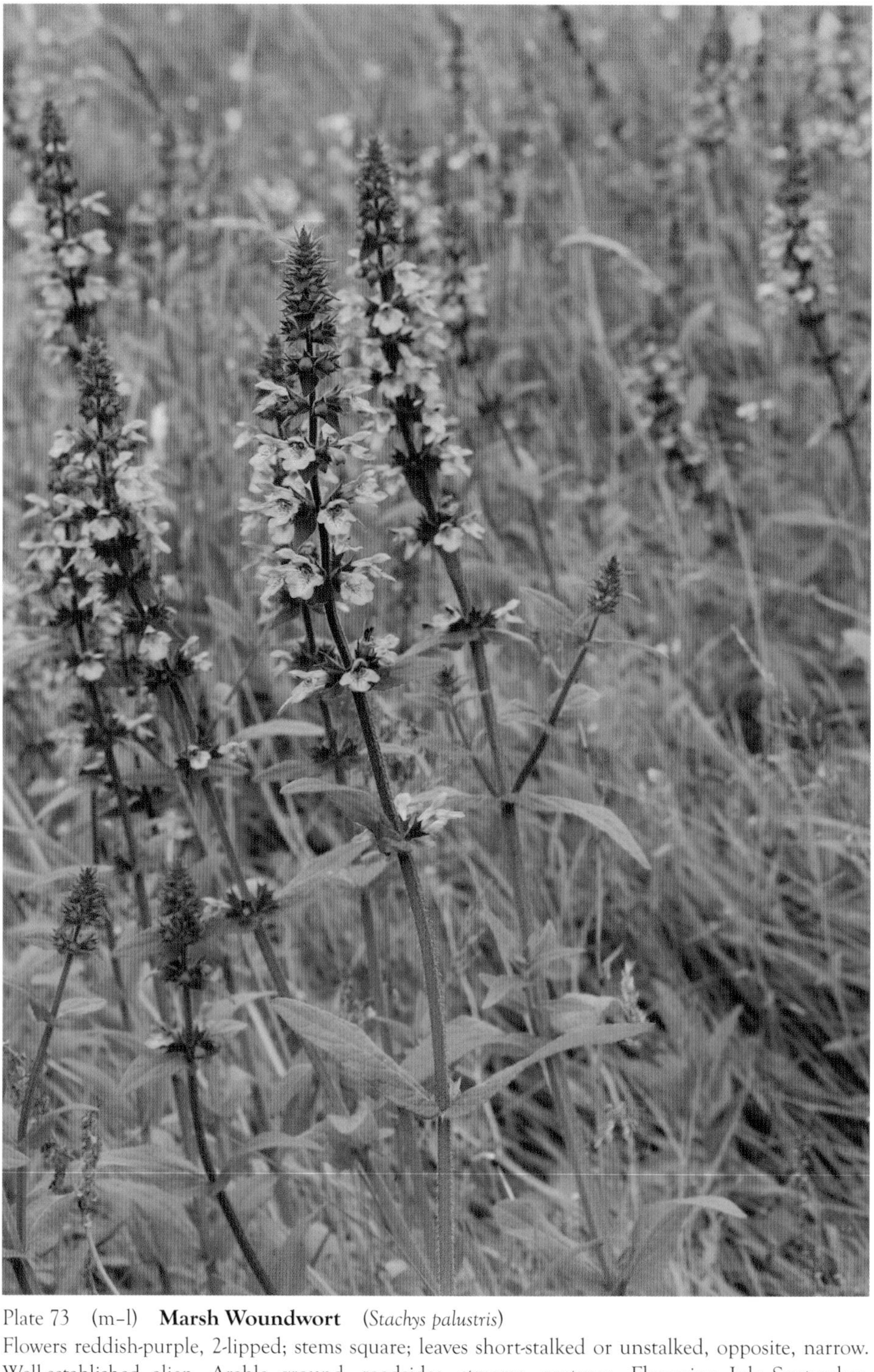

Plate 73 (m–l) **Marsh Woundwort** (*Stachys palustris*)
Flowers reddish-purple, 2-lipped; stems square; leaves short-stalked or unstalked, opposite, narrow. Well-established alien. Arable ground, roadsides, streams, pastures. Flowering July–September. Photograph: rough pasture above Scarfa Taing, Muckle Roe.

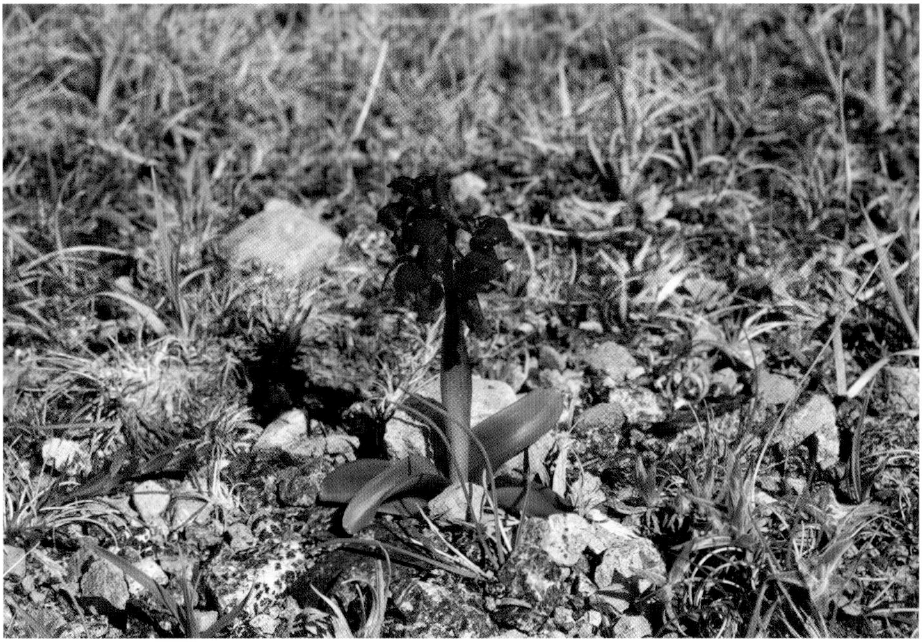

Plate 74 (s) **Early-purple Orchid** (*Orchis mascula*)
Flowers purplish, with long spur; leaves oblong, mostly at the base of the plant; stems with small sheathing leaves. Native. Serpentine gravel in Unst and very rarely in limestone grassland elsewhere. Flowering late May–early June. Photograph: Keen of Hamar, Unst.

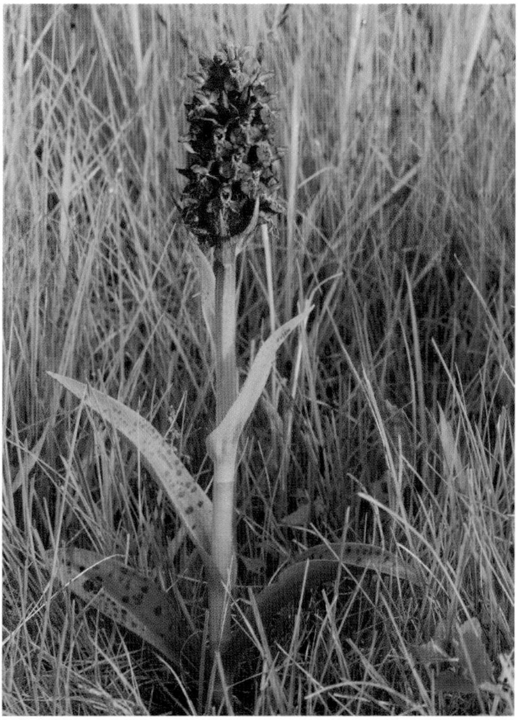

Plate 75 (s–m)
Northern Marsh-orchid
(*Dactylorhiza purpurella*)
Flowers rich purple, in spikes; leaves spotted. Native. Marshes and damp pastures, but also occasionally on dry roadside verges. Flowering late May–July. Photograph: damp meadow, Tingwall.

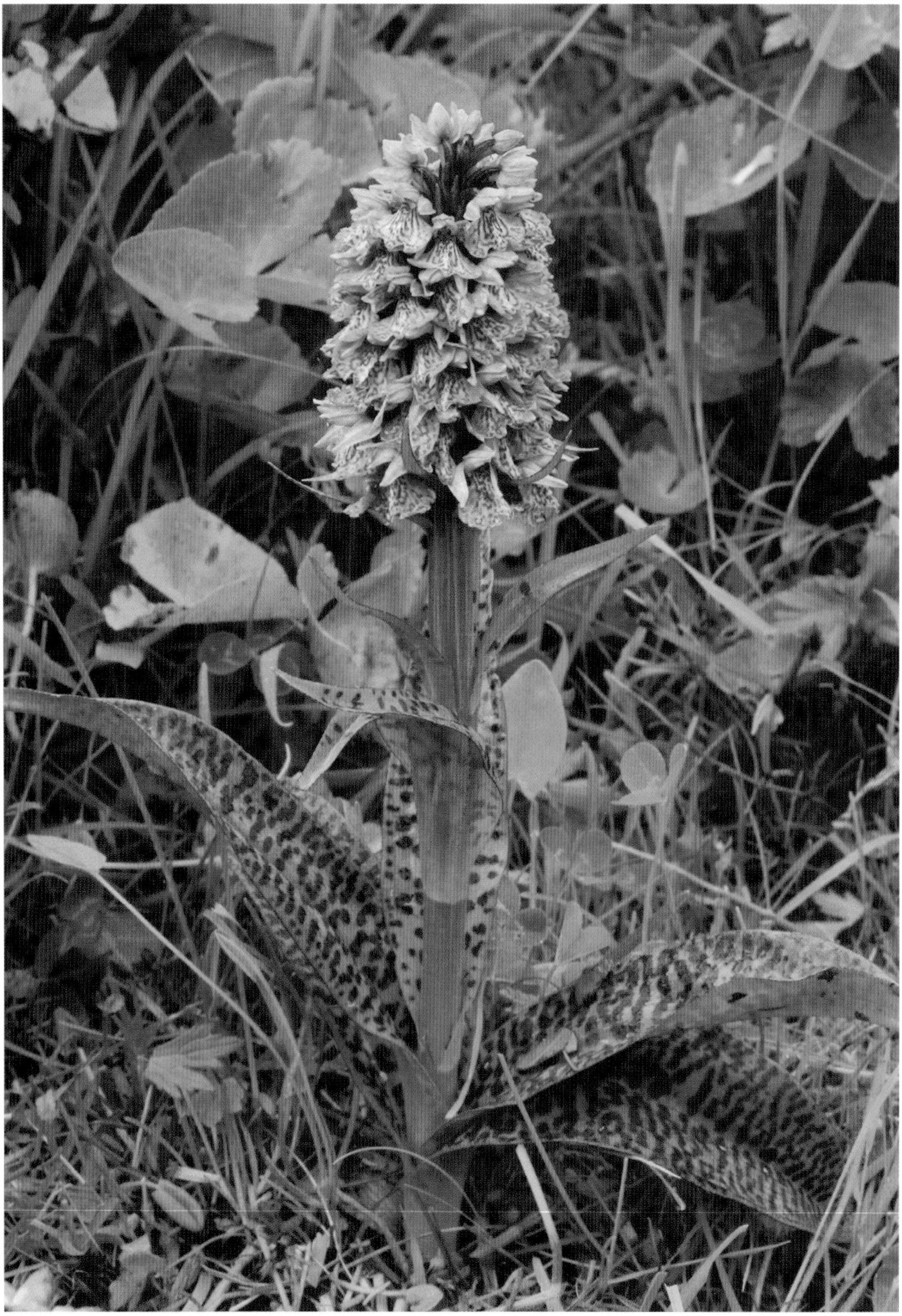

Plate 76 (m) **Dactylorhiza × formosa**

Flowers variable in colour but usually bright purplish-lilac. A tall, showy plant, a hybrid between heath spotted-orchid and northern marsh-orchid. It usually grows alongside or near the parent plants and has a clear preference for the wetter ground favoured by the latter parent. Flowering late May–July. Photograph: marsh, Burland, Trondra.

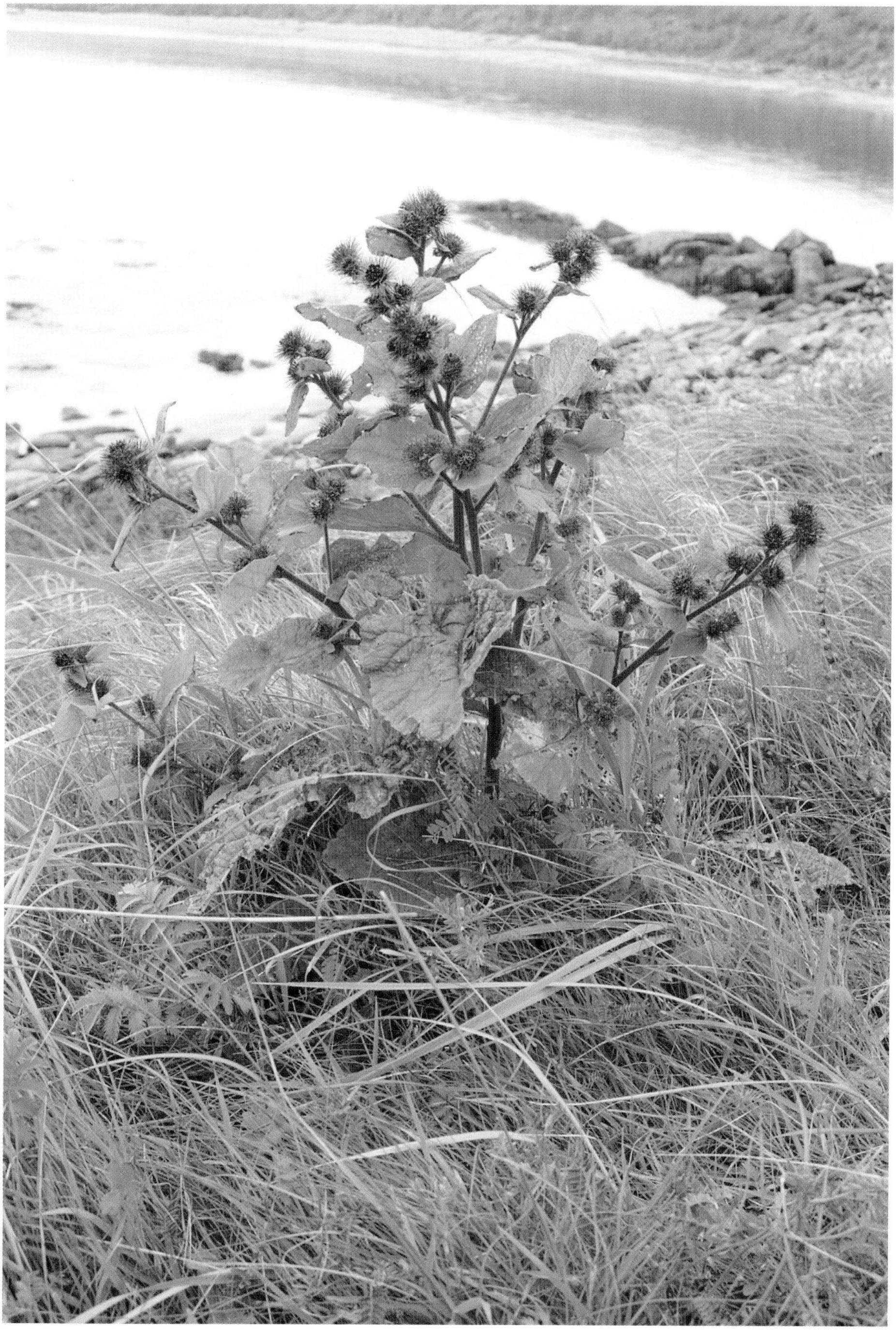

Plate 77 (l) **Wood Burdock** (*Arctium nemorosum*)
Flowerheads reddish-purple, 3–4 cm wide; stems robust. Very rare native, also a very rare casual. Sandy ground. Flowering late August–September. Photograph: boat-ramp at the north side of Grutness Voe, Sumburgh.

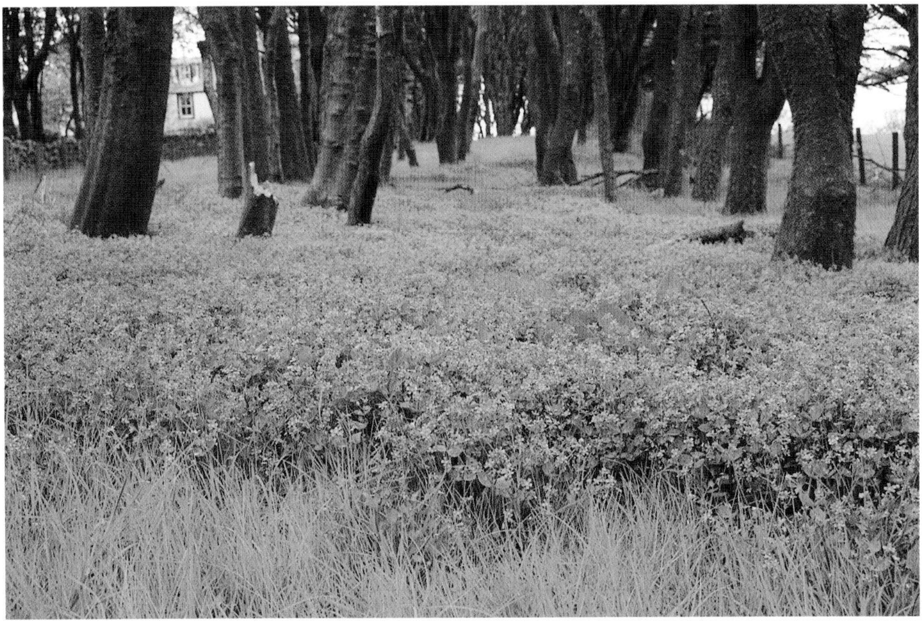

Plate 78 (m) **Pink Purslane** (*Claytonia sibirica*)
Flowers pink, sometimes white, petals 5, deeply notched; stems hairless; leaves rounded, fleshy, unstalked. Well-established alien. Garden outcast. Abundant in the roadside wood near Kergord House. Flowering late May–August. Photograph: woodland, Kergord, Weisdale.

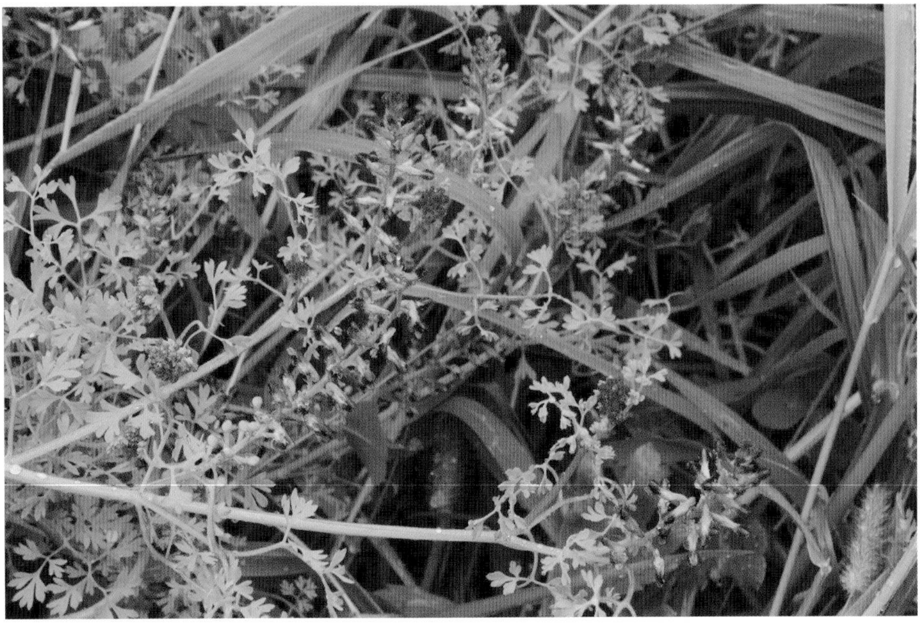

Plate 79 (m) **Common Fumitory** (*Fumaria officinalis* subsp. *officinalis*)
Flowers pinkish, in spikes, tubular, tips tinged purple, spur rounded; stems weak, straggly, hairless; leaves pinnately lobed, fern-like, smoky-green. Well-established alien. In or near arable land. Flowering June–early October. Photograph: cultivated field, Scalloway.

Plate 80 (s) **Purple Saxifrage** (*Saxifraga oppositifolia*)
Flowers rosy-purple, petals 5; leaves small, opposite, unstalked. A rare plant of rocky, mainly coastal areas of Northmavine, extremely scarce elsewhere. Native. Flowering late March–June. Photograph: Snarraness peninsula, West Mainland.

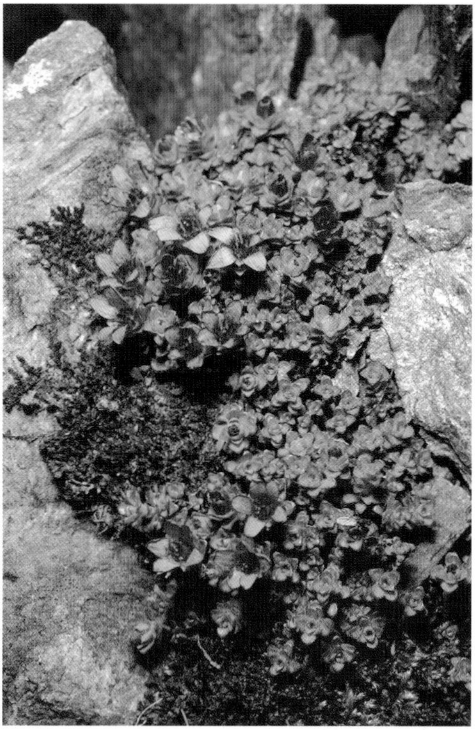

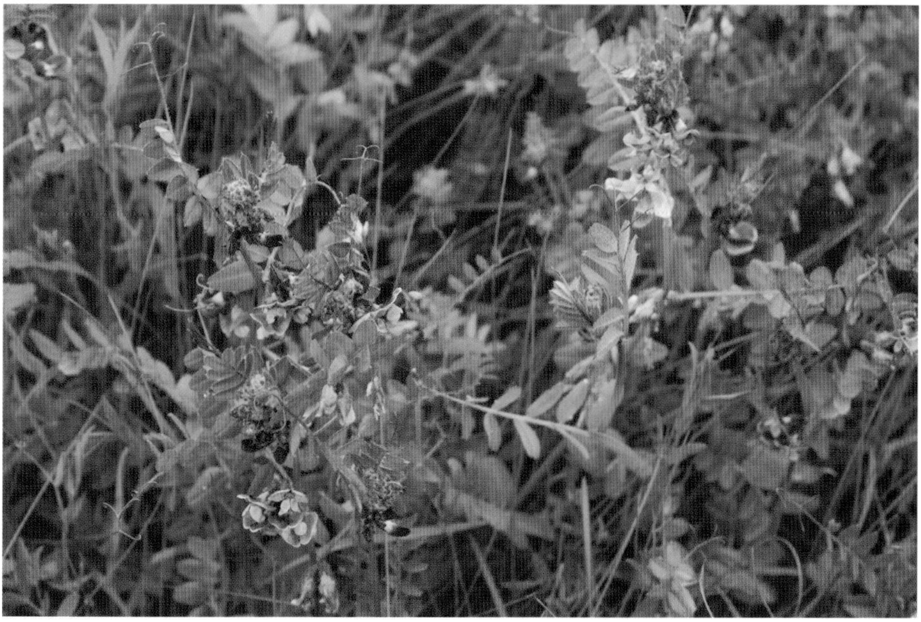

Plate 81 (m) **Bush Vetch** (*Vicia sepium*)
Flowers purplish, in spikes of 2–6 blooms; stems weak, clambering; leaves pinnate, ending in tendrils, leaflets oval, stipules 2-lobed. Native, possibly alien in some places. Grassy roadside verges, arable land. Flowering late June–August. Photograph: grassy sides of ditch by roadside, Quendale.

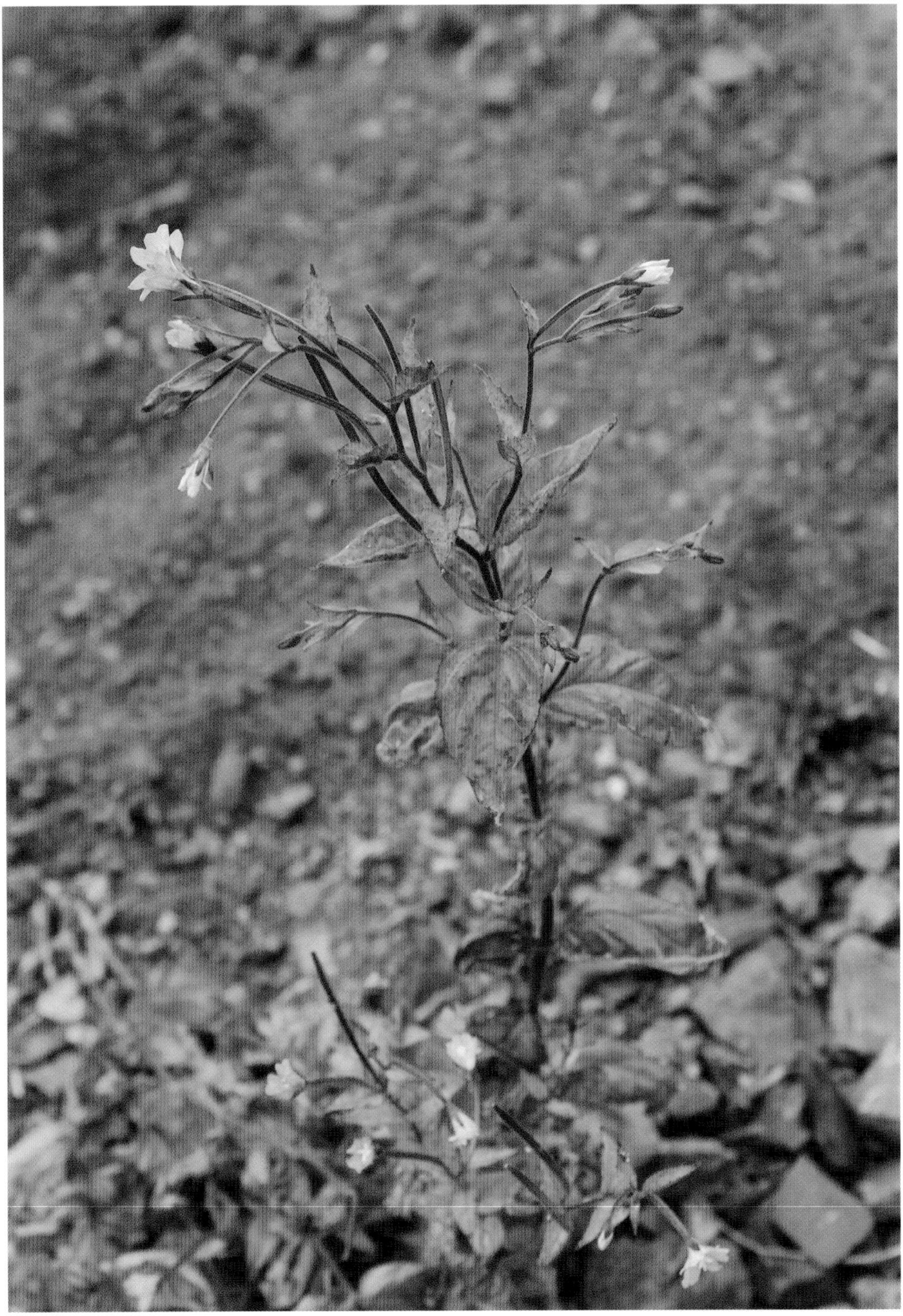

Plate 82 (m) **Broad-leaved Willowherb** (*Epilobium montanum*)
Flowers pinkish-purple, 6–9 mm wide, in spikes, petals 4, well-notched; leaves broadly lanceolate, opposite. Apparently native in one or two places; otherwise a well-established alien of gardens, and waste and rubbly places. Flowering July–early October. Photograph: waste ground, Port Arthur, Scalloway.

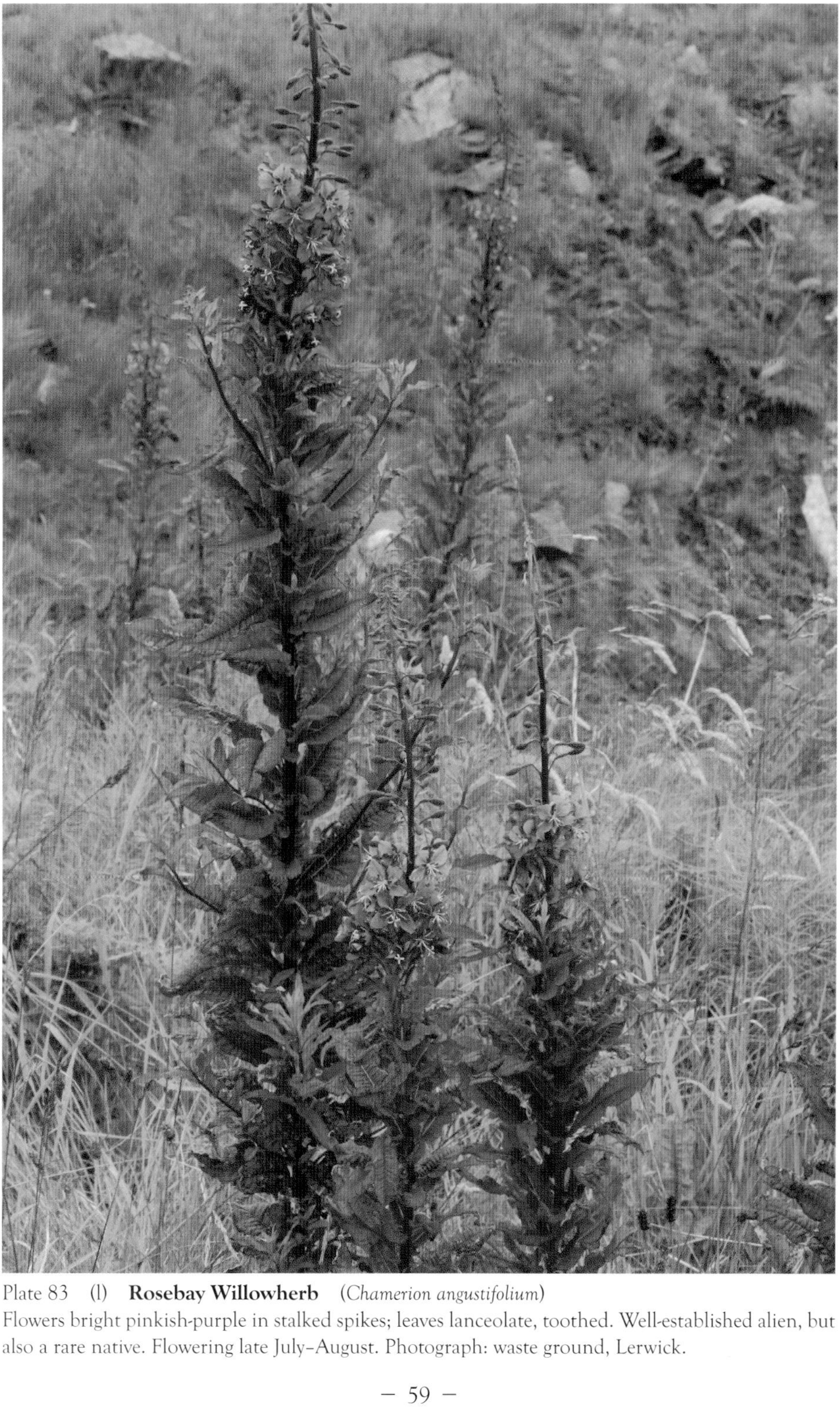

Plate 83 (l) **Rosebay Willowherb** (*Chamerion angustifolium*)
Flowers bright pinkish-purple in stalked spikes; leaves lanceolate, toothed. Well-established alien, but also a rare native. Flowering late July–August. Photograph: waste ground, Lerwick.

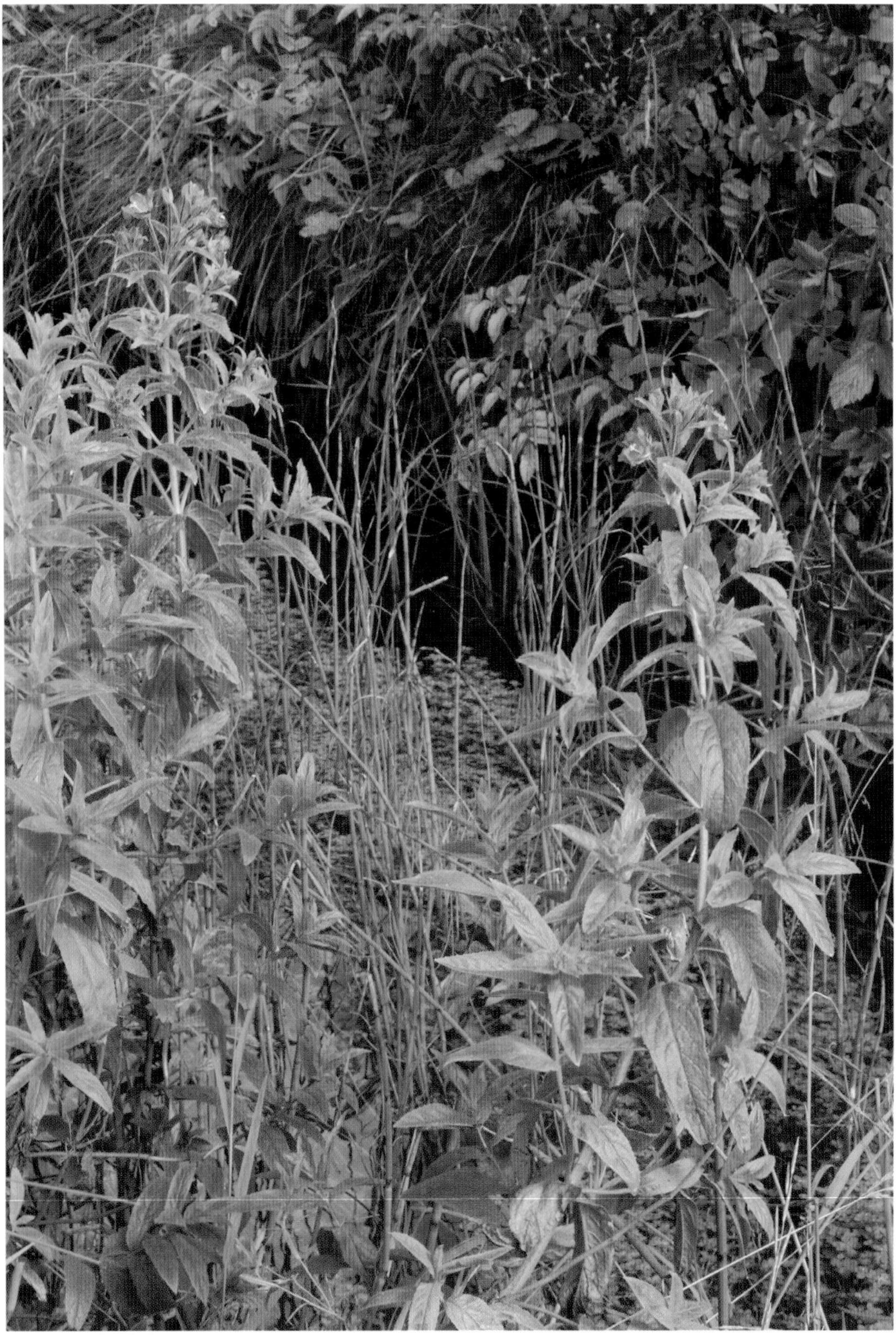

Plate 84 (l) **Great Willowherb** (*Epilobium hirsutum*)
Flowers purplish-pink, petals 5, in stalked spikes; stems hairy; leaves lanceolate, opposite, toothed, unstalked. Well-established alien. Streams, ditches, waste ground. Flowering August–September. Photograph: burn running into Strand Loch, Tingwall.

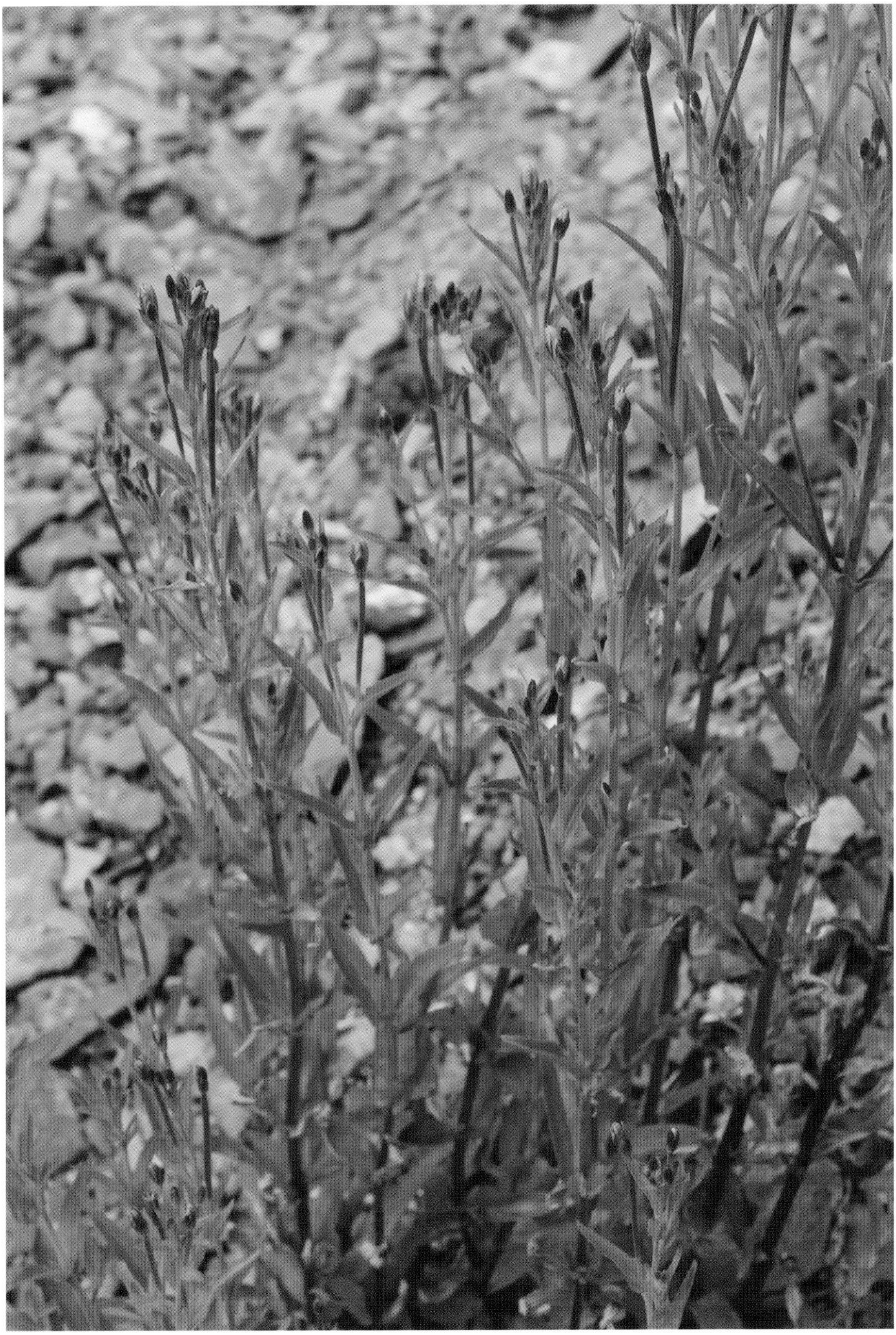

Plate 85 (m–l) **Short-fruited Willowherb** (*Epilobium obscurum*)
Flowers deep rose, petals 4, notched; leaves lanceolate, toothed, unstalked. Well-established alien. Ditches, old walls, waste ground. Flowering July–early September. Photograph: waste ground, Port Arthur, Scalloway.

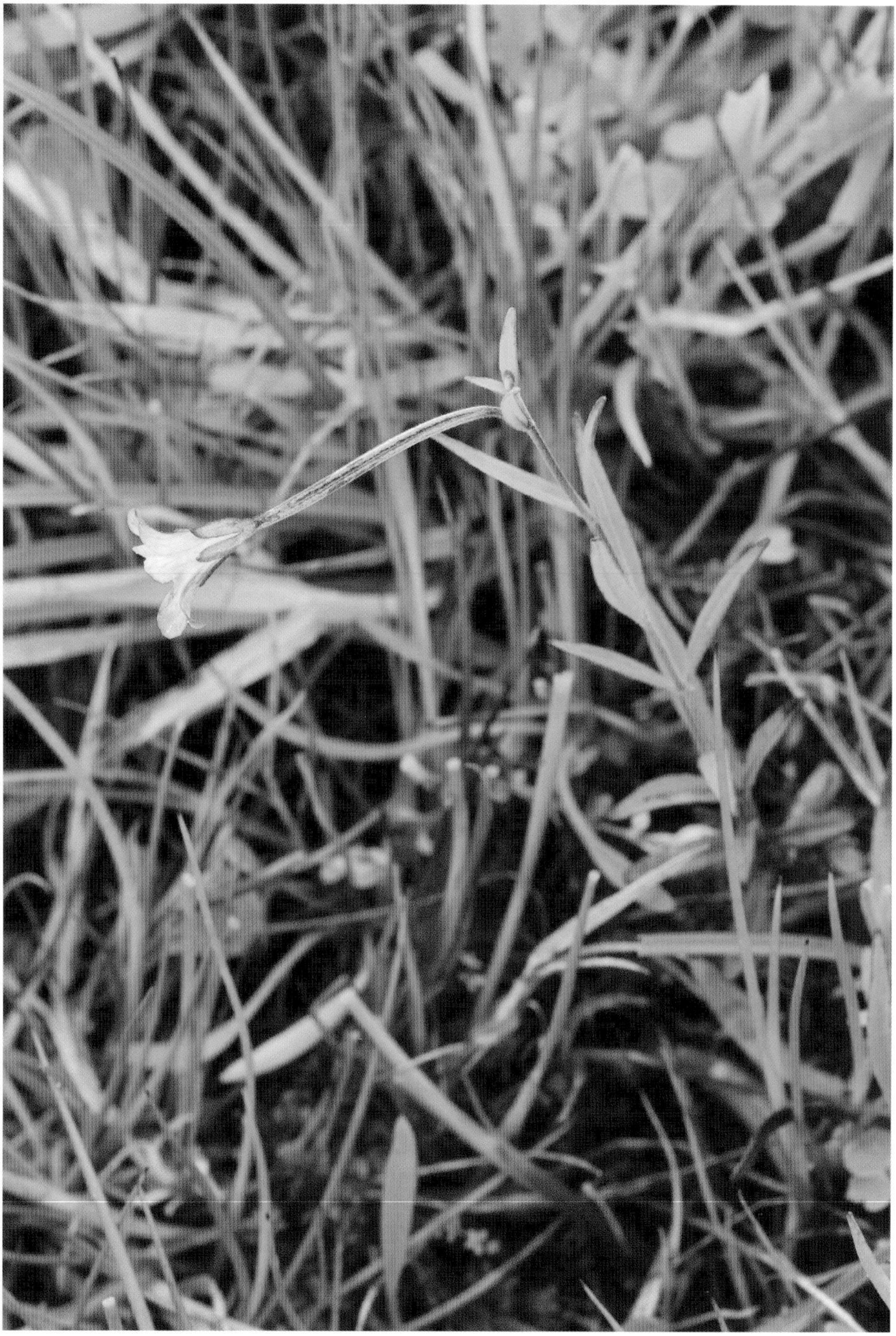

Plate 86 (m) **Marsh Willowherb** (*Epilobium palustre*)

Flowers violet-pink, nodding when open, petals 4, notched; stems hairy; leaves lanceolate, opposite. Native. Streams, ditches, marshes. Flowering July–September. Photograph: damp pasture, Whiteness.

Plate 87 (s) **Frog Orchid**
(*Coeloglossum viride*)
Flowers greenish or brownish, in short spikes; stems angled; lowest leaves almost round, upper becoming narrower. Native. An inconspicuous orchid of dry, sandy, coastal pastures, cliff-tops sward, limestone grassland and stony ground. Flowering late May–early August. Photograph: Keen of Hamar, Unst.

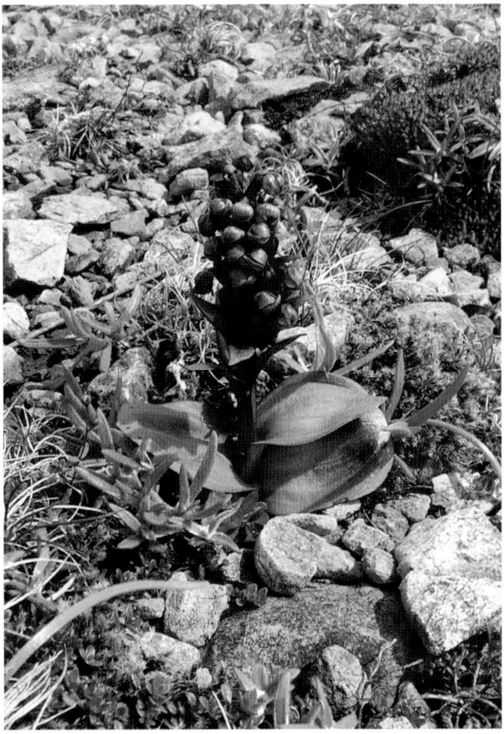

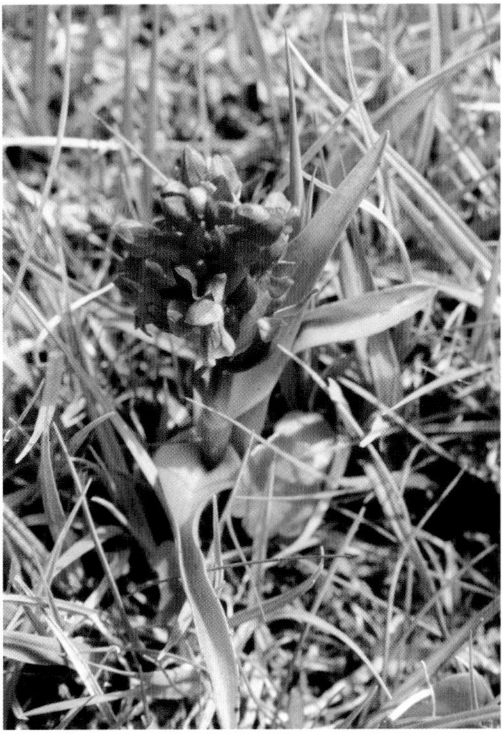

Plate 88 (s) **Early Marsh-orchid**
(*Dactylorhiza incarnata*)
Flowers in spikes, usually flesh-pink but often darker on sandy ground at the south end of Shetland; leaves unspotted, hooded at the tip. Native. Rich marshy pastures, damp sandy dune pastures. Flowering late May–July. Photograph: damp limestone pasture, Whiteness.

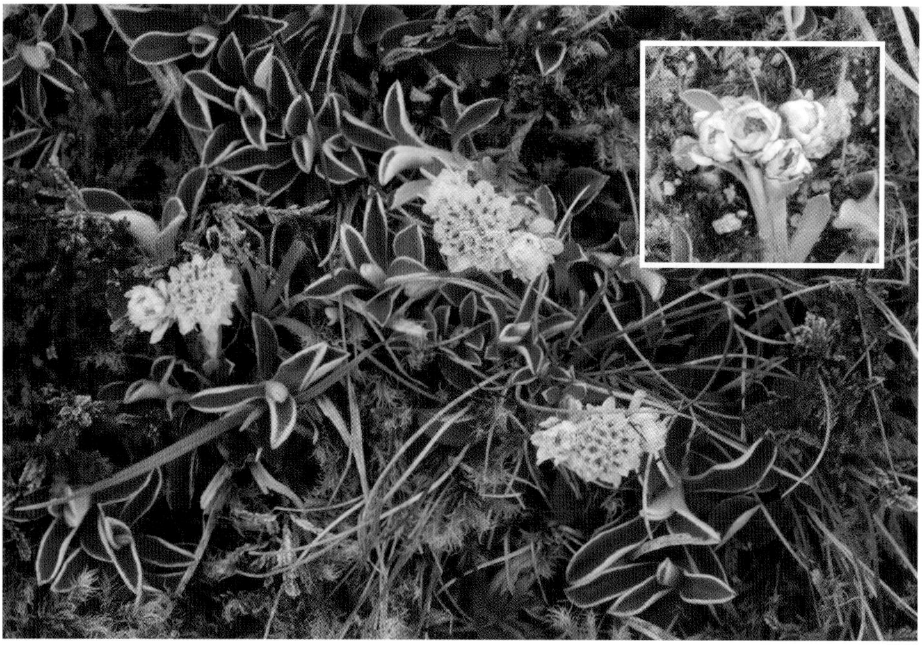

Plate 89 (s) **Mountain Everlasting** (*Antennaria dioica*)
Flowerheads white in male plants, rose-pink in female plants (see inset); leaves in rosettes, dark green above, covered in white woolly hairs below. Native. A creeping plant of stony or rocky heaths. Flowering late May–July. Photograph: eastern slopes of Ronas Hill.

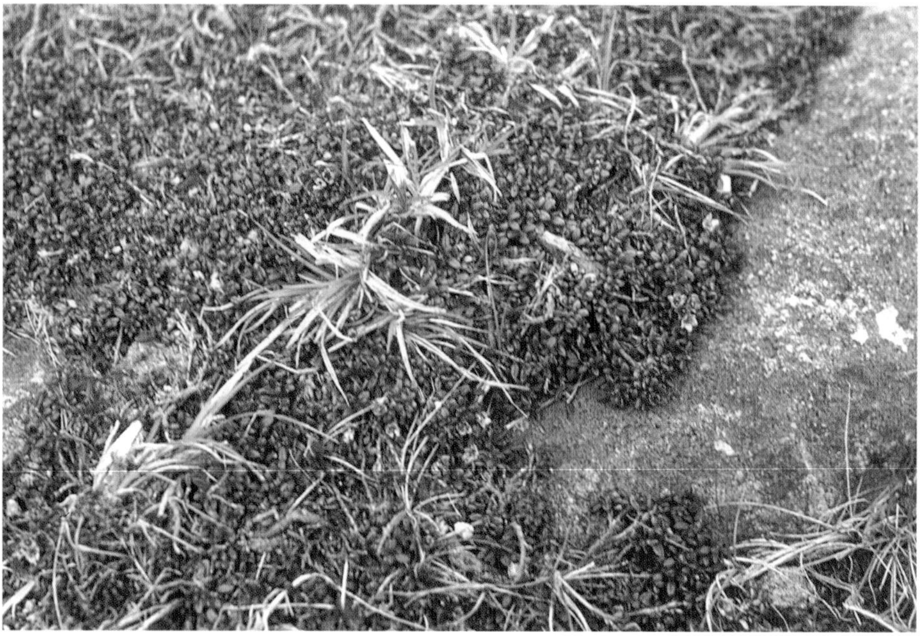

Plate 90 (s) **Trailing Azalea** (*Loiseleuria procumbens*)
Flowers pink, small, petals 5; leaves numerous, oblong, opposite. Native. Very rare evergreen shrub found only on Ronas Hill. Flowering late May–June. Photograph: Ronas Hill.

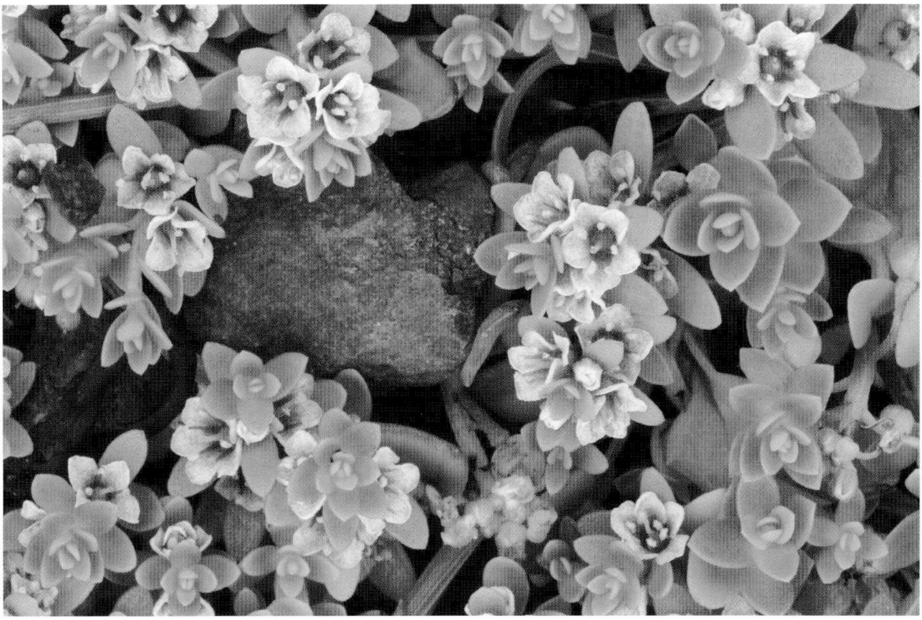

Plate 91 (s) **Sea-milkwort** (*Glaux maritima*)
Flowers consist of a 5-lobed pinkish or whitish calyx, no petals; plant creeping, hairless and fleshy. Native. Rocky shores, saltmarshes or saltmarshy turf. Flowering June–early September. Photograph: stony beach, East Voe of Scalloway.

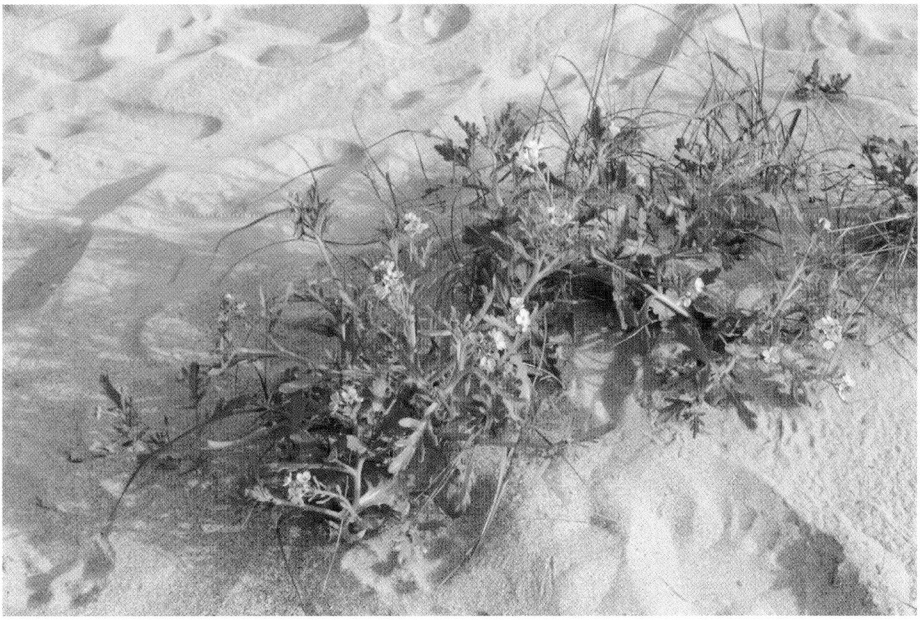

Plate 92 (s–l) **Sea Rocket** (*Cakile maritima*)
Flowers pinkish-lilac, sometimes white, fragrant, petals 4; stems succulent, branching; leaves pinnately lobed, fleshy. Native. Shingly and sandy beaches. Flowering June–early October. Photograph: sandy beach, St Ninian's Bay.

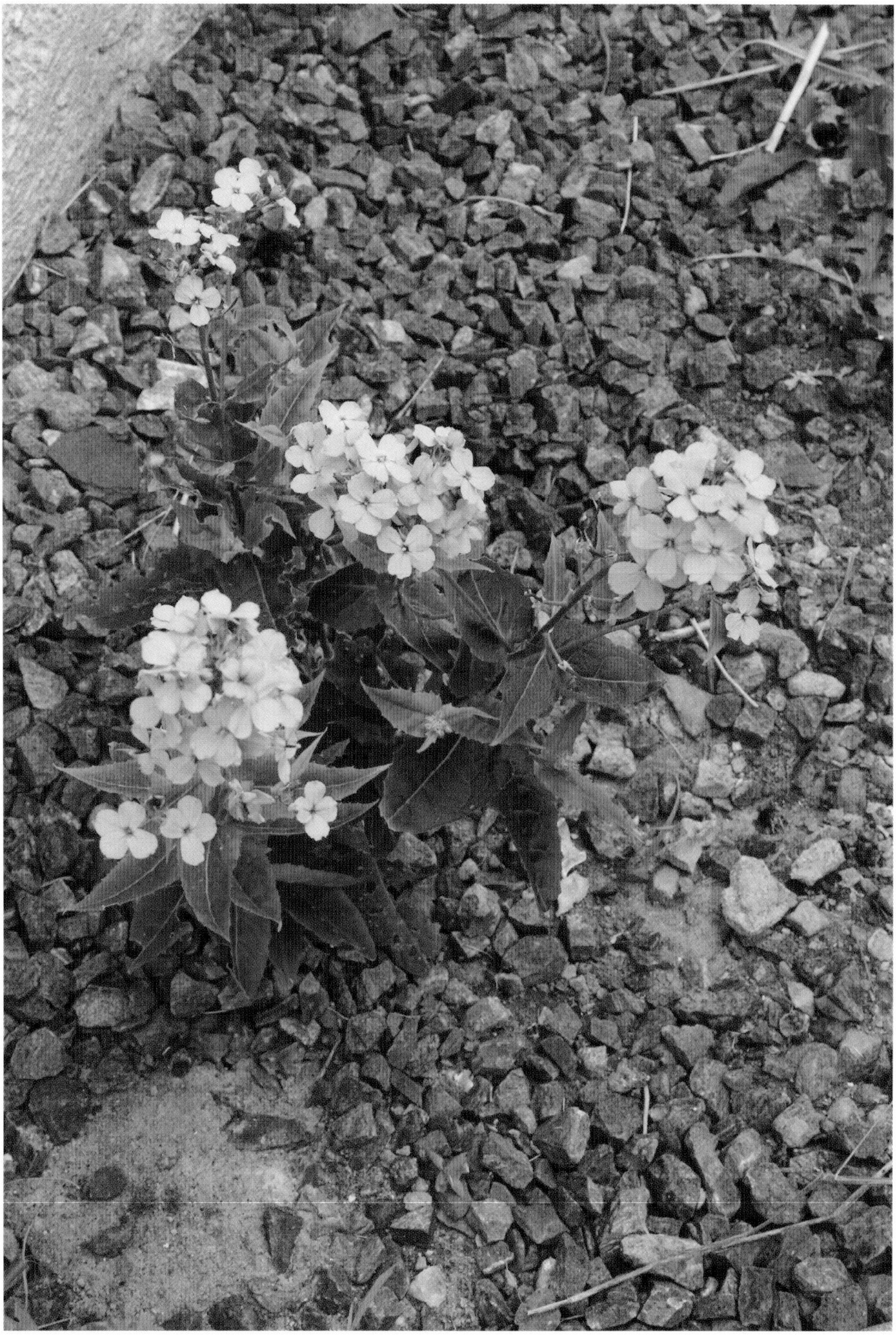

Plate 93 (m–l) **Dame's-violet** (*Hesperis matronalis*) 'Sweet Rocket'
Flowers white to violet, very fragrant; stems hairy; leaves lanceolate, toothed, short-stalked. Casual. Outcast on waste ground, rubbish tips and in the vicinity of gardens. Flowering late May–early October. Photograph: by wall of an old house, Scalloway.

Plate 94 (m) **Sea Aster**
(*Aster tripolium*)
Flowerheads very similar to those of michaelmas-daisies, up to 2.0 cm wide, whitish-mauve to pale purple, with yellow centres; stems stout, branched above; leaves fleshy, undivided, the upper oblong to linear, the lower broader. An unmistakable, hairless maritime plant found only on sea-cliffs and steep sea-banks on Isbister Holm, east of Whalsay, and at Yoxie Geo on the east side of Whalsay itself. Photograph: steep-sided geo, Isbister Holm. This species, which occurs on most of the British coastline, was first recorded from Shetland on 7 August, 1968, by J. G. Roger, W. Scott and W. L. N. Tickell on Isbister Holm. The image is the first known photograph of this plant to be taken in Shetland.

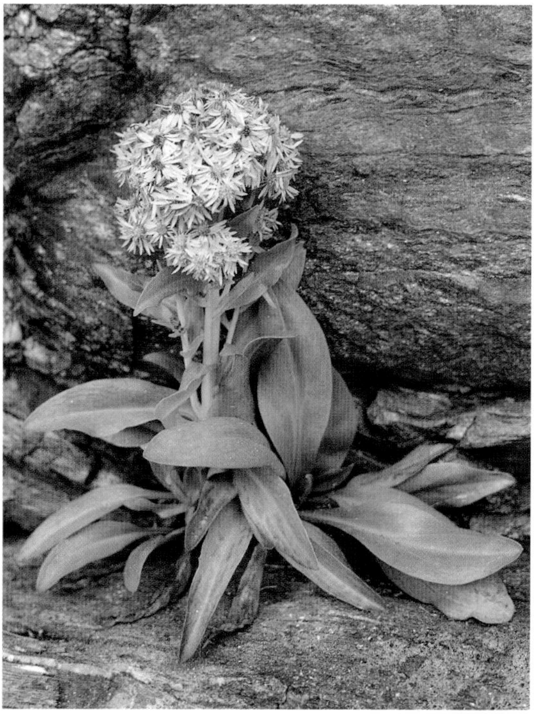

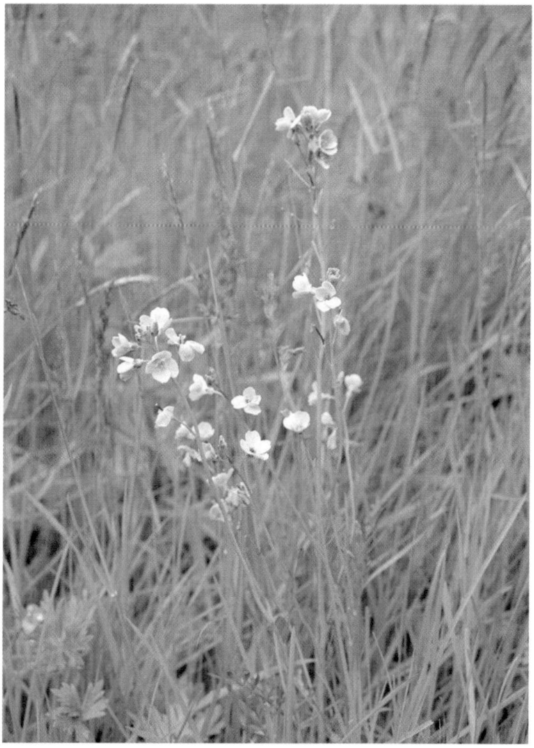

Plate 95 (m) **Cuckooflower**
(*Cardamine pratensis*)
Flowers pinkish-lilac, sometimes white, petals 4; stems hairless; leaves pinnate, basal leaves long-stalked, broader than the stem leaves. Native. Damp pastures, ditches. Flowering May-August. Photograph: ditch, Asta, near Scalloway.

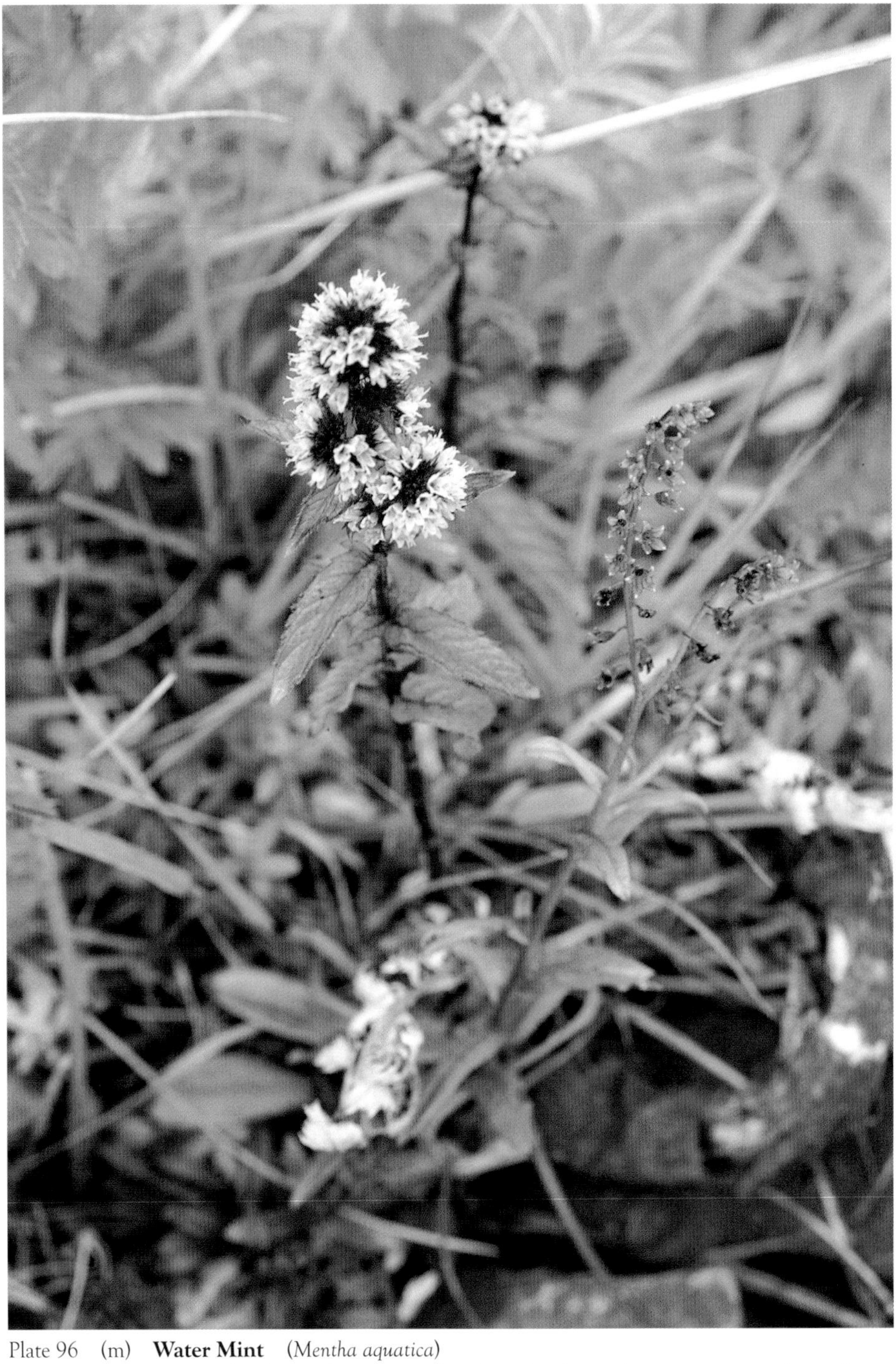

Plate 96 (m) **Water Mint** (*Mentha aquatica*)
Flowers lilac, tiny, densely clustered in a rounded flowerhead, petals 4; stems erect, hairy; leaves opposite, short-stalked, toothed. An aromatic native. Burns, ditches, sides of lochs. Flowering August–October. Photograph: by a burn, Houlland, Scalloway.

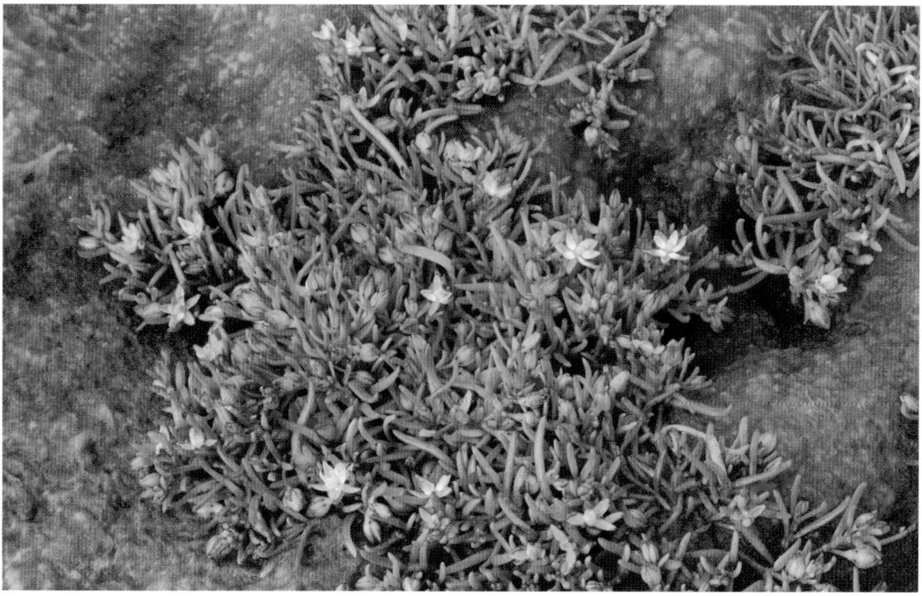

Plate 97 (s) **Greater Sea-spurrey** (*Spergularia media*)
Flowers whitish-pink, 9–12 mm wide, petals equal to or exceeding sepals; leaves opposite, linear. Native. Saltmarshes and muddy saltmarshy turf. Flowering June–August. Photograph: saltmarsh at the head of Whiteness Voe.

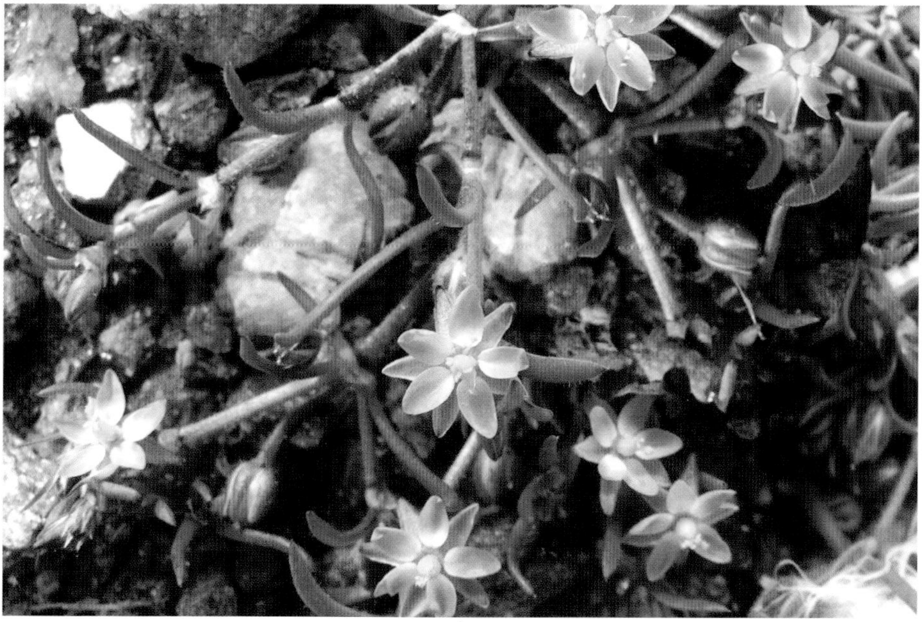

Plate 98 (s) **Lesser Sea-spurrey** (*Spergularia marina*)
Flowers deep pinkish-rose, almost white in very exposed places, 6–8 mm wide, petals shorter than sepals. Native. Coastal rocks, especially holms and skerries, less often in saltmarshy turf, and occasionally inland on gravelly roadside verges. Flowering June–August. Photograph: roadside verge, Gutcher, Yell.

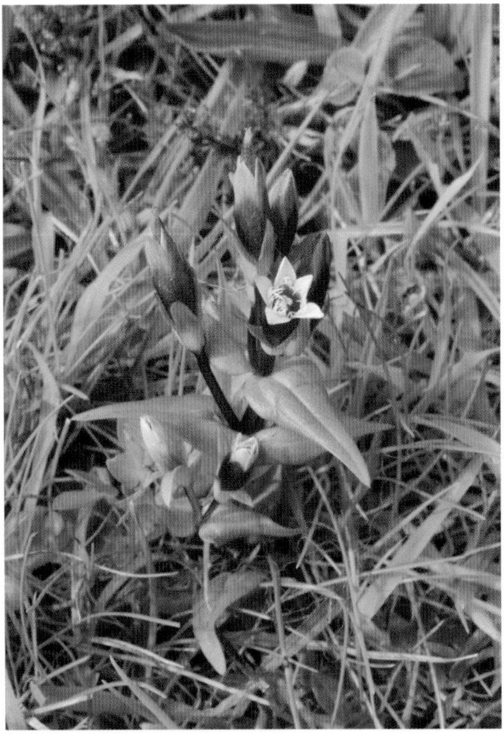

Plate 99 (s–m) **Autumn Gentian**
(*Gentianella amarella* subsp. *septentrionalis*)
Flowers bell-shaped, whitish inside, reddish outside, petals 4 or 5, fringed inside with white hairs; sepals 4 or 5; leaves opposite. Native. Sandy dune pastures, very rarely elsewhere. Flowering late July–early September. Photograph: sandy coastal turf, Tresta, Fetlar.

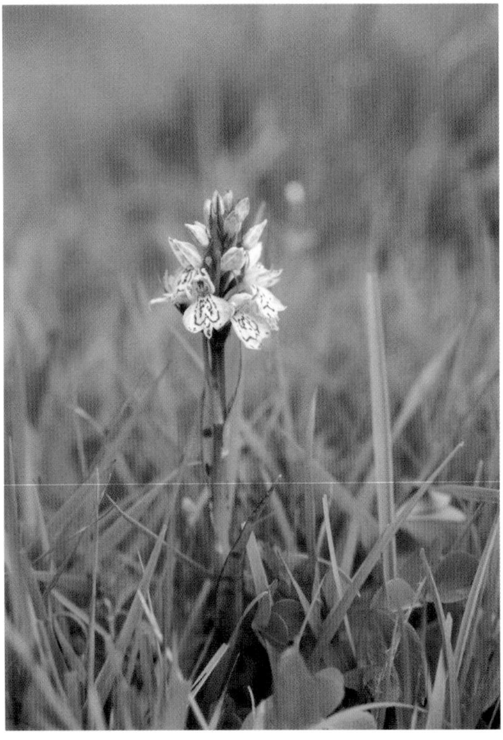

Plate 100 (s–m)
Heath Spotted-orchid
(*Dactylorhiza maculata*)
Flowers pinkish-lilac, sometimes white, in spikes; leaves lanceolate, often spotted. Native. Damp heathy pastures, moorland, etc., on all but the richest soils. Flowering late May–July. Photograph: damp pasture, Utnabrake, Scalloway.

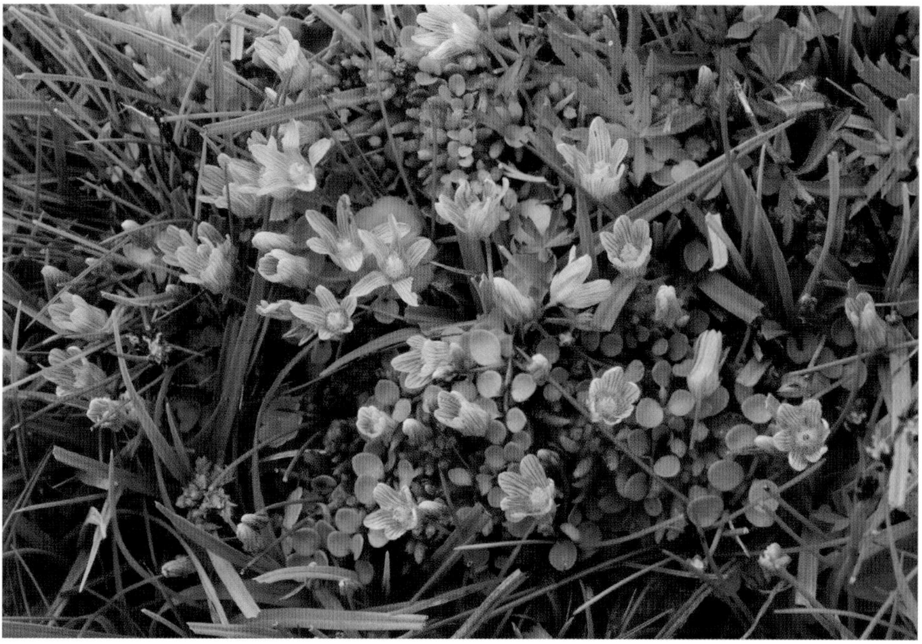

Plate 101 (s) **Bog Pimpernel** (*Anagallis tenella*)
Flowers pink, bell-like; mat-forming, hairless. Native. Damp turf by lochs and burns, sphagnous bogs, marshes. Flowering late July–early September. Photograph: Loch of Setter, Clousta.

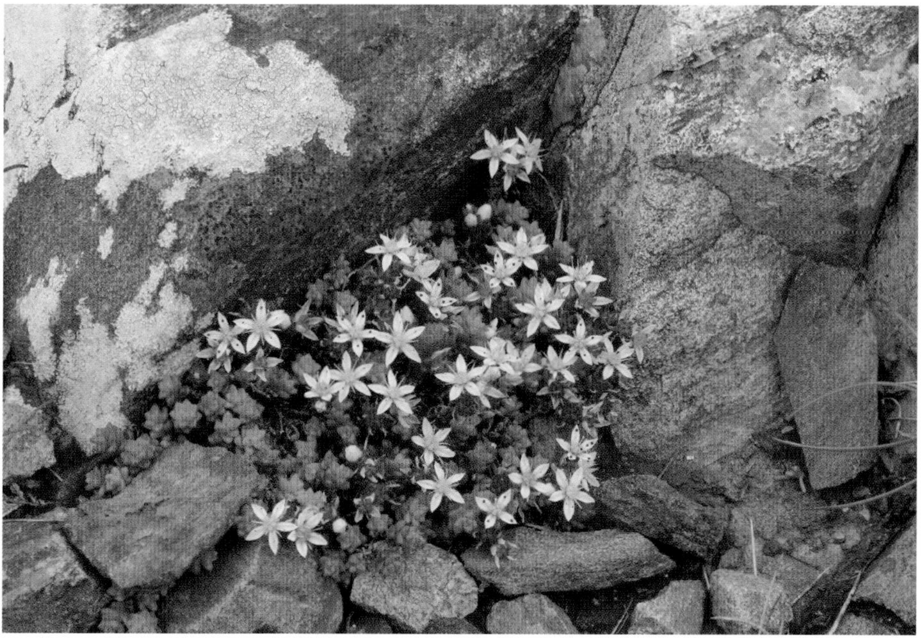

Plate 102 (s) **English Stonecrop** (*Sedum anglicum*)
Flowers white above, pink below, about 12 mm wide; mat-forming plant; leaves cylindrical and fleshy. Native. Rare. Dry rocky-heathy grassland and rocky outcrops. Flowering June–September. Photograph: Ward of Bruray, Out Skerries.

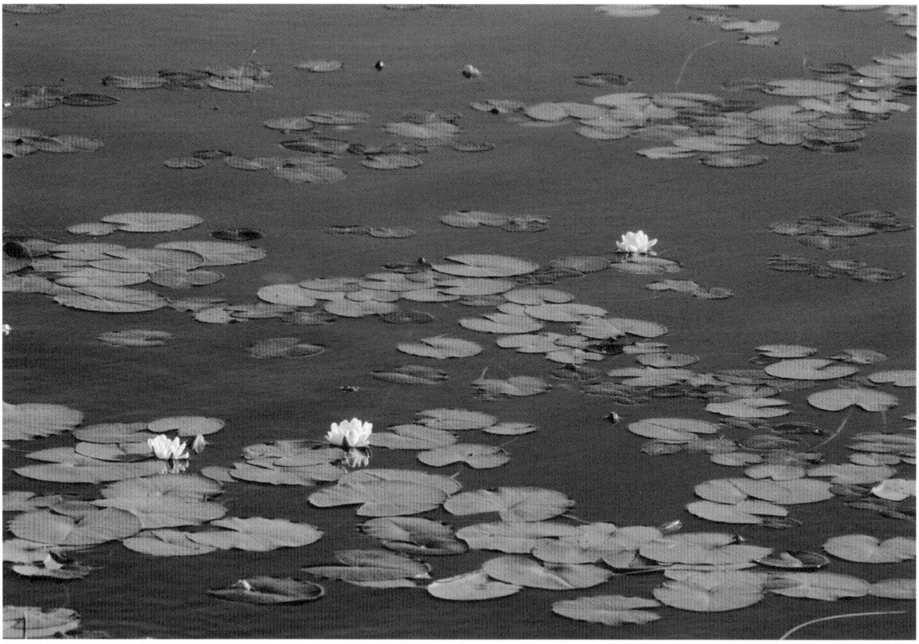

Plate 103 (l) **White Water-lily** (*Nymphaea alba* subsp. *occidentalis*)
Flowers white, very large, opening fully on sunny days; leaves circular, large, floating. An unmistakable native plant confined to a few lochs in the West Mainland. Flowering July–August. Photograph: Lunga Water, West Mainland.

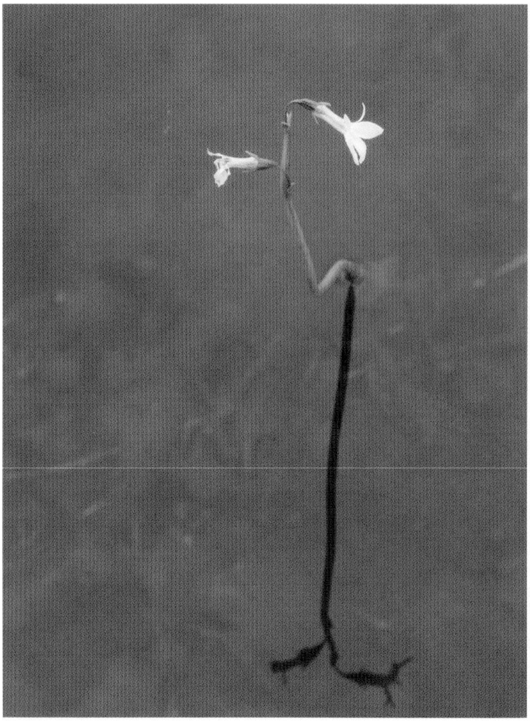

Plate 104 (m) **Water Lobelia**
(*Lobelia dortmanna*)
Flowers pale whitish-lilac, drooping, 2-lipped, held above the water on hollow, leafless stems; leaves in a submerged rosette. Native. Shallow water at the edge of stony lochs and pools. Flowering July–August. Photograph: North Loch of Hostigates, Vementry.

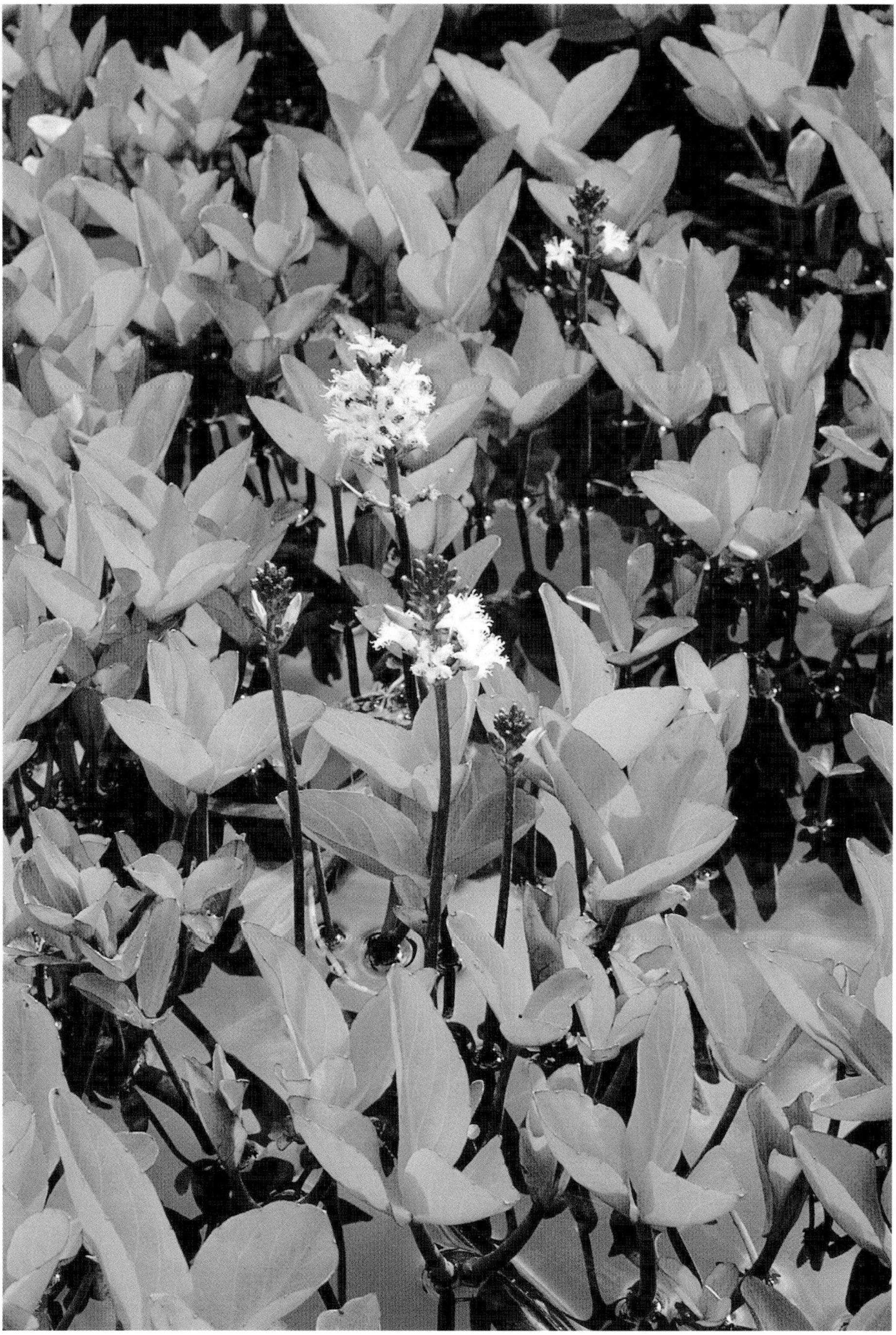

Plate 105 (m–l) **Bogbean** (*Menyanthes trifoliata*)
Flowers white inside, pink outside, in spikes, petals 5, fringed with white hairs on the inside; leaves divided into three large somewhat oval leaflets. Native. Deep peaty bog-pools, lochs, streams. Flowering late May–early June. Photograph: burn from the Loch of Asta, near Scalloway.

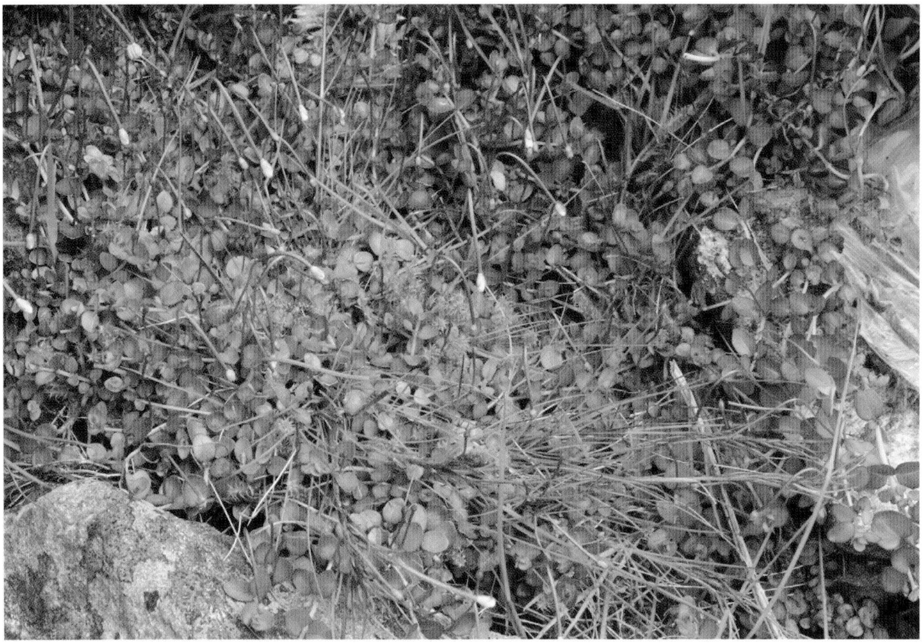

Plate 106 (s) **New Zealand Willowherb** (*Epilobium brunnescens*)
Flowers pinkish-white, small, long-stalked; prostrate, creeping plant; leaves stalked, rounded, often bronzy. Well-established alien. Gravelly roadside verges, quarries, at the bottom of or on walls. Flowering June–August. Photograph: disused quarry north-north-east of the Ward of Scousburgh.

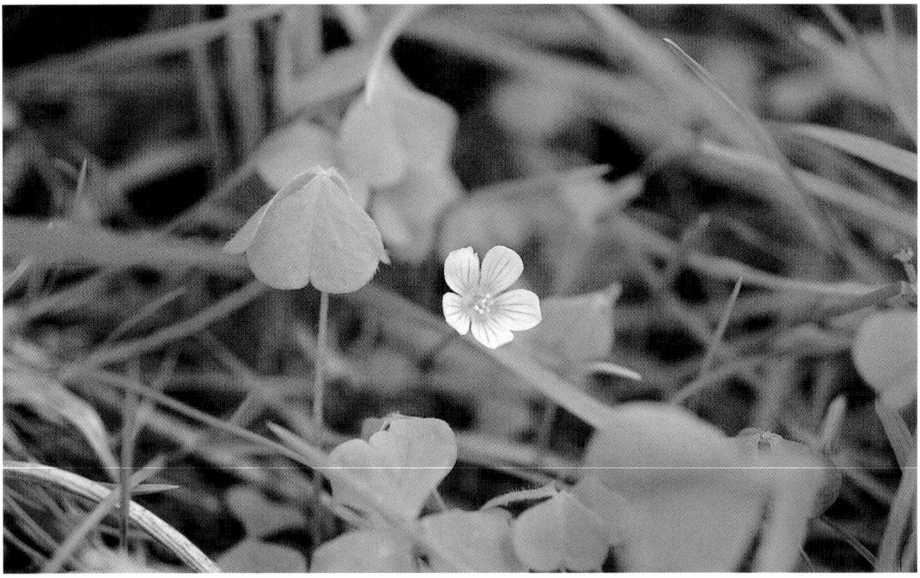

Plate 107 (s) **Wood-sorrel** (*Oxalis acetosella*)
Flowers pale whitish-pink, solitary, petals 5; stems finely hairy; leaves trifoliate, leaflets heart-shaped. Very rare as a native in damp shady places, but a well-established alien in the Kergord Plantations, Weisdale, especially in the Lindsay Lee wood. Flowering May–July. Photograph: Lindsay Lee plantation, Kergord.

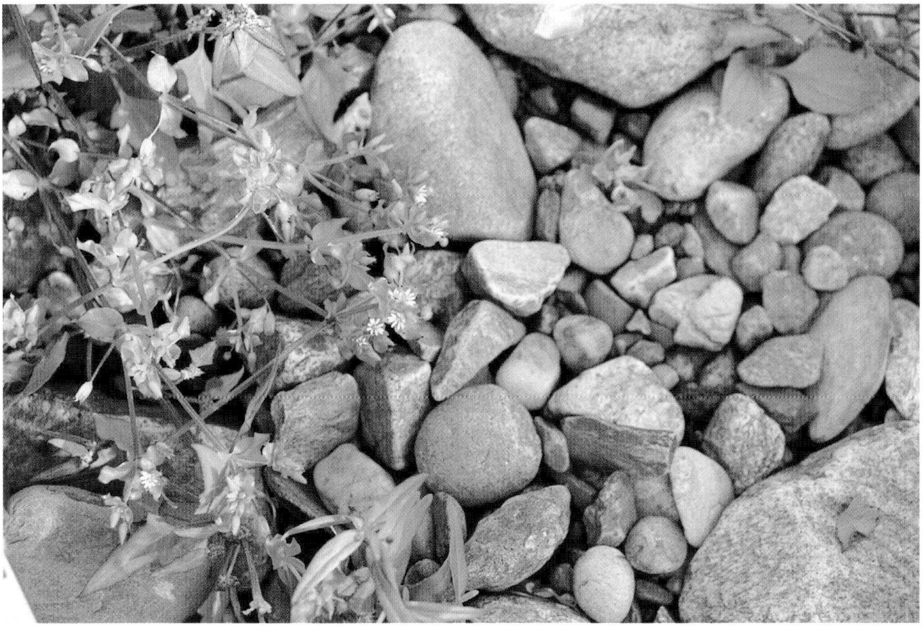

Plate 108 (s) **Common Chickweed** (*Stellaria media*) 'Ervi'
Flowers white, petals 5, cleft to base; sepals equal to or longer than the petals; stems with a line of white hairs down one side; leaves oval, opposite, wavy, untoothed. Native. Arable land, waste ground, shingly beaches, sea-cliffs. Flowering April–September. Photograph: shingly beach, Easter Quarff.

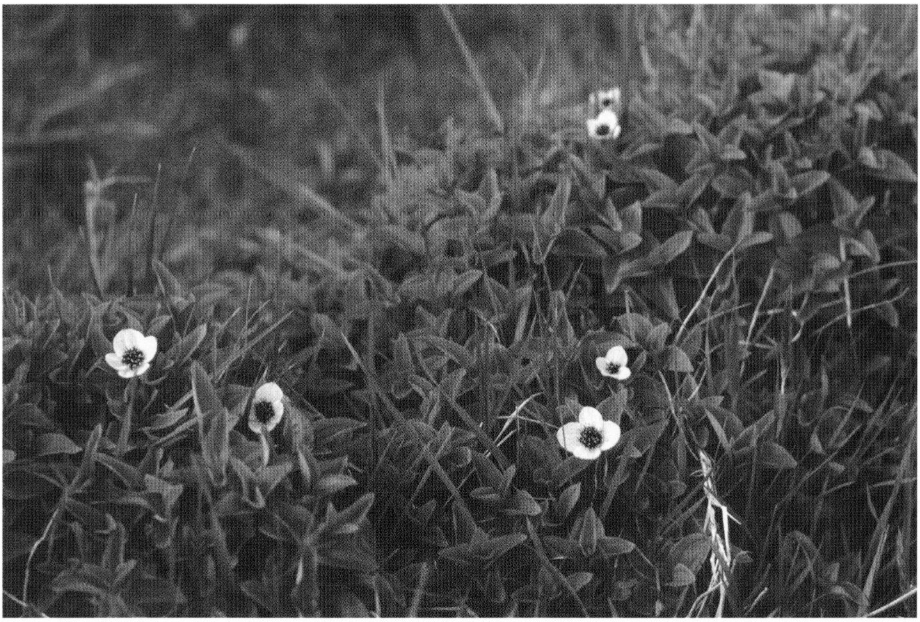

Plate 109 (s) **Dwarf Cornel** (*Cornus suecica*)
Flowers dark purplish, tiny, surrounded by 4 large, white and very obvious petal-like bracts; creeping plant; leaves oval, pointed, unstalked. Native. Heathy places. Very rare. Flowering June. Photograph: Otterswick, Yell.

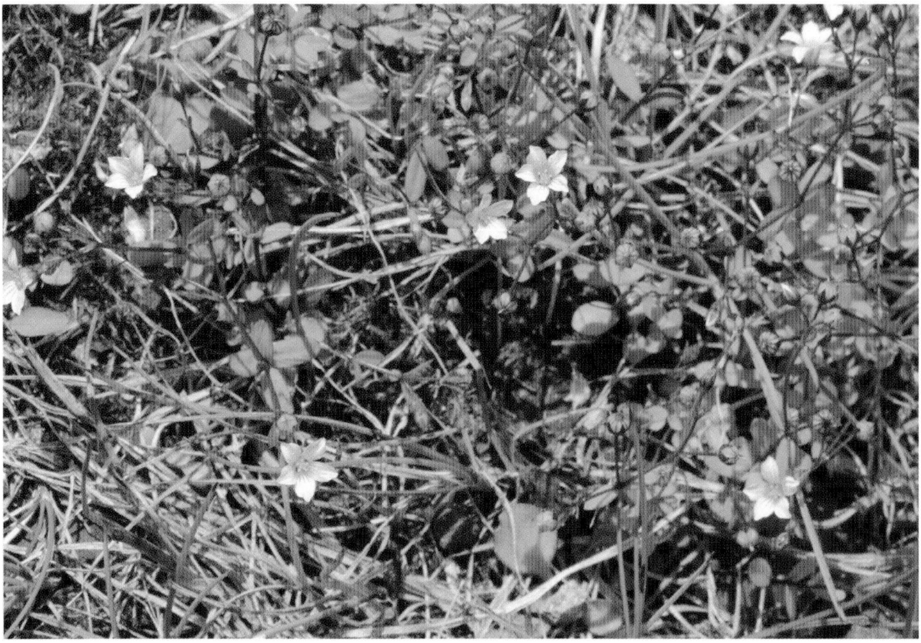

Plate 110 (s) **Fairy Flax** (*Linum catharticum*)
Flowers white, small, solitary, petals 5; leaves oblong, opposite, untoothed, distinctly one-veined. Native. Heaths, dry grassland, sandy coastal turf, stony places. Flowering late April–August. Photograph: gravelly roadside verge, Tingwall.

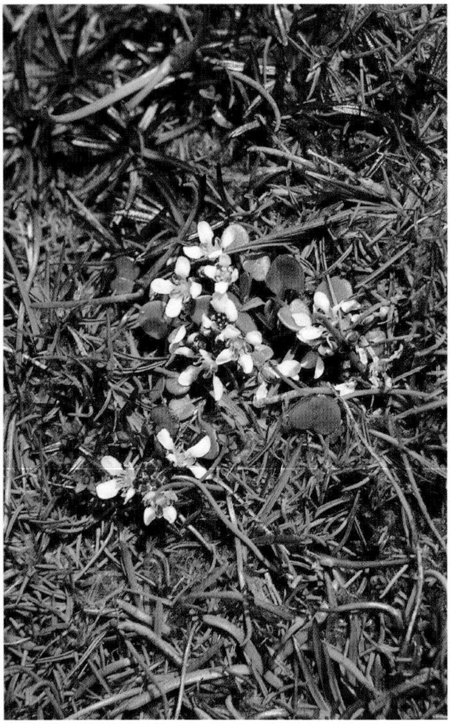

Plate 111 (s–m) **Common Scurvygrass** (*Cochlearia officinalis*)
Flowers white, sometimes lilac or mauve, in clusters, petals 4; leaves fleshy, heart-shaped, lower stalked, upper clasping stem. Native. Sea-cliffs, sandy or shingly beaches, coastal grassland, serpentine gravel. Flowering late April–August. Photograph: coastal turf, Whiteness Voe.

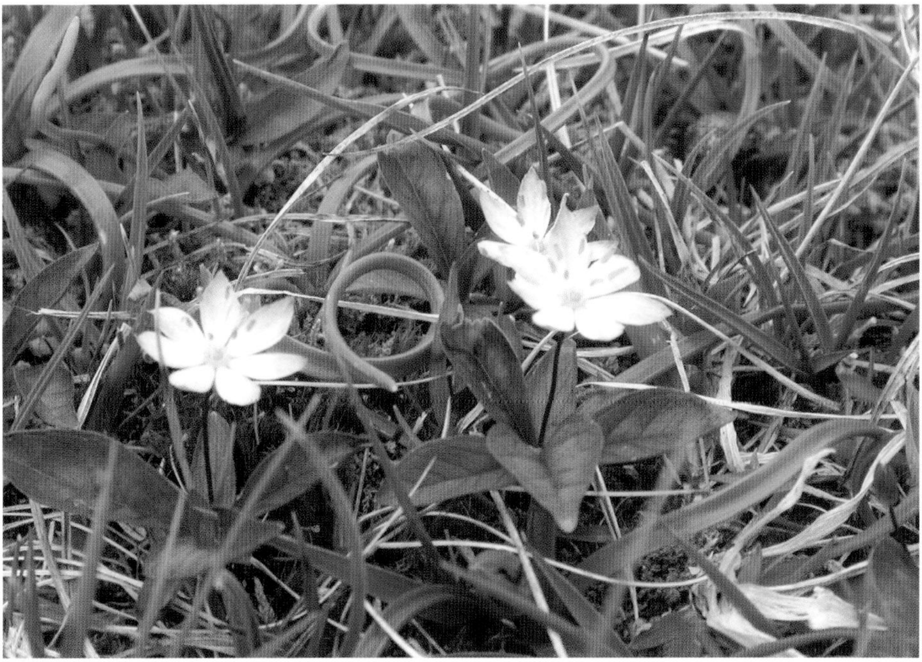

Plate 112 (s) **Chickweed-wintergreen** (*Trientalis europaea*)
Flowers white, star-like, on slender stalks, petals 5–9; leaves lanceolate, mostly in a single whorl near the top of the stem. Native. Dry or slightly damp heathy pastures. Flowering June–early July. Photograph: Foula.

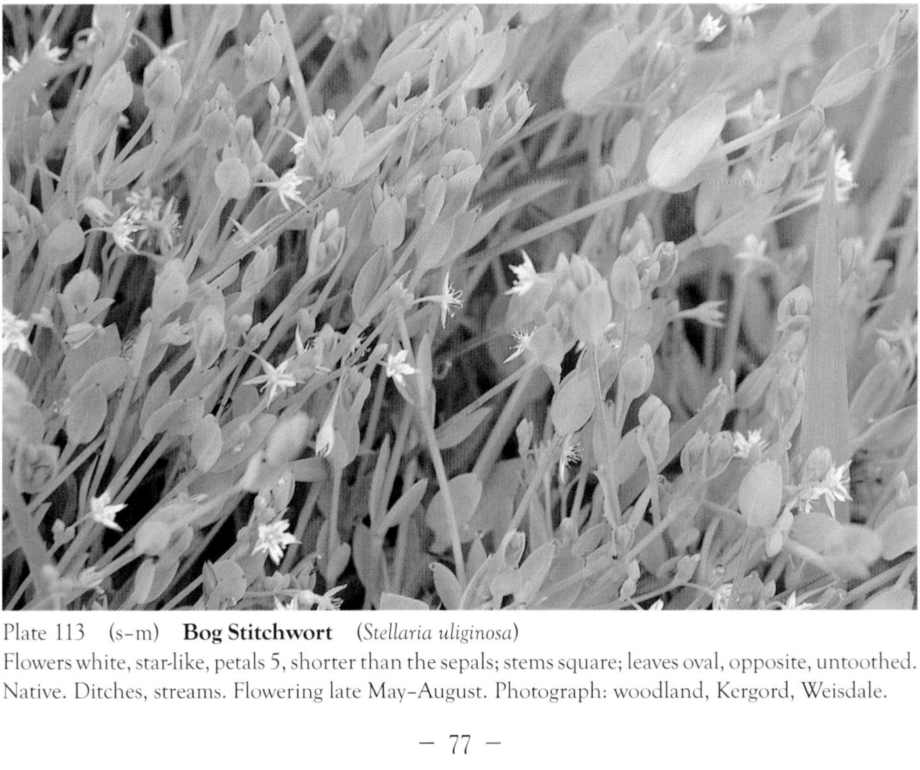

Plate 113 (s–m) **Bog Stitchwort** (*Stellaria uliginosa*)
Flowers white, star-like, petals 5, shorter than the sepals; stems square; leaves oval, opposite, untoothed. Native. Ditches, streams. Flowering late May–August. Photograph: woodland, Kergord, Weisdale.

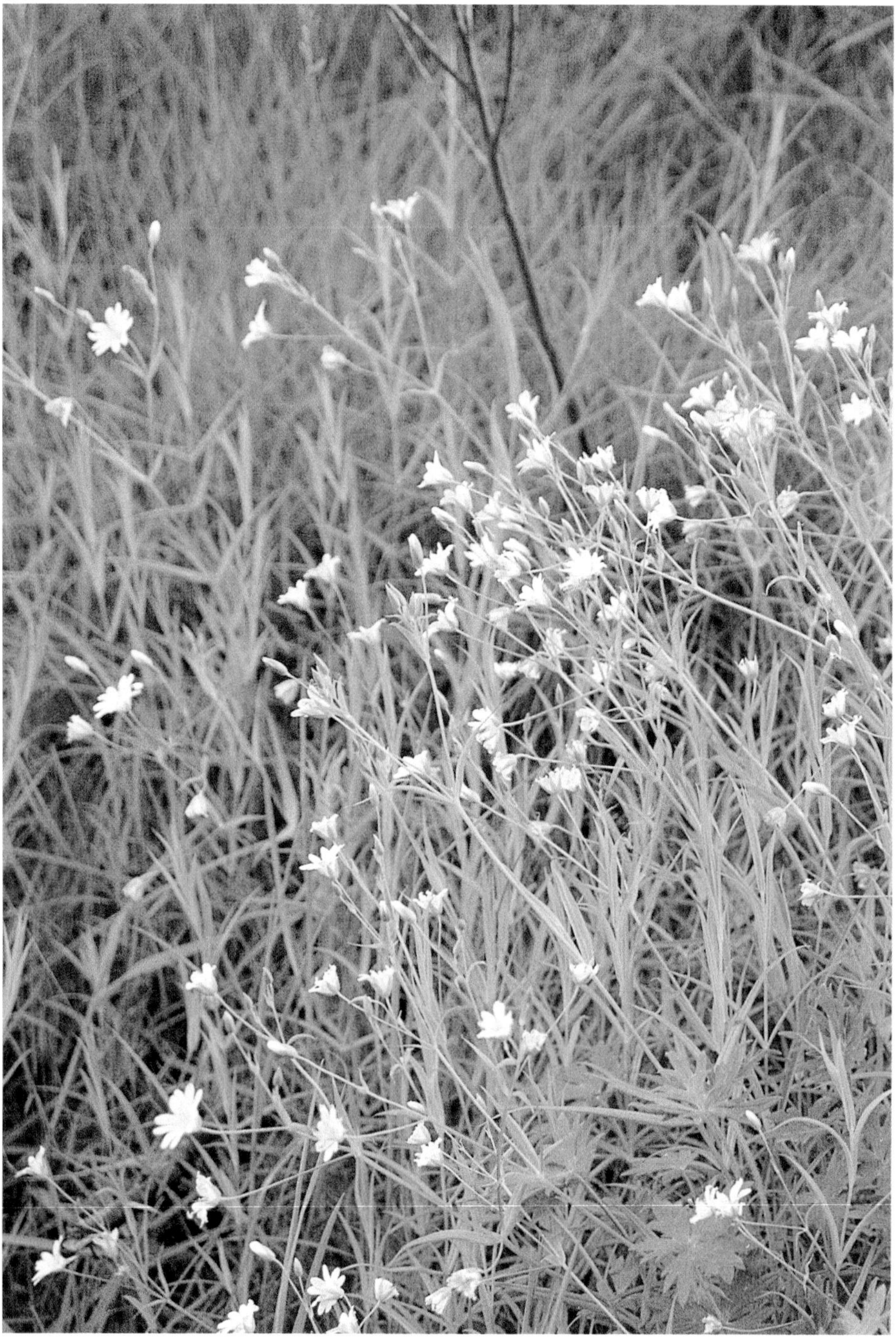

Plate 114 (m-l) **Greater Stitchwort** (*Stellaria holostea*)
Flowers white, 15–18 mm wide, petals 5, deeply notched; stems slender, hairless; leaves lanceolate, opposite, pointed. Well-established alien. Found only in some of the Kergord Plantations. Flowering May–July. Photograph: Lindsay Lee wood, Kergord, Weisdale.

Plate 115 (m) **Lesser Stitchwort**
(*Stellaria graminea*)
Flowers white, petals 5, cleft more than half-way, 5–12 mm wide, petals and sepals of equal length; stems smoothly 4-angled; leaves linear–lanceolate. Well-established alien in one place in South Mainland, probably merely casual elsewhere. Flowering June–September. Photograph: wet pasture by a stone wall, Boddam, present since at least 1957.

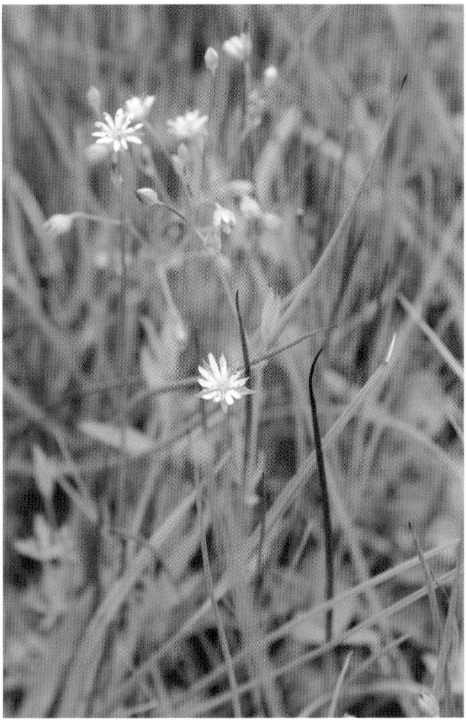

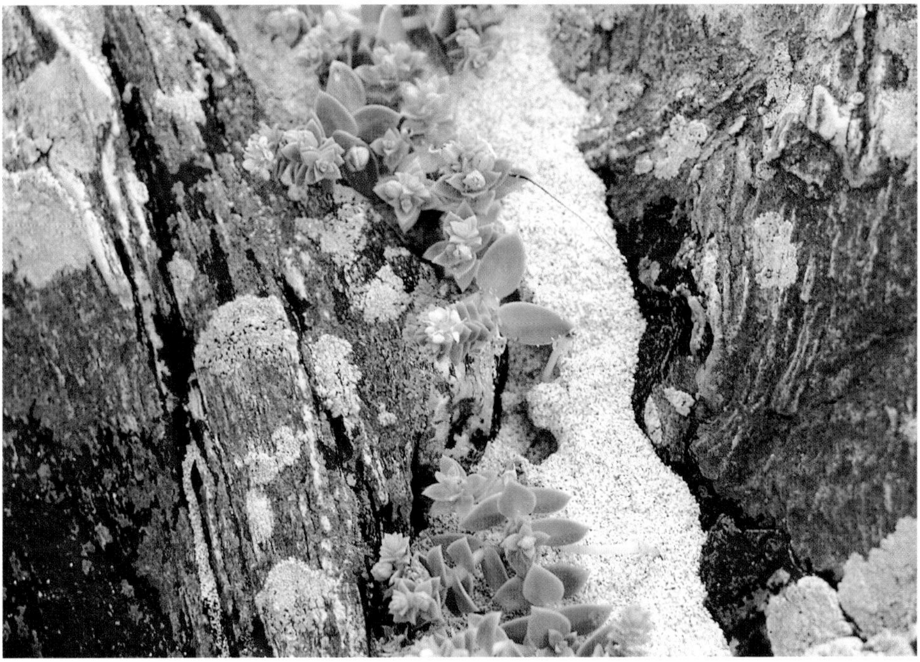

Plate 116 (s) **Sea Sandwort** (*Honckenya peploides*)
Flowers greenish-white, petals 5; leaves paired, broad, fleshy, untoothed. Native. Sandy beaches. Flowering late May–July. Photograph: Sand of Meal, West Burra.

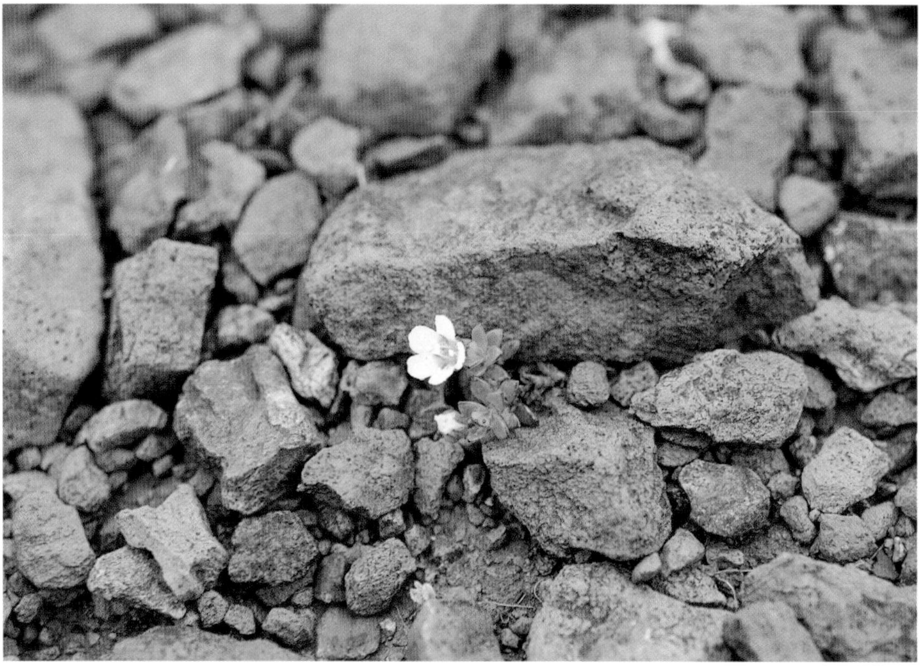

Plate 117 (s) **Arctic Sandwort** (*Arenaria norvegica* subsp. *norvegica*)
Flowers white, petals 5; leaves oval, opposite, fleshy. Native. A national rarity confined to the serpentine gravel of Unst. Flowering late May–September. Photograph: Keen of Hamar, Unst.

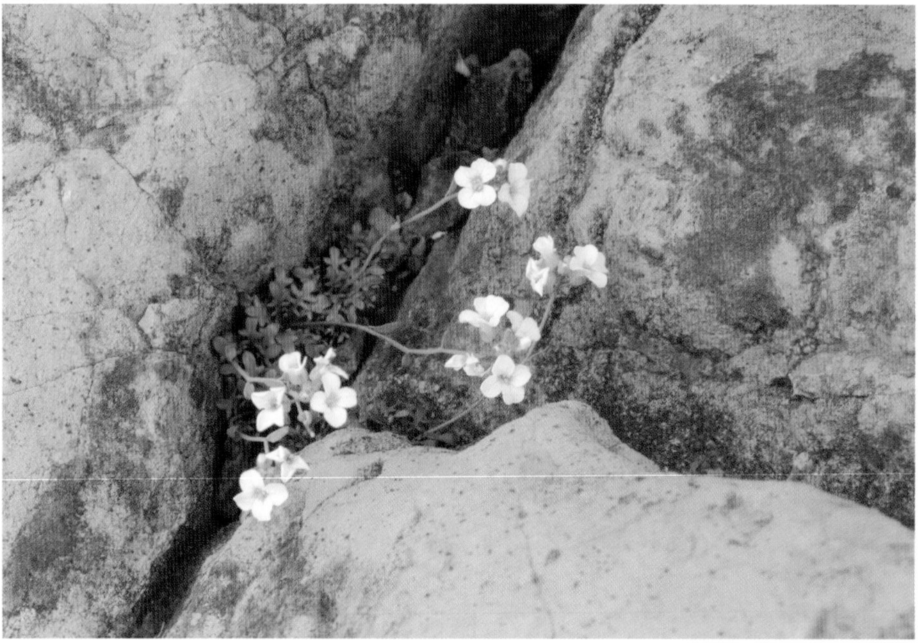

Plate 118 (s) **Northern Rock-cress** (*Arabis petraea*)
Flowers white, petals 4; stems slender; lower leaves pinnately lobed, long-stalked. Native. Serpentine gravel. Flowering May–August. Photograph: Keen of Hamar, Unst.

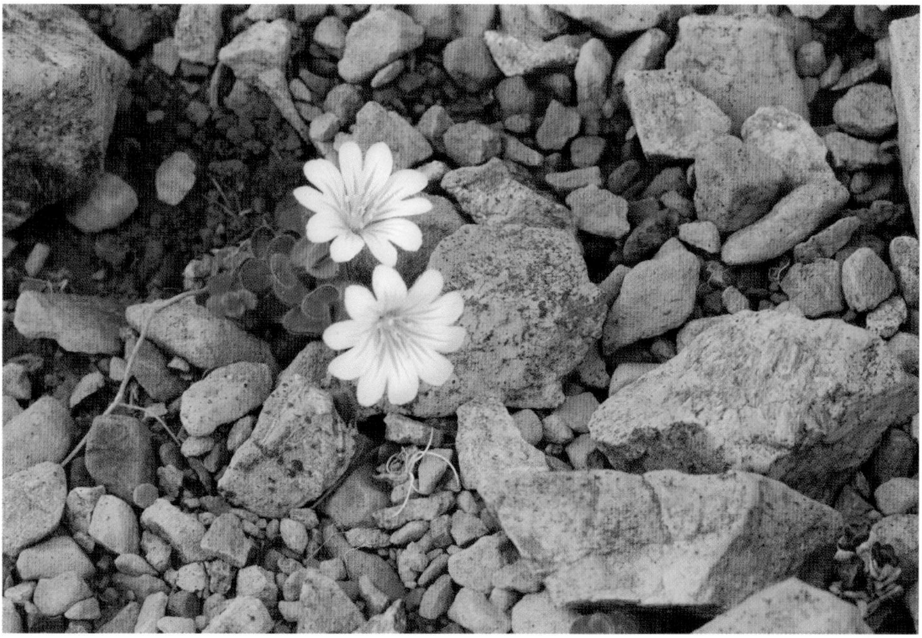

Plate 119 (s) **Shetland Mouse-ear** (*Cerastium nigrescens* var. *nigrescens*)
Flowers white, large, petals 5, deeply cleft; leaves round, fleshy, purplish, hairy. Native, endemic at the level of a variety. Confined to the Unst serpentine gravel. Flowering late May–early August. Photograph: Keen of Hamar, Unst.

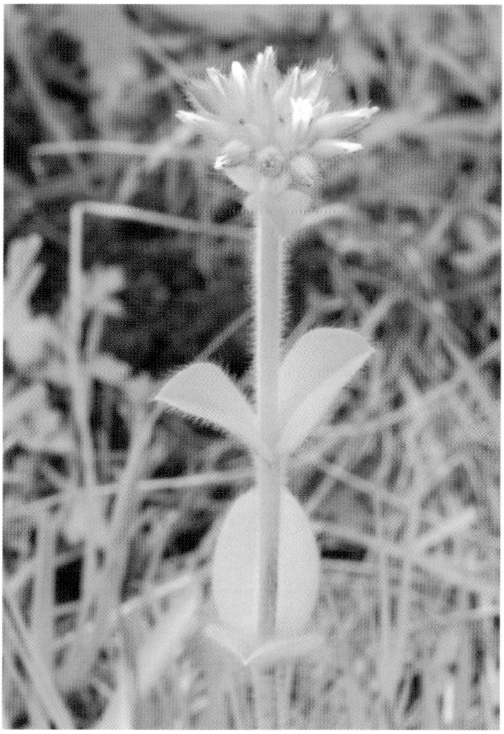

Plate 120 (s–m) **Sticky Mouse-ear** (*Cerastium glomeratum*)
Flowers white, in tight clusters; stems covered with sticky, glandular hairs; leaves hairy. Well-established alien. Crofting and farming areas, arable ground. Flowering May–September. Photograph: cultivated field, Berry Farm, Scalloway.

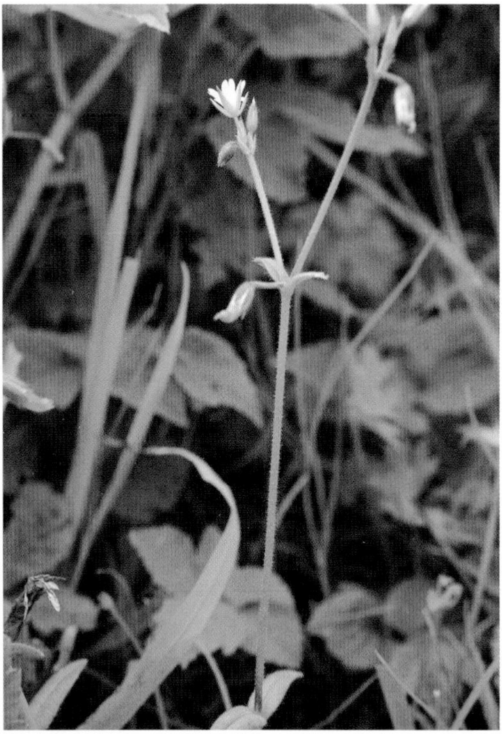

Plate 121 (s–m)
Common Mouse-ear
(*Cerastium fontanum*)
Flowers white, petals 5, notched; sepals pointed, slightly shorter than the petals; stems hairy; leaves lanceolate, opposite, untoothed, hairy. Native. Grows in many habitats. Flowering late April–September. Photograph: meadow, Fladdabister.

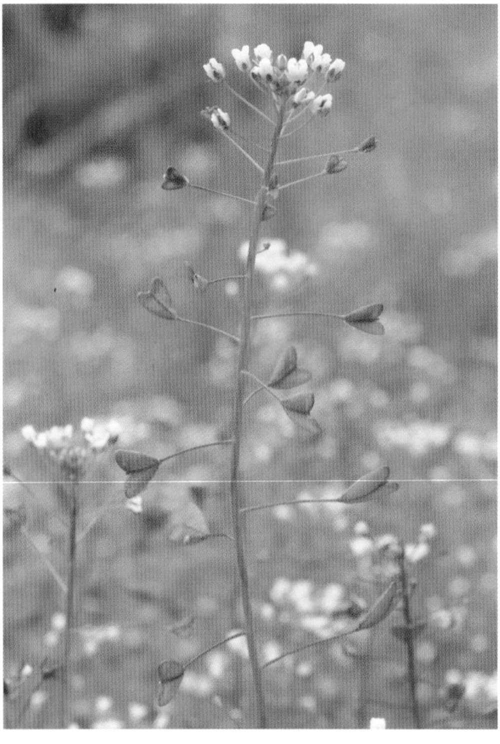

Plate 122 (s–m) **Shepherd's-purse**
(*Capsella bursa-pastoris*)
Flowers white, 2–3 mm wide; stems slender, erect; leaves lanceolate, pinnately-lobed, mainly in a basal rosette; pods triangular, notched. Well-established alien. Arable ground, roadsides, waste places. Flowering late April–early October. Photograph: cultivated field, Berry Farm, Scalloway.

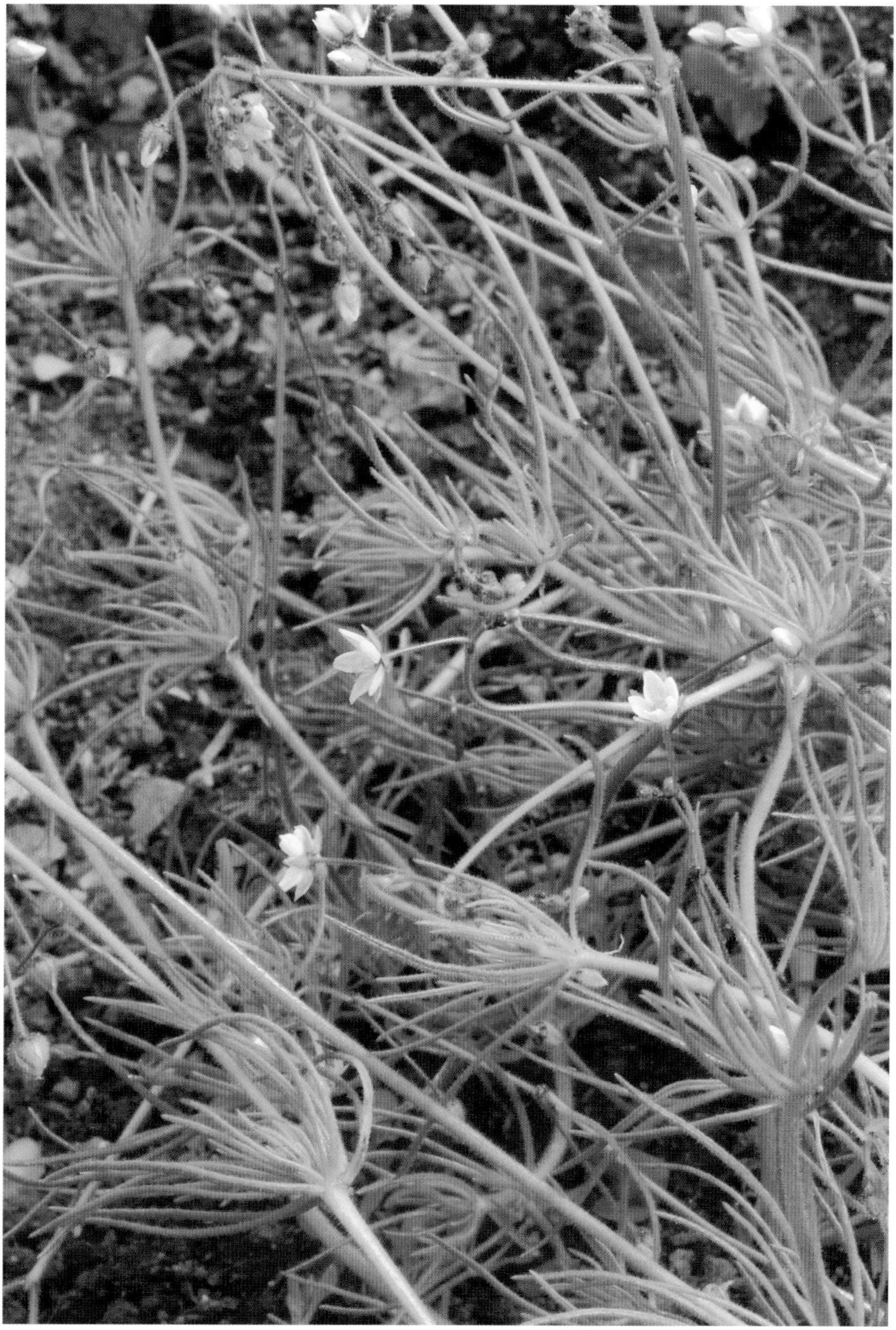

Plate 123 (s–m) **Corn Spurrey** (*Spergula arvensis*) 'Meldie'
Flowers white, 4–10 mm wide, petals 5; stems branching, sticky, hairy; leaves linear, blunt-tipped, in whorls. Well-established alien. Arable ground, and about crofts and farms. Flowering late May–October. Photograph: margin of cornfield, Burland, Trondra.

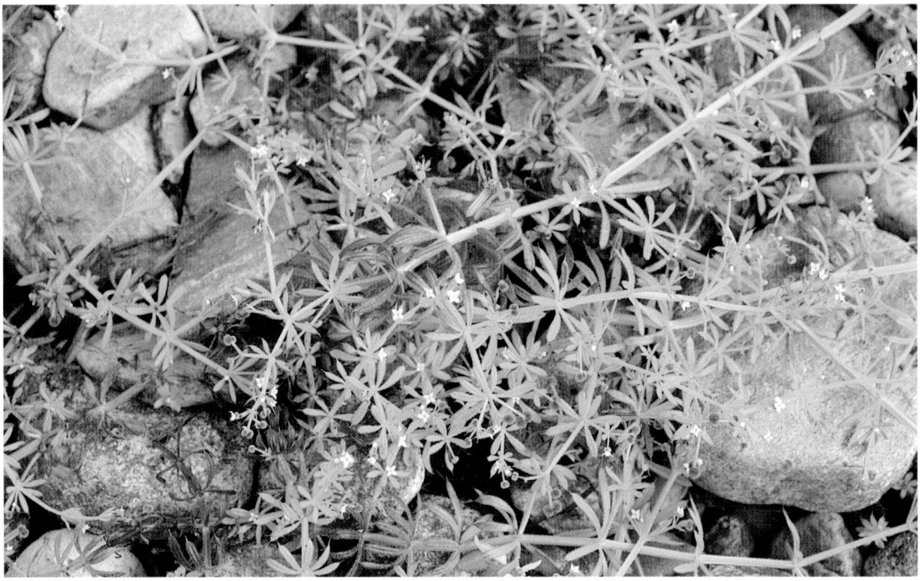

Plate 124 (m–l) **Cleavers** (*Galium aparine*)
Flowers white, minute, petals 4; stems square; leaves lanceolate in whorls of 6–9. Native. A straggling plant covered in down-turned prickles which make the stems adhere to clothing. Shingly beaches. Flowering July–September. Photograph: shingly beach, Easter Quarff.

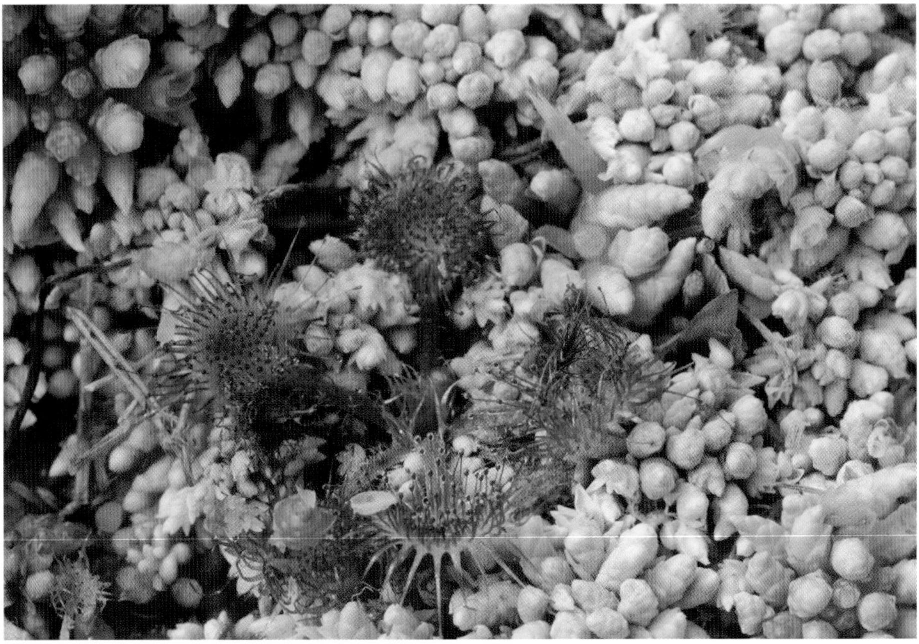

Plate 125 (s) **Round-leaved Sundew** (*Drosera rotundifolia*)
Flowers white, 5 mm wide, very rarely opening fully, borne on a shortly stalked stem arising from a flat rosette of round, long-stalked, yellowish-green leaves which bear red, sticky, gland-tipped, insect-catching hairs. Native. Boggy or mossy moors. Flowering July–August. Photograph: (leaves only), boggy moorland by the Burn of Roerwater, Northmavine.

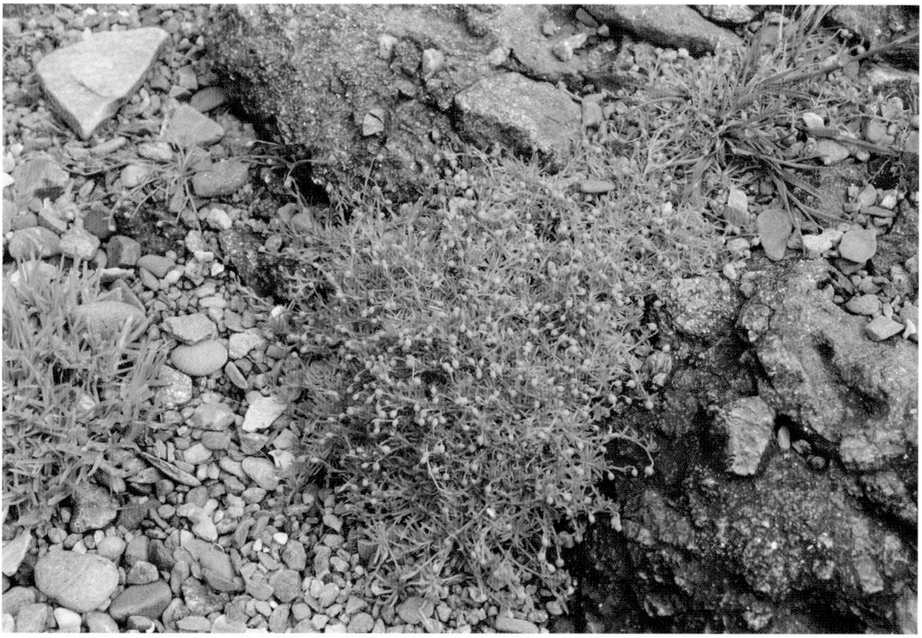

Plate 126 (s) **Procumbent Pearlwort** (*Sagina procumbens*)
Flowers greenish-white, tiny, 1–2 mm wide, petals much smaller than sepals; dense mat-forming plant. Native. Rocky or stony places, shingly beaches, saltmarshes, ditches, and a weed in gardens. Flowering May–September. Photograph: among rocks by beach, Easter Quarff.

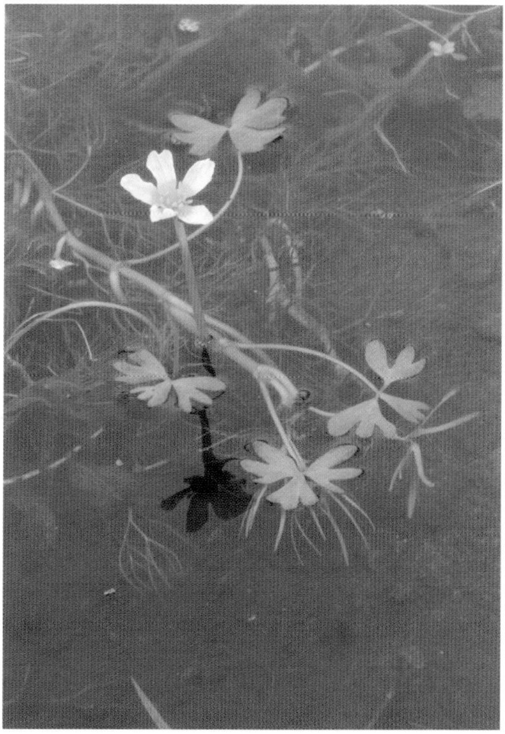

Plate 127 (m)
Brackish Water-crowfoot
(*Ranunculus baudotii*)
Flowers white, 12–18 mm wide, petals 5, sepals often with bluish tips, reflexed or spreading, petals up to twice as long as sepals or more; leaves floating. Native. Lochs and pools. Flowering June–early September. Photograph: Loch of Gards, Scatness.

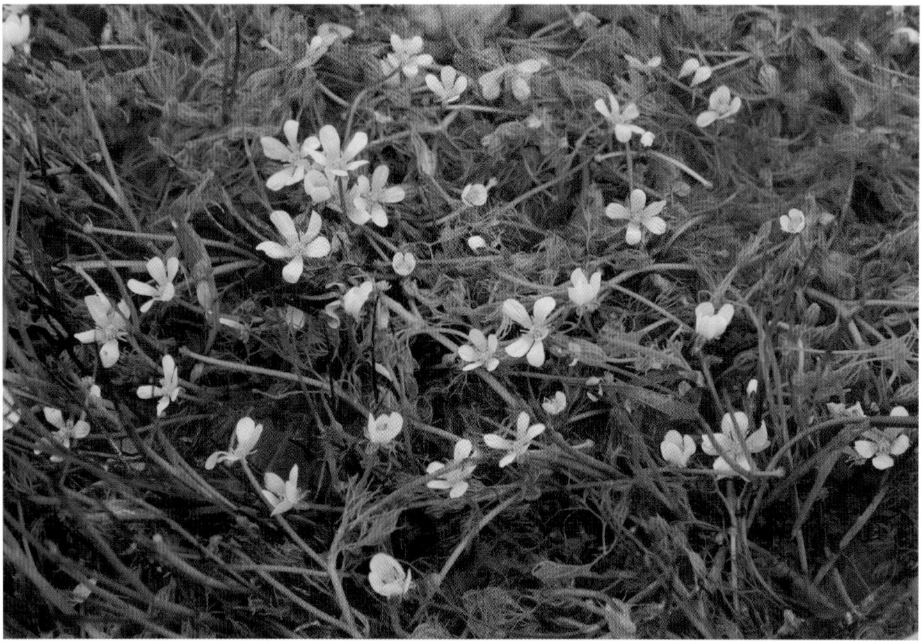

Plate 128 (m) **Thread-leaved Water-crowfoot** (*Ranunculus trichophyllus*)
Flowers white, 5–10 mm wide, petals 5; leaves all submerged. Native. Lochs and pools. Flowering late May–August. Photograph: small pond near Sumburgh Hotel.

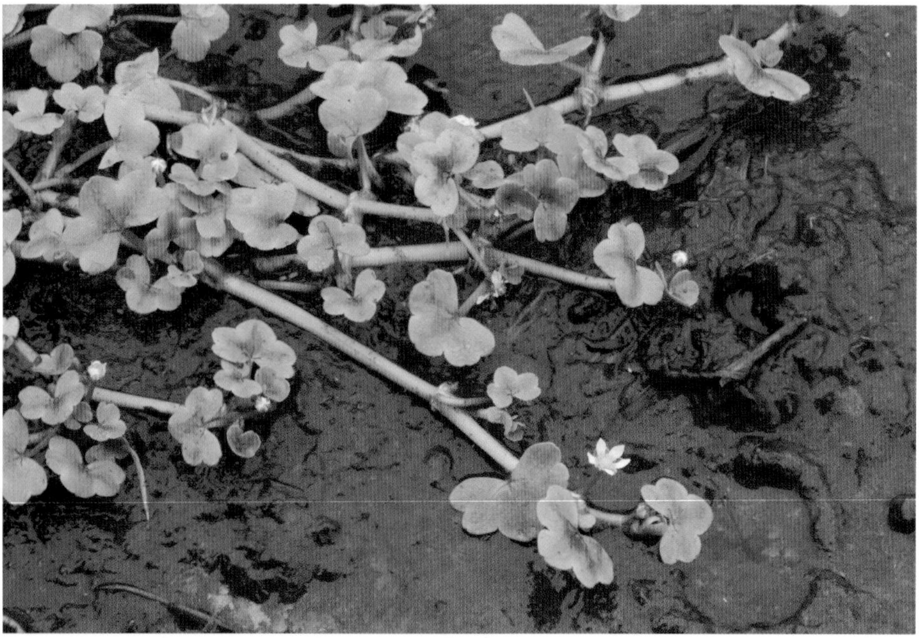

Plate 129 (m) **Ivy-leaved Crowfoot** (*Ranunculus hederaceus*)
Flowers white, 4–8 mm wide, petals 5, sepals not reflexed, petals equalling sepals; leaves ivy-shaped. Native. Small streams, ditches, sandy or muddy loch margins. Flowering June–early September. Photograph: Loch of Gards, Scatness.

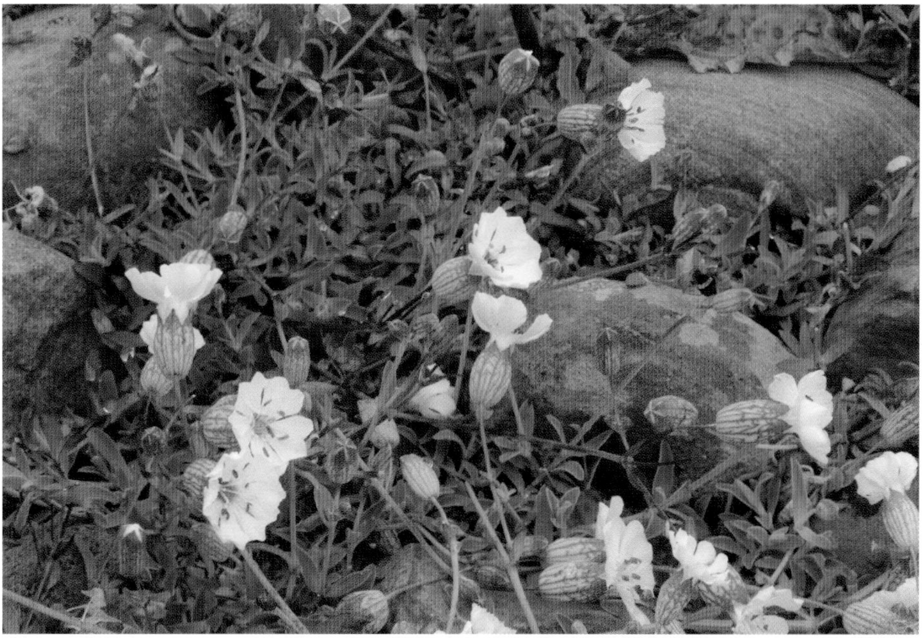

Plate 130 (s–m) **Sea Campion** (*Silene uniflora*)
Flowers white, petals 5, deeply cleft; sepal tube inflated; stems numerous, spreading; leaves narrow, opposite, blue-green, hairless. Native. Shingly beaches, sea-cliffs, serpentine gravel. Flowering late May–August. Photograph: Grutness Voe, Sumburgh.

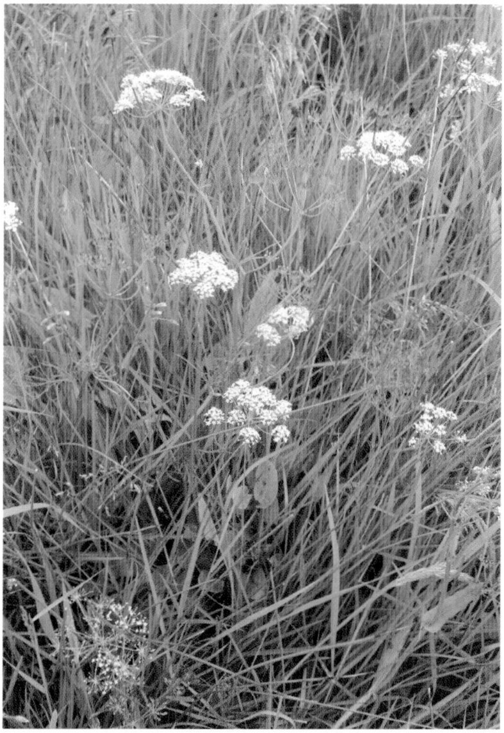

Plate 131 (m) **Pignut**
(*Conopodium majus*)
Flowers white, tiny, in umbels, petals 5; stems slender, arising from a small, brown, edible, underground tuber; leaves pinnate. Well-established alien. Pastures, roadsides. Flowering June–July. Photograph: rich grassy field, Easter Quarff.

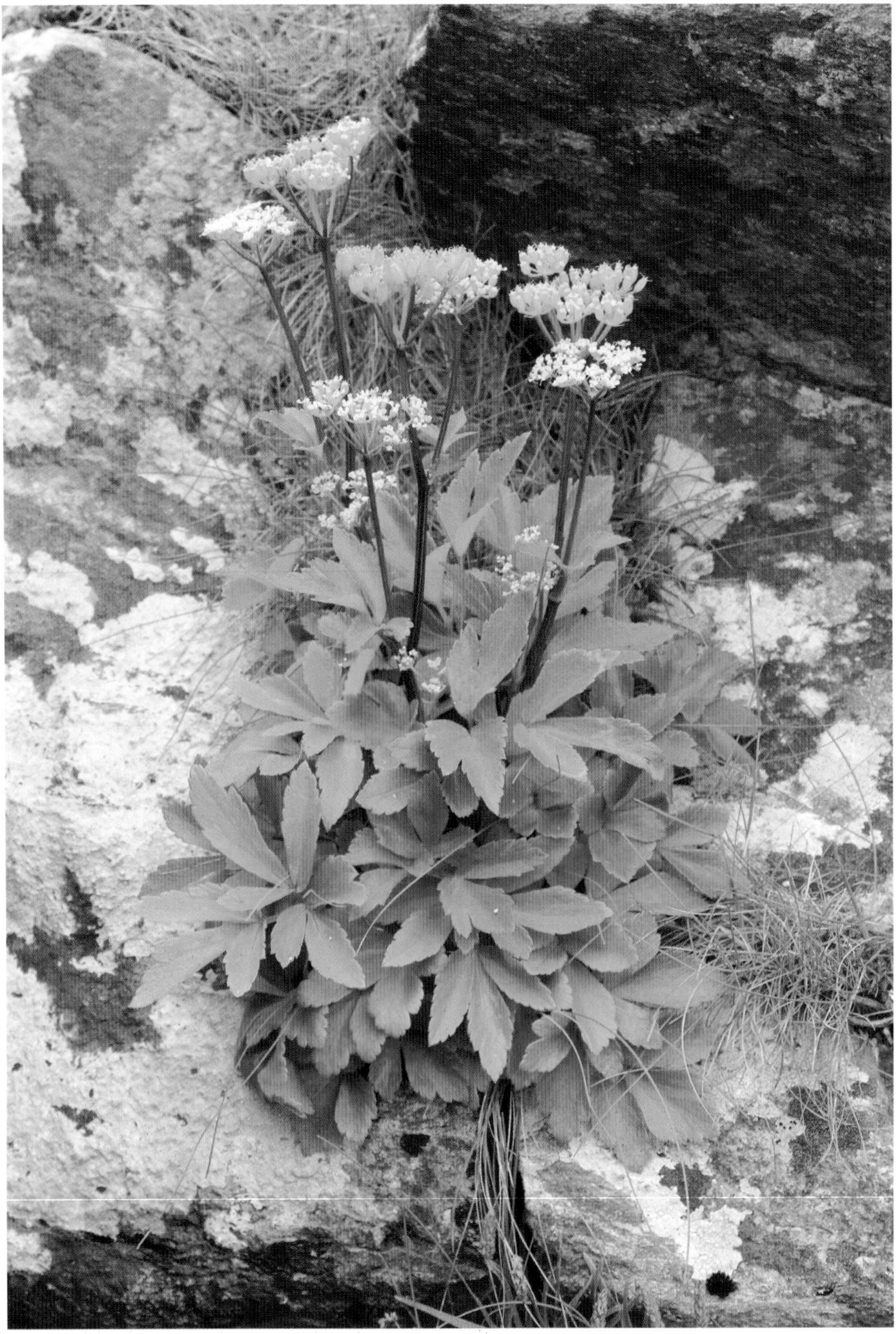

Plate 132 (m–l) **Scots Lovage** (*Ligusticum scoticum*)
Flowers white, in umbels 4.0–6.0 cm wide; stems hairless, often magenta; leaves divided into 3 long-stalked, lobed leaflets; leaf-stalk broadly sheathing at the base. Native. Sea-cliffs, rocky geos, beaches, stonework of old piers. Flowering July–early September. Photograph: sea-banks, Lunna Ness.

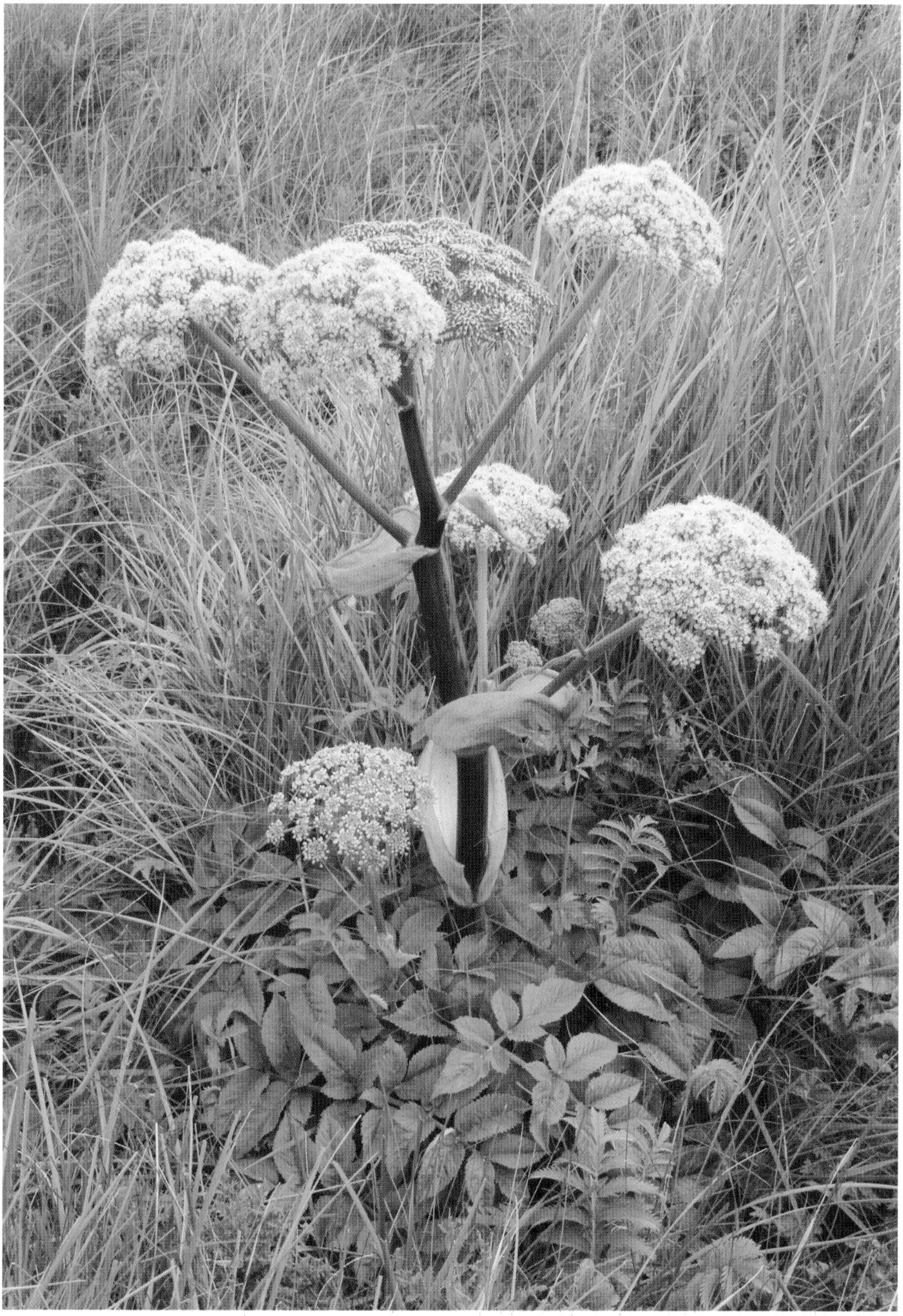

Plate 133 (l) **Wild Angelica** (*Angelica sylvestris*)
Flowers whitish-pink, in large flowerheads up to 14.0 cm wide, composed of many smaller, rounded umbels; stems stout almost hairless; leaves pinnate, leaf-stalk expanded to form an inflated sheath. Native. Damp meadows, pastures, streamsides, etc. Flowering late July–September. Photograph: landward side of sand-dunes, Bay of Quendale.

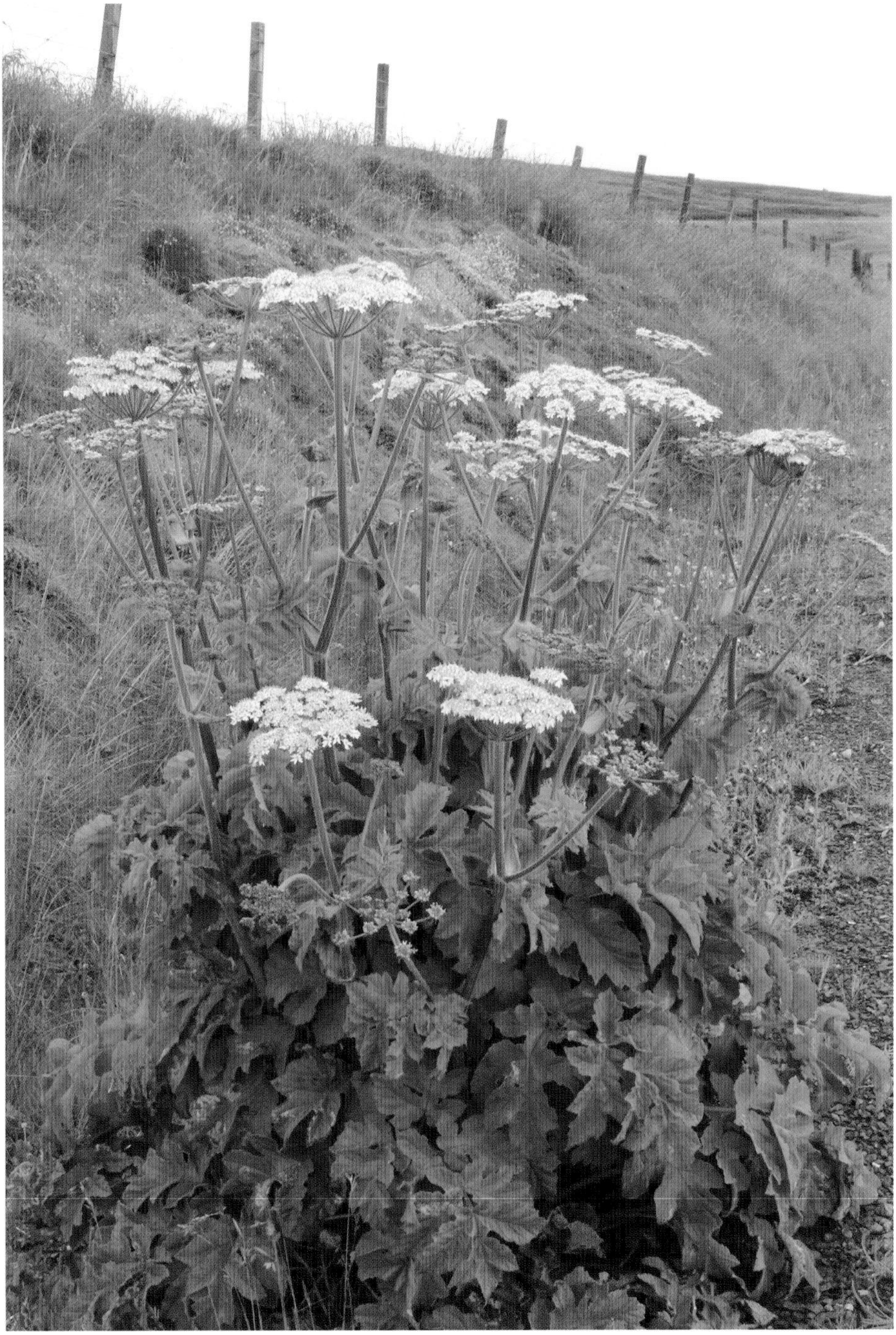

Plate 134 (l) **Hogweed** (*Heracleum sphondylium*) 'Keksi'
Flowers whitish-pink, in umbels, petals 5, notched; stems hairy; leaves pinnate, leaflets broad, hairy, lobed, leaf-stalk expanded into a large sheath. Well-established alien. Rough grassy places, sandy pastures, churchyards. Flowering July–August. Photograph: roadside verge near Fladdabister.

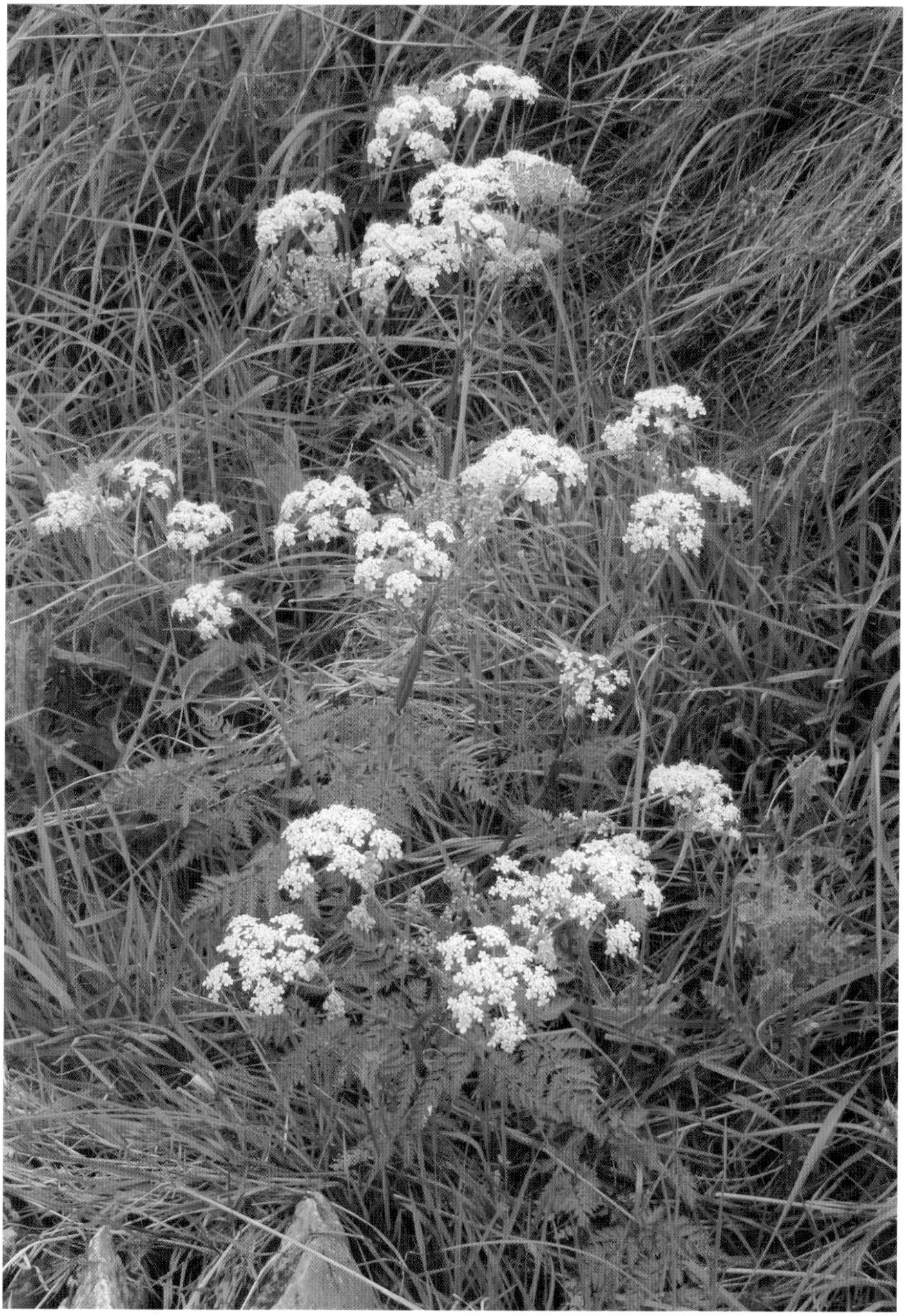

Plate 135 (l) **Cow Parsley** (*Anthriscus sylvestris*)
Flowers white, clustered in 6–12 umbels, 2.0–6.0 cm wide; stems downy, often purple; leaves much divided and thus fern-like in appearance. Well-established alien. Rough grassy places, banks, waste ground, almost always near dwellings. Flowering late May–July. Photograph: grassy bank by the East Voe of Scalloway.

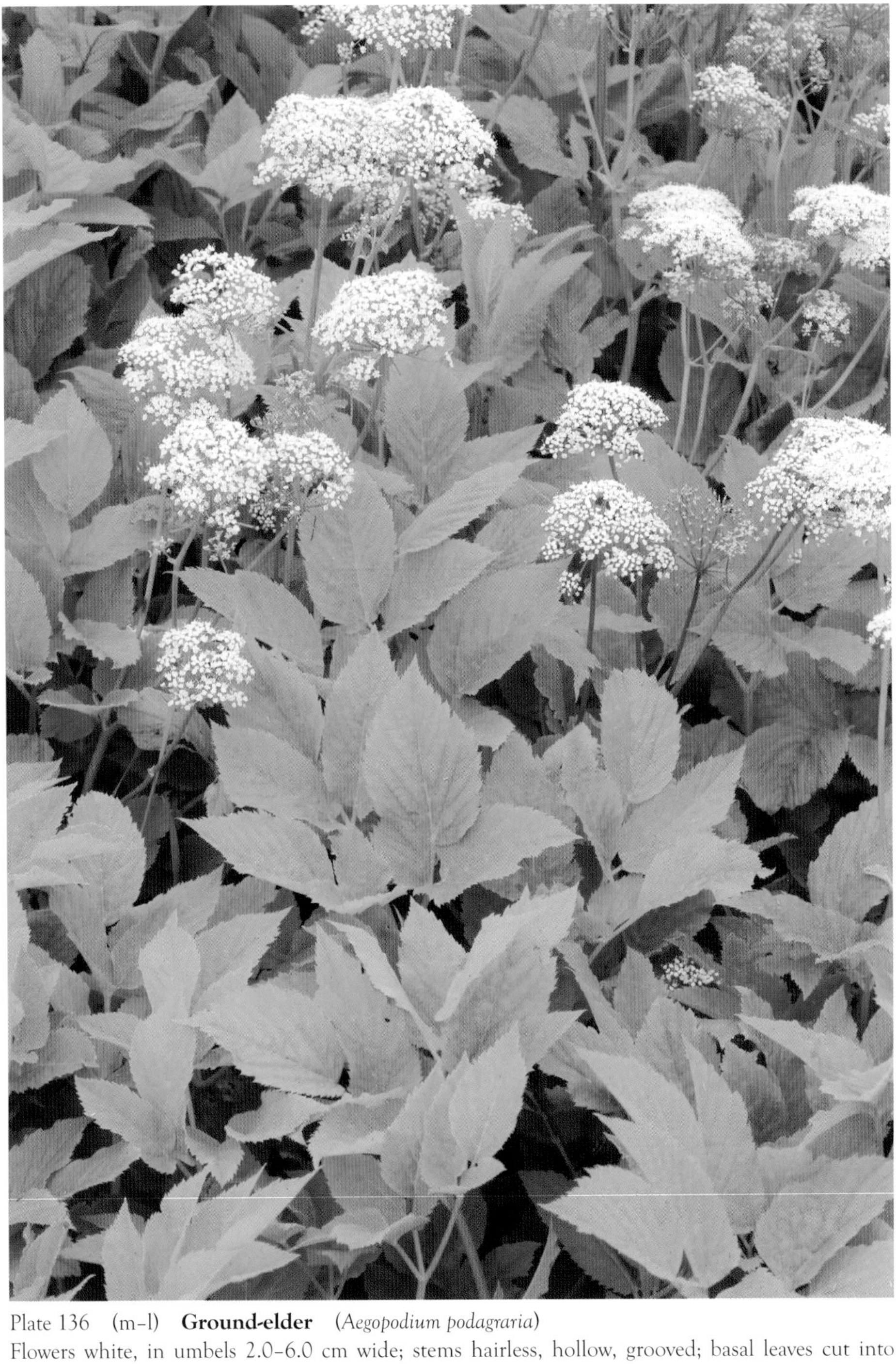

Plate 136 (m–l) **Ground-elder** (*Aegopodium podagraria*)
Flowers white, in umbels 2.0–6.0 cm wide; stems hairless, hollow, grooved; basal leaves cut into three segments each having three lanceolate to ovate lobes. Well-established alien. Garden outcast, waste ground, rubbish dumps. Flowering late June–early August. Photograph: grassy area by roadside, Sandwick, South Mainland.

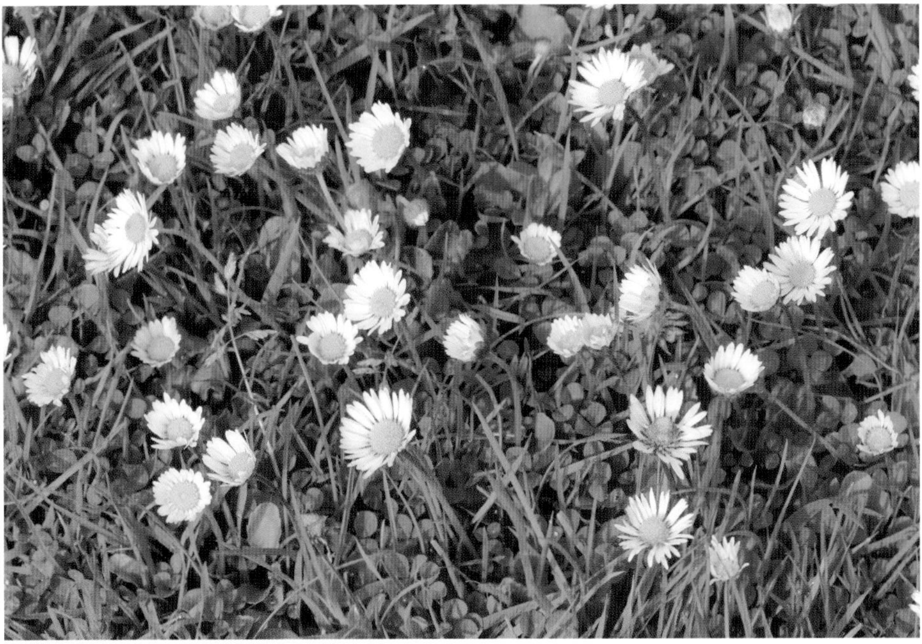

Plate 137 (s) **Daisy** (*Bellis perennis*) 'Kokkeloori'
Flowerheads solitary, composed of numerous tiny flowers, the central ones yellow, the outer white, conspicuous and often tinged crimson, especially beneath; stems hairy; leaves in a basal rosette, spoon-shaped, hairy. Native. Short grassland. Flowering March–October and during mild winters in favoured spots. Photograph: grassy roadside verge, Tingwall.

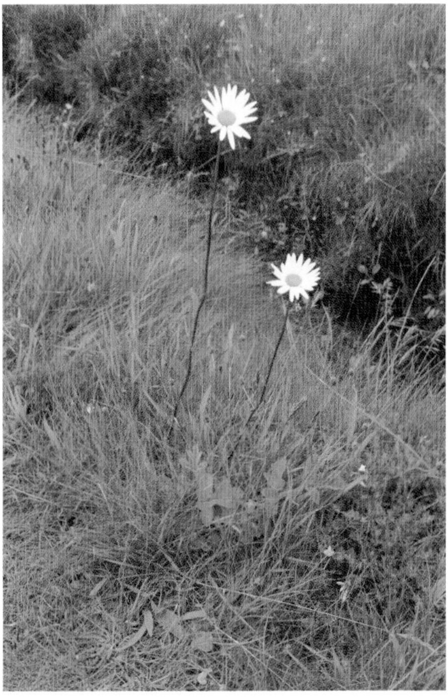

Plate 138 (m) **Oxeye Daisy**
(*Leucanthemum vulgare*)
Flowerheads daisy-like, 2.5–5.0 cm wide, solitary; leaves dark green, the basal long-stalked. Casual. Roadside verges, dry grassland, meadows, pastures. Flowering July–August. Photograph: roadside verge, Fladdabister.

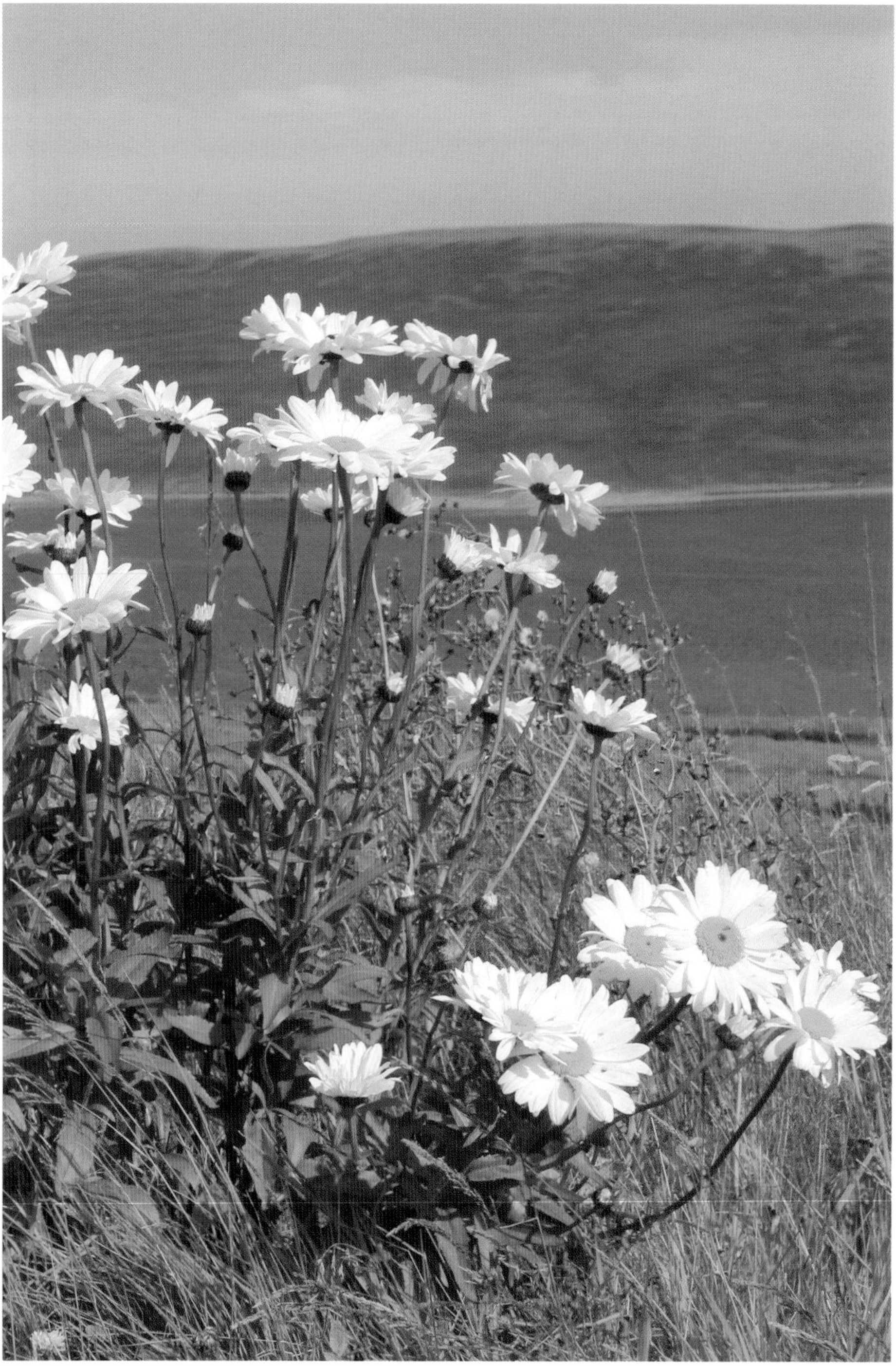

Plate 139 (l) **Shasta Daisy** (*Leucanthemum × superbum*)
Flowerheads daisy-like, large, 6.0–9.0 cm wide. Casual. Garden outcast or deliberately introduced. Flowering August–early October. Photograph: rough pasture, Laxfirth, Tingwall.

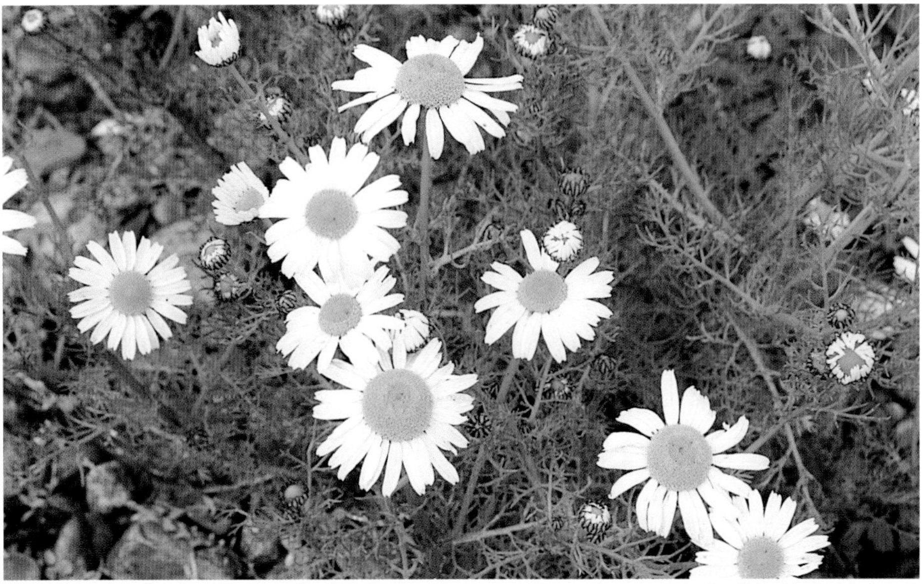

Plate 140 (m–l) **Sea Mayweed** (*Tripleurospermum maritimum* subsp. *nigriceps*) 'Muckle Kokkeloori'
Flowerheads daisy-like, up to 5.0 cm wide; stems stout, usually prostrate; leaves fleshy, feathery. Native. Shingly beaches and sea-bird cliffs. Flowering late June–September. Photograph: stony beach, Easter Quarff.

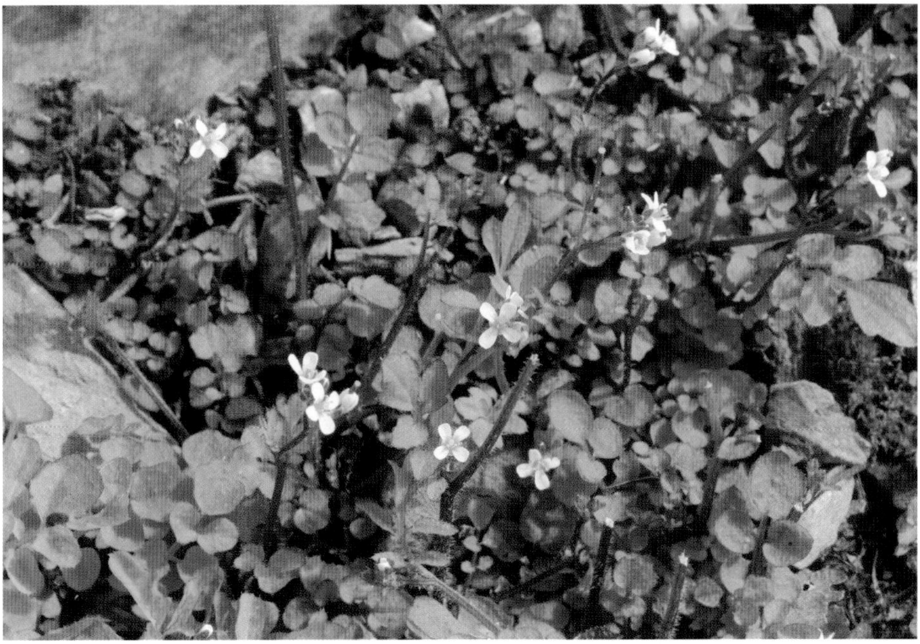

Plate 141 (s) **Wavy Bitter-cress** (*Cardamine flexuosa*)
Flowers white, 5–8 mm wide; stems wavy; basal leaves in a lax rosette with 3–6 pairs of lateral leaflets, stem leaves narrower than basal leaves. Well-established alien in the Kergord Plantations, Weisdale, otherwise a garden outcast on dumped soil, open waste places, etc. Flowering late April–August. Photograph: gravelly area in a farmyard, Tresta, Fetlar.

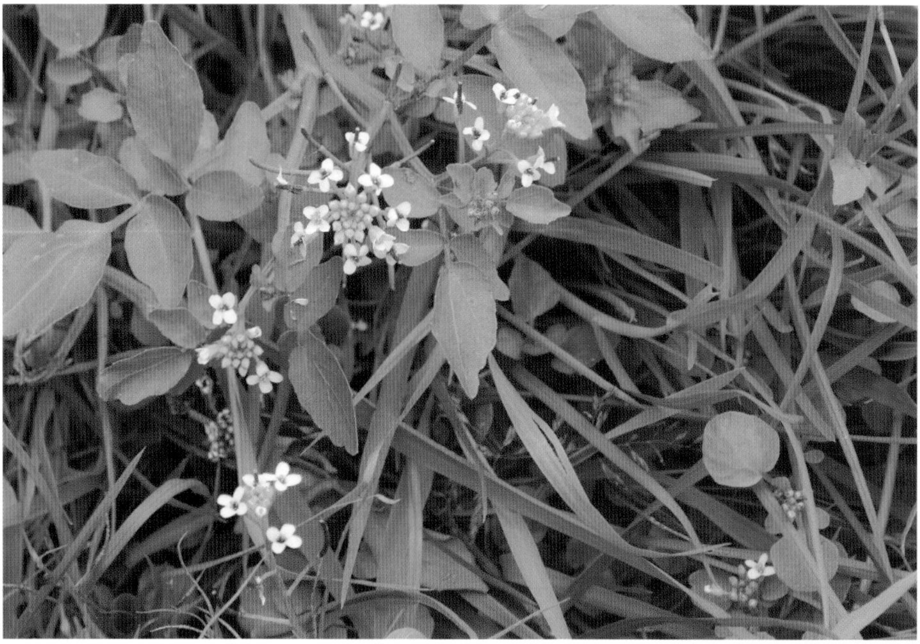

Plate 142 (s) **Water-cress** (*Rorippa nasturtium-aquaticum*)
Flowers white, about 6 mm wide; leaves dark green, glossy, pinnate with rounded leaflets. Well-established alien. Nutrient-rich ditches, streams and lochs. Flowering June–September. Photograph: ditch near Sumburgh Hotel.

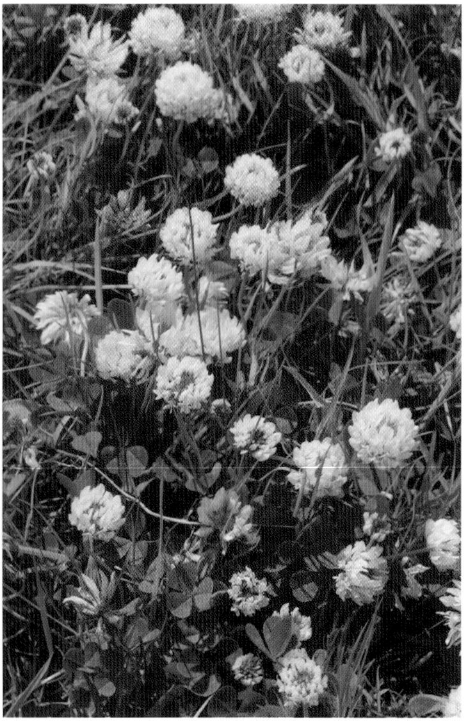

Plate 143 (s–m) **White Clover** (*Trifolium repens*)
Flowers white, tiny, in globular flowerheads; stems creeping; leaves trifoliate, often with a pale or dark band near the base of each leaflet. Native and alien. Pastures, grassy places, roadsides. Flowering late May–August. Photograph: grassy roadside verge near Scalloway.

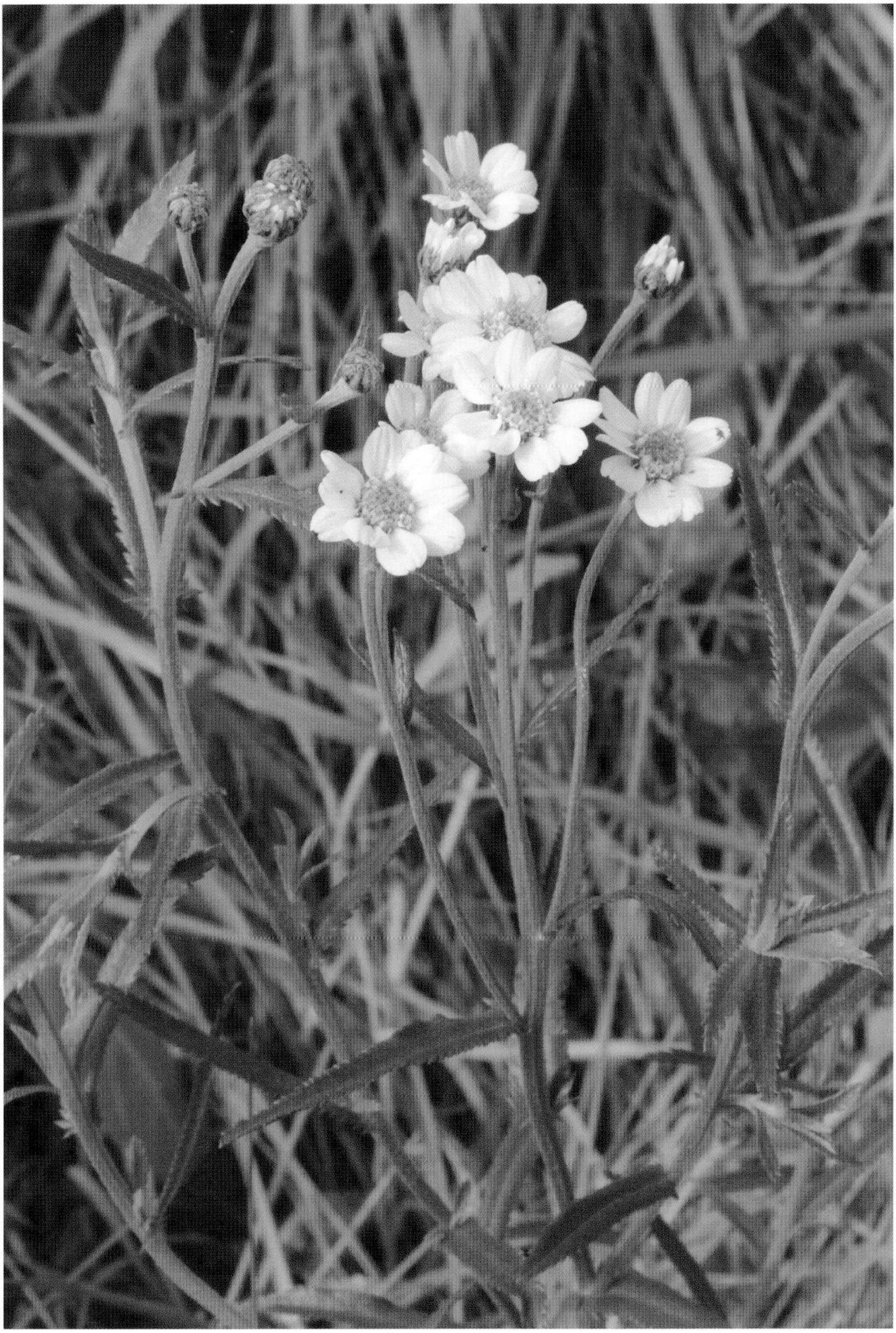

Plate 144 (m) **Sneezewort** (*Achillea ptarmica*)
Flowerheads greenish-white; stems finely hairy; leaves long, narrow, minutely saw-toothed. Native. Meadows, streamsides, loch margins, roadsides. Flowering late July–September. Photograph: landward side of sand-dunes, Bay of Quendale.

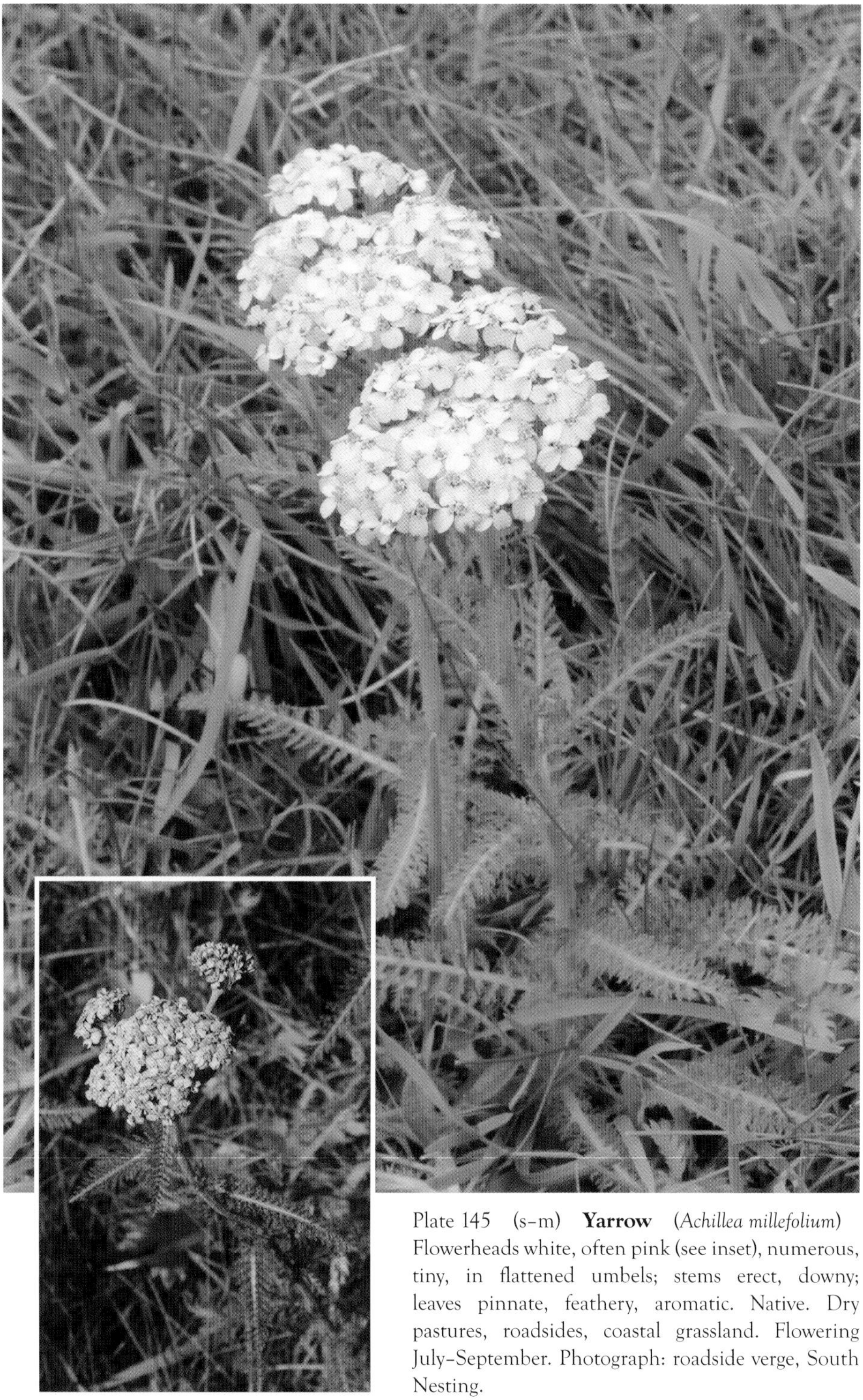

Plate 145 (s–m) **Yarrow** (*Achillea millefolium*) Flowerheads white, often pink (see inset), numerous, tiny, in flattened umbels; stems erect, downy; leaves pinnate, feathery, aromatic. Native. Dry pastures, roadsides, coastal grassland. Flowering July–September. Photograph: roadside verge, South Nesting.

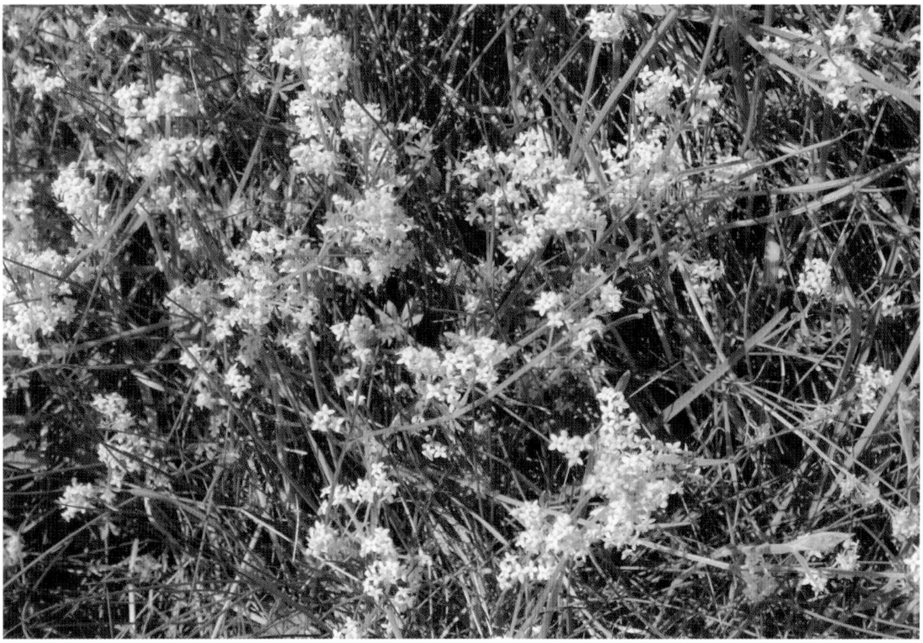

Plate 146 (s–m) **Heath Bedstraw** (*Galium saxatile*)
Flowers white, tiny, petals 4; stems straggly; leaves pointed, arranged in whorls of 6–8. Native. Dry heaths, gravelly roadside verges. Flowering June–August. Photograph: grassy roadside bank near Green Head, north of Lerwick.

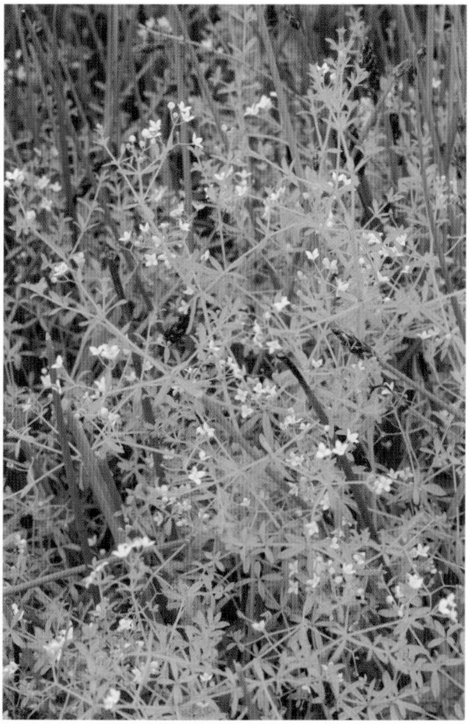

Plate 147 (s–l)
Common Marsh-bedstraw
(*Galium palustre* subsp. *palustre*)
Flowers white, tiny, petals 4; stems straggly; leaves, blunt-tipped, in whorls of 4–6. Native. Marshes, sides of burns, ditches. Flowering June–August. Photograph: marsh, Burland, Trondra.

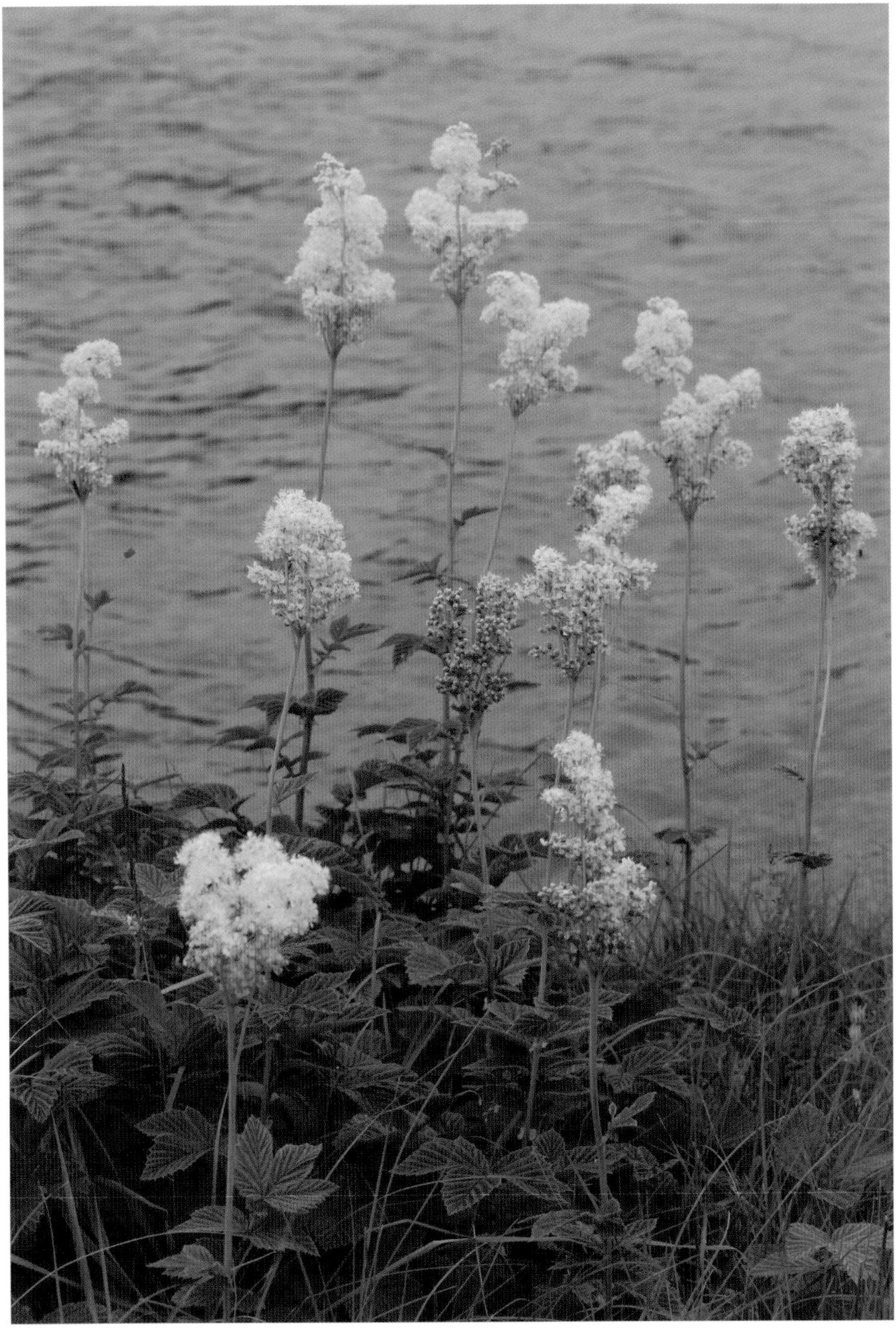

Plate 148 (l) **Meadowsweet** (*Filipendula ulmaria*) 'Yölgirse'
Flowers in dense cream-coloured clusters; stems square, stiff; leaves pinnate, leaflets toothed, green above, silvery below. Native. A sweetly fragrant plant of streamsides, margins of lochs, damp pastures. Flowering late July–August. Photograph: margin of the Loch of Tingwall.

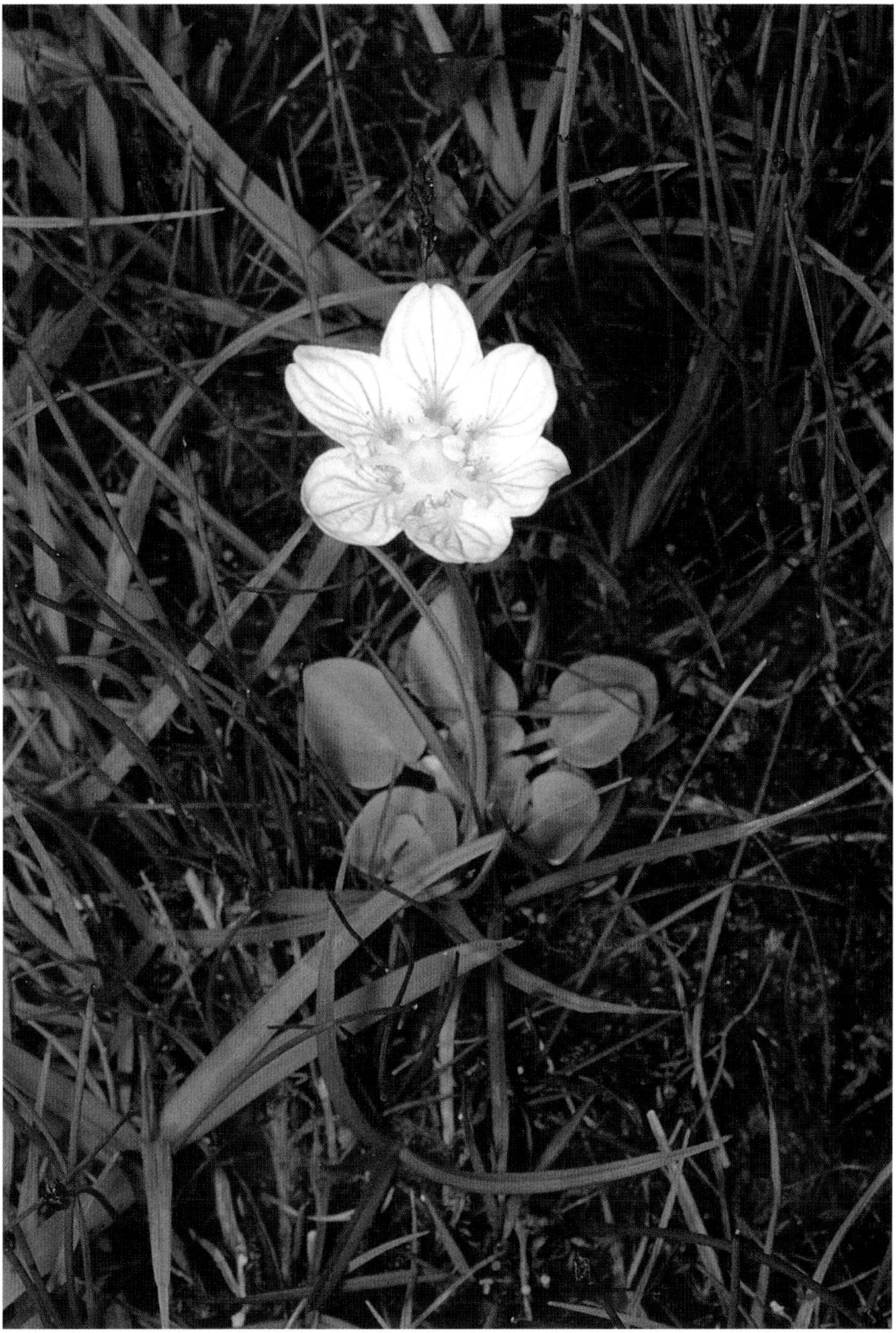

Plate 149 (s–m) **Grass-of-Parnassus** (*Parnassia palustris*)
Flowers white, 2.0 cm wide, solitary, petals 5, veined; stems slender, clasped by a single leaf; other leaves in a basal rosette, stalked. Native. Damp pastures, marshes, stony lochsides. Flowering July–September. Photograph: Quoys, Lerwick.

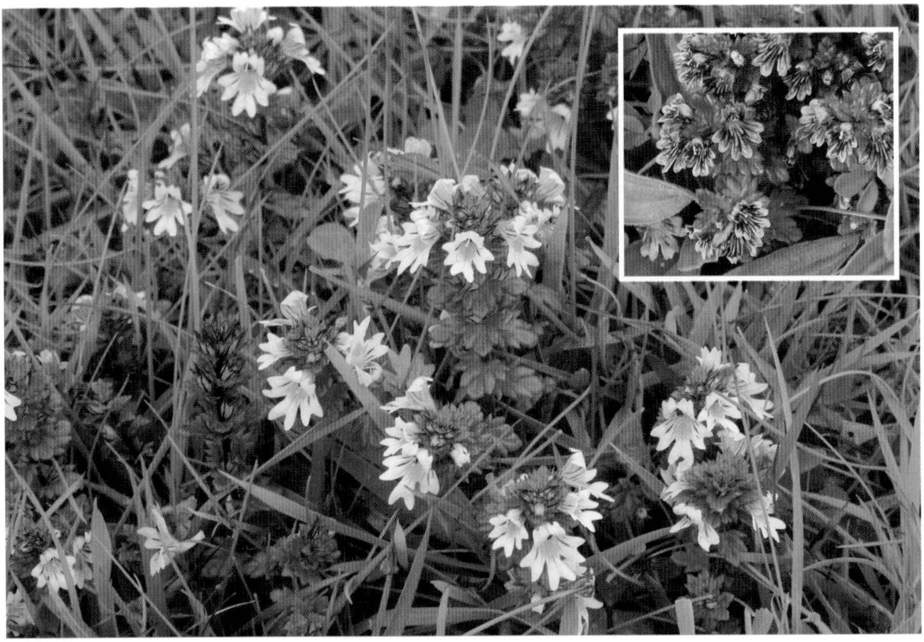

Plate 150 (s) **Eyebright** (*Euphrasia* sp.)
A genus with many closely related species and hybrids. In general the flowers are whitish-lilac, often much darker (see inset), 2-lipped, with a yellow spot and purple lines on the lower lip; stems, and sometimes the leaves, hairy; leaves deeply toothed. Native. Eyebrights occur in many habitats from coastal turf to upland heaths; damp pastures to serpentine gravel. Flowering late May–July. Photograph: coastal grassland, Tresta, Fetlar.

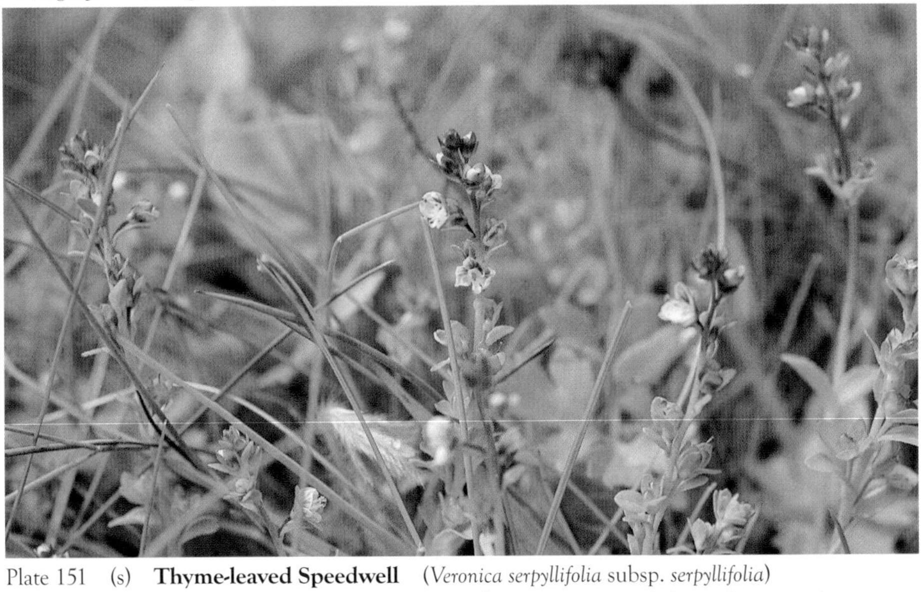

Plate 151 (s) **Thyme-leaved Speedwell** (*Veronica serpyllifolia* subsp. *serpyllifolia*)
Flowers bluish-lilac with darker veins, in spikes, petals 4; stems minutely hairy, leaves oval, opposite, unstalked, barely toothed. Native. Damp grassy places, roadside verges. Flowering May–July. Photograph: damp pasture, Fladdabister.

Plate 152 (s) **Slender Speedwell**
(*Veronica filiformis*)
Flowers pale lilac-blue, on long slender stalks; mat-forming plant. Well-established alien in and around Tingwall churchyard. Grassy roadside verges, churchyards, lawns. Flowering late April–July. Photograph: grassy roadside verge by Tingwall churchyard.

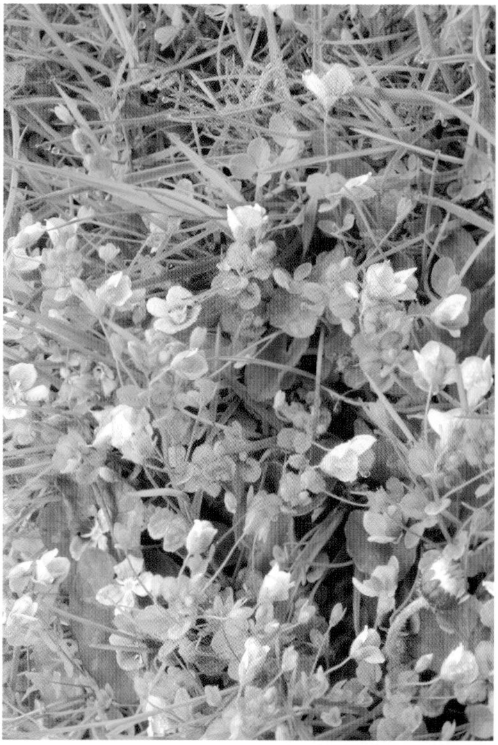

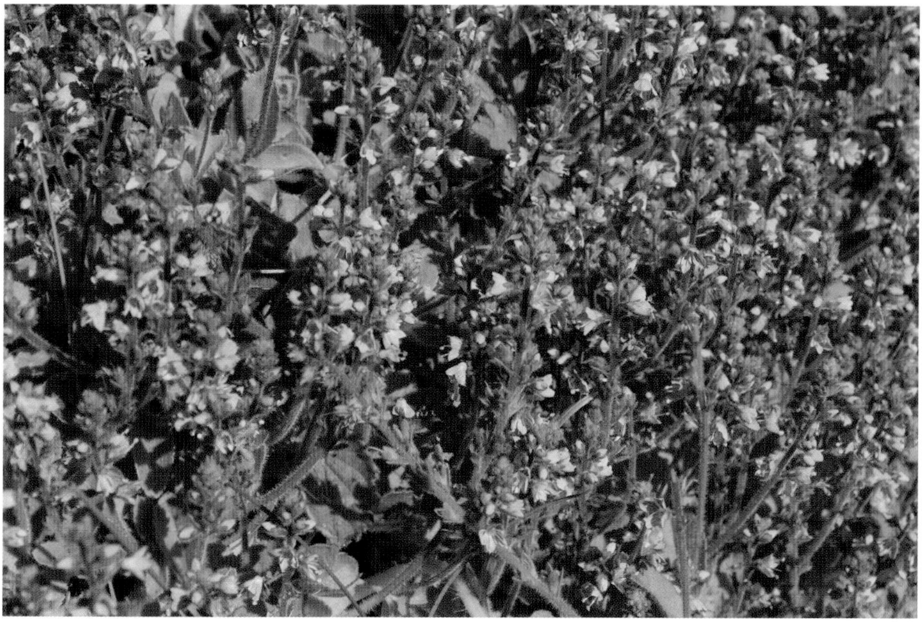

Plate 153 (s) **Heath Speedwell** (*Veronica officinalis*)
Flowers lilac, veined dark blue, in erect spikes, petals 4; stems hairy, creeping; leaves oval, opposite, toothed, hairy. Native. Heathland, dry grassy places. Flowering June–August. Photograph: grassy roadside bank, Asta, near Scalloway.

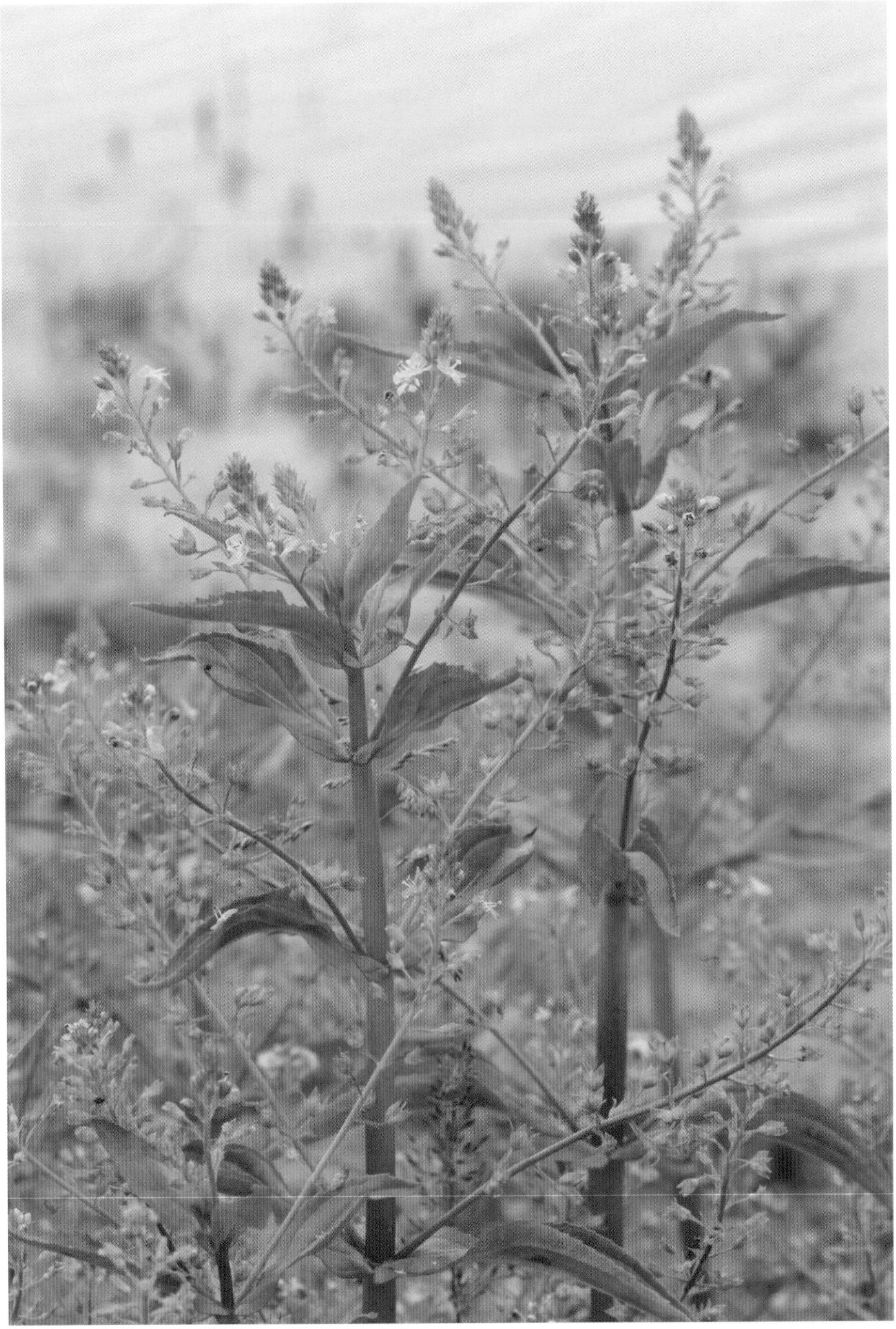

Plate 154 (m–l) **Blue Water-speedwell** (*Veronica anagallis-aquatica*)
Flowers bluish-lilac, in opposite spikes, petals 4, stems succulent; leaves lanceolate, opposite, wavy, scarcely toothed. Native. Ditches and streams. Flowering July–September. Photograph: pond behind the Bay of Quendale.

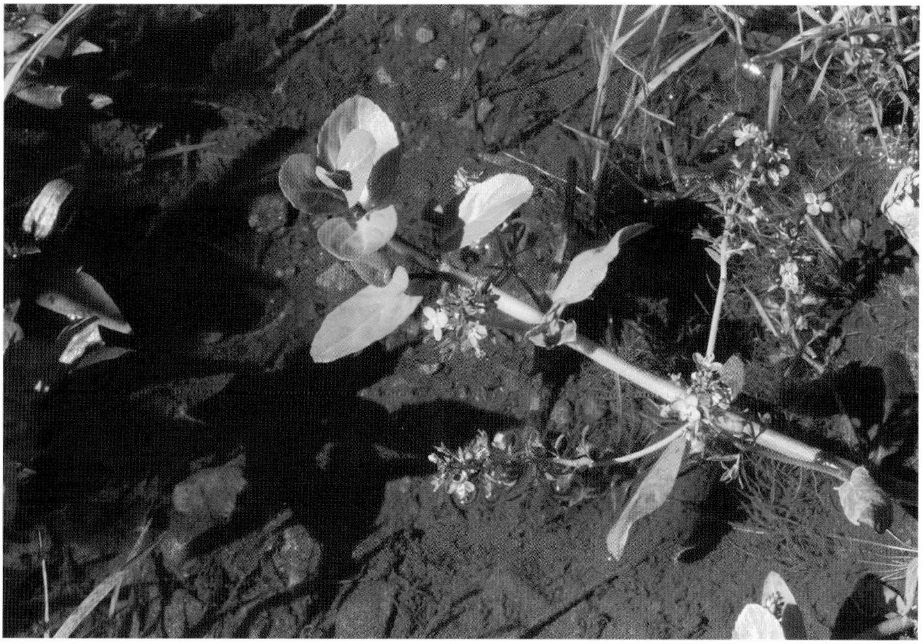

Plate 155 (m) **Brooklime** (*Veronica beccabunga*)
Flowers blue, 7–8 mm wide, in opposite stalked spikes at base of upper leaves; stems hairless; leaves oval, thick, stalked, fleshy. Native. Ditches, burns, marshes, and with a preference for limestone areas. Flowering June–early August. Photograph: burn running into Strand Loch, Tingwall.

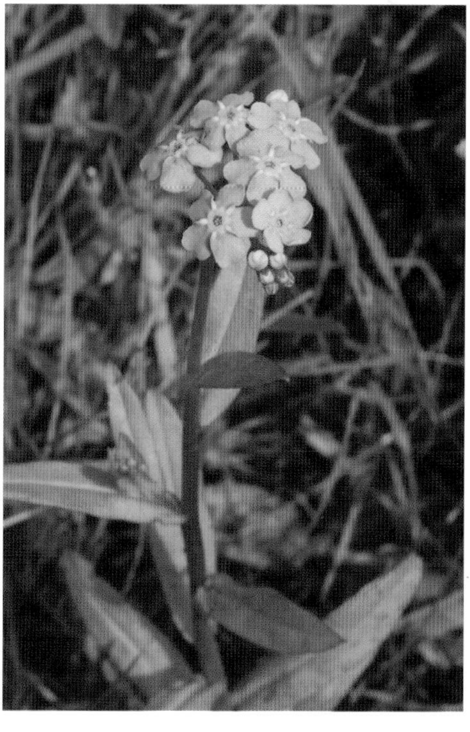

Plate 156 (m) **Water Forget-me-not** (*Myosotis scorpioides*)
Flowers 4–10 mm wide, blue, pink at first; petals notched; calyx teeth broadly triangular; hairs closely pressed to stems and calyces; leaves oblong-lanceolate, up to 10 cm long. Well-established alien. Ditches, burns, marshes, swampy vegetation by lochs. Flowering late June–September. Photograph: burn, Easter Quarff.

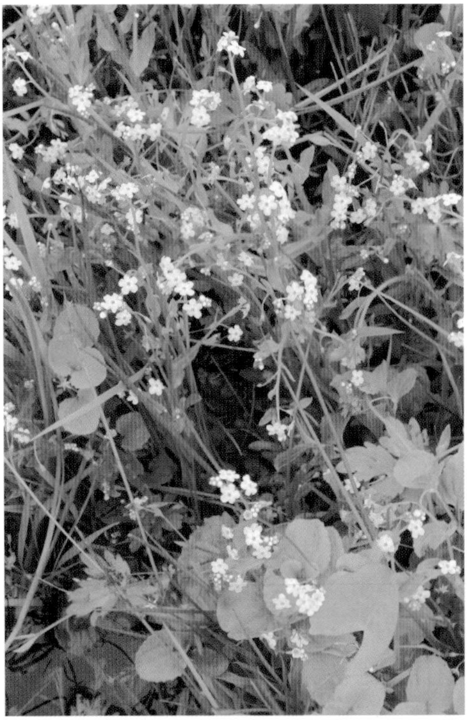

Plate 157 (s–m)
Creeping Forget-me-not (*Myosotis secunda*)
Flowers characteristically sky-blue, pink at first, 6–7 mm wide, petals 5; stems hairy; leaves oval, alternate. Native. Streams, ditches, marshes. Flowering late June–August. Photograph: stream, Easter Quarff.

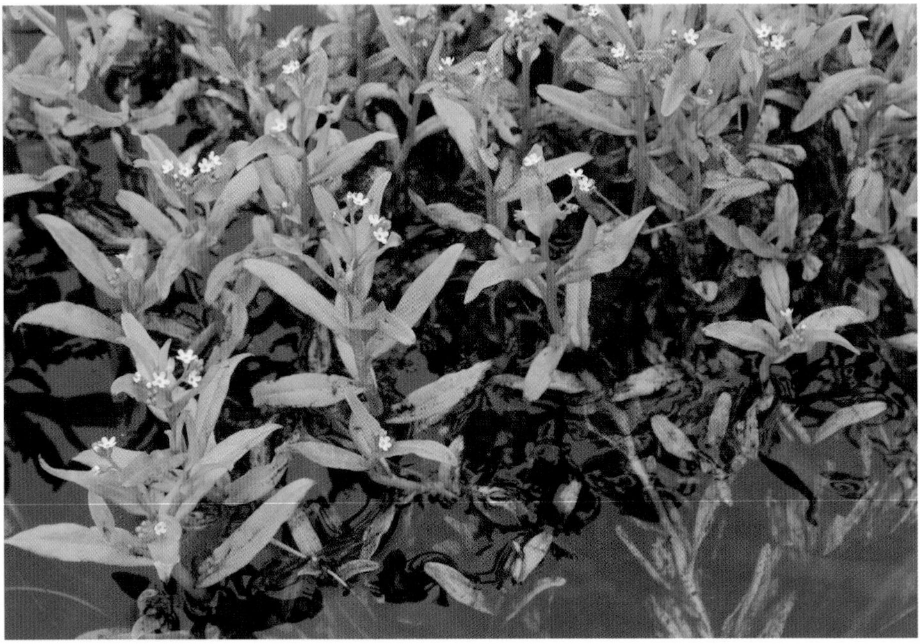

Plate 158 (m) **Tufted Forget-me-not** (*Myosotis laxa*)
Flowers blue, pink at first, small, 2–4 mm wide, petals not notched, calyx teeth narrowly triangular. Native. Ditches, burns, marshes. Flowering late June–early August. Photograph: burn running into Strand Loch, Tingwall.

Plate 159 (s)
Changing Forget-me-not
(*Myosotis discolor*)
Flowers initially whitish or creamy, becoming blue, tiny (2 mm wide), in curving spikes; stems hairy; leaves lanceolate, alternate, hairy. Probably native. Dry grassland, arable ground. Flowering May–August. Photograph: meadow, Fladdabister.

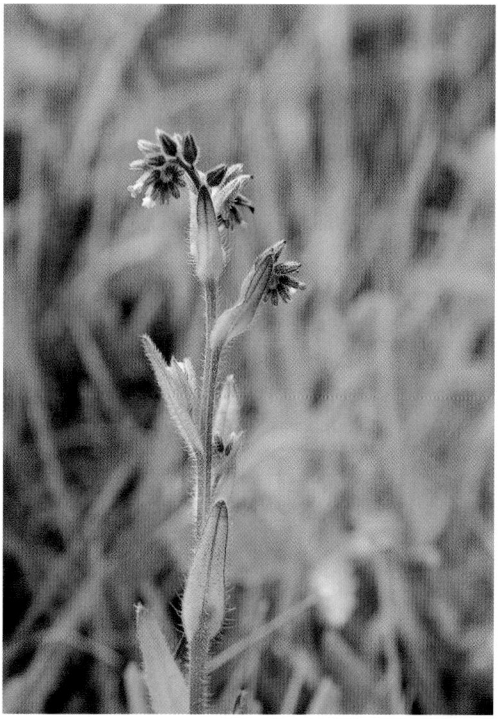

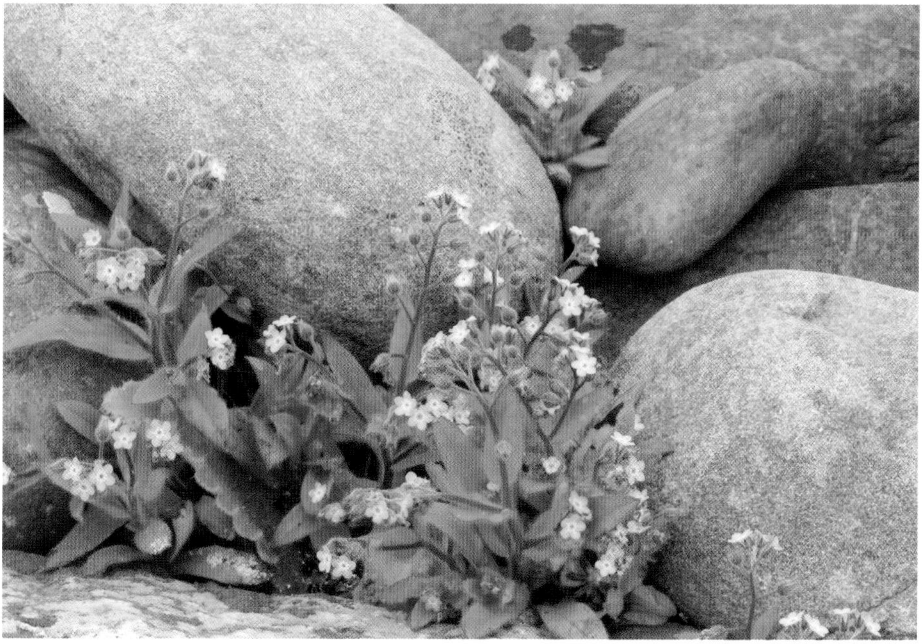

Plate 160 (s–m) **Field Forget-me-not** (*Myosotis arvensis*)
Flowers blue, pink at first, petals 5; leaves oblong, softly hairy. Well-established alien. Dry arable land, waste ground, sometimes on foreshores. Flowering late May–August. Photograph: Grutness Voe, Sumburgh.

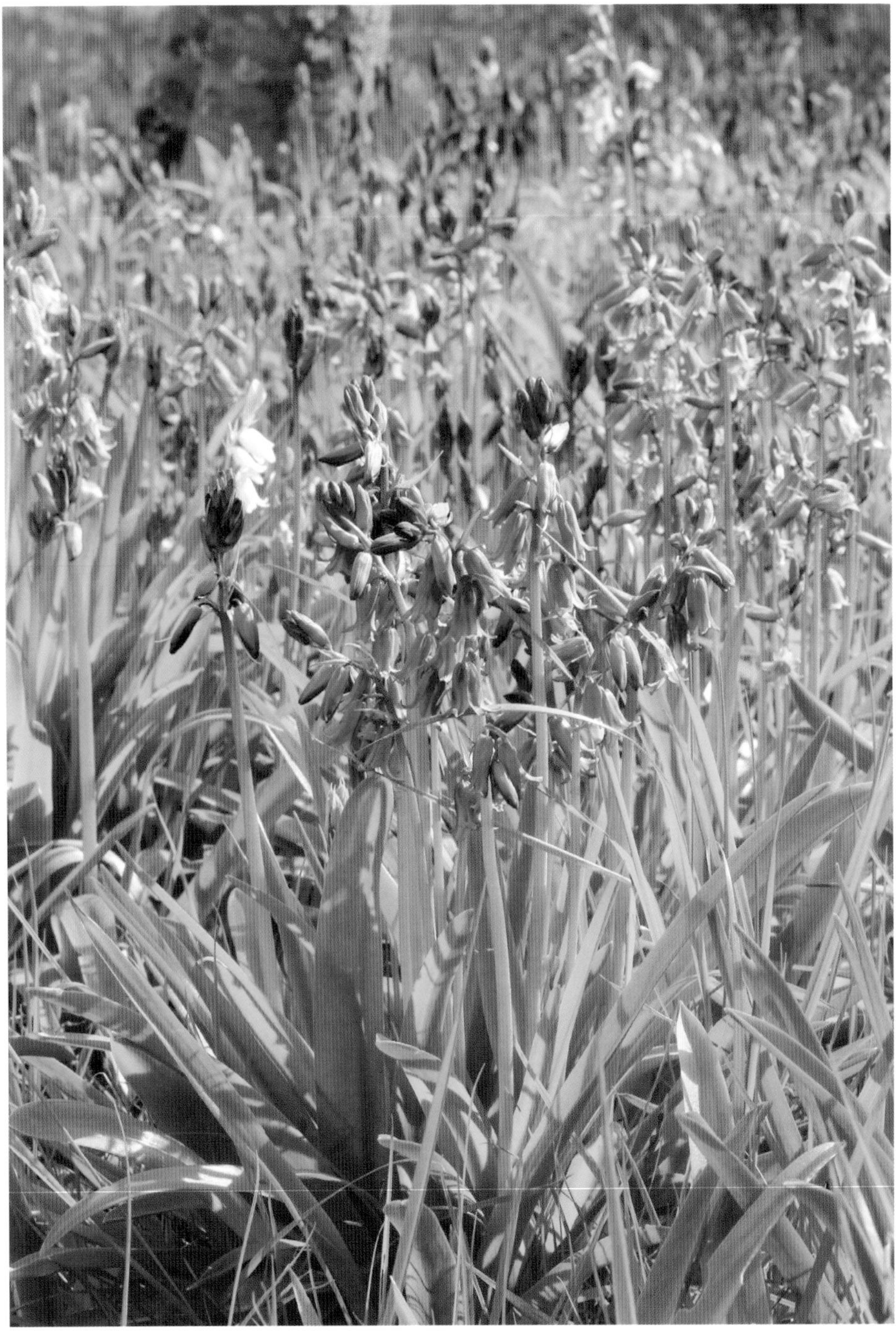

Plate 161 (m) **Bluebell** (*Hyacinthoides* × *massartiana*)
Flowers bluish-violet, sometimes white or pink, in spikes, bell-shaped; leaves long, narrow, all from the base of the plant. Well-established alien of garden origin. Grassy places near houses. Flowering late May–early June. Photograph: wooded area, Asta, near Scalloway.

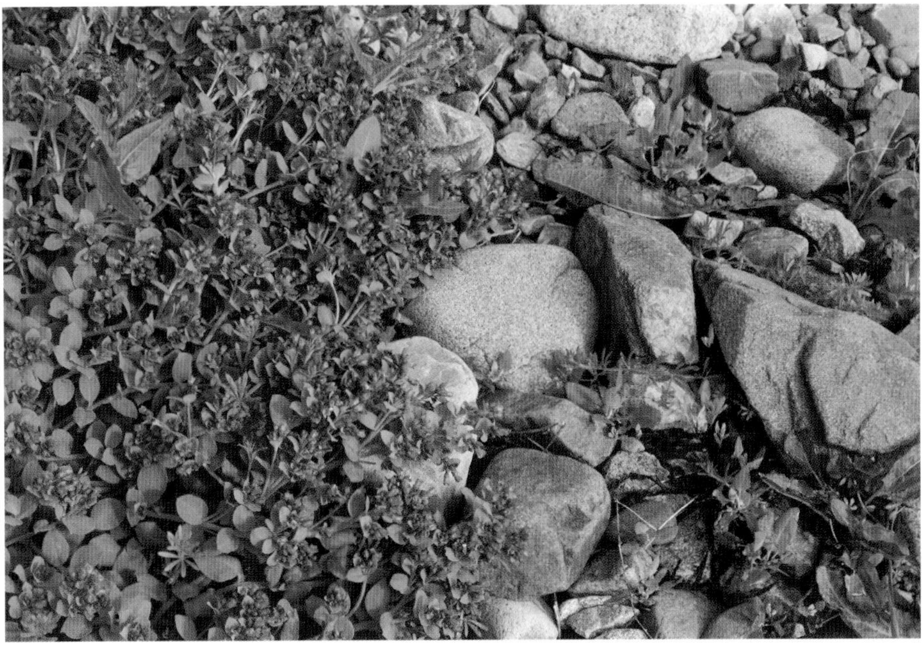

Plate 162 (m–l) **Oysterplant** (*Mertensia maritima*)
Flowers pink, becoming blue, bell-shaped, petals 5; stems sprawling, branching, succulent; leaves oval, bluish-green. Native. Rare and found on only a few shingly beaches. Flowering June–August. Photograph: shingly beach, head of Ura Firth, Northmavine.

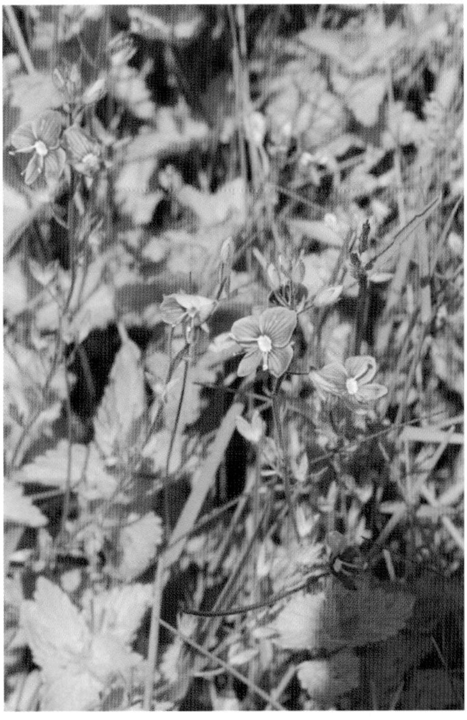

Plate 163 (s–m) **Germander Speedwell** (*Veronica chamaedrys*)
Flowers bright blue with a whitish eye, in spikes, petals 4; stems weak, with lines of hairs on opposing sides; leaves oval, opposite, toothed, hairy. Well-established alien on grassy roadside banks and verges between Utnabrake, north of Scalloway, north to the Tingwall churchyard. Flowering June–August. Photograph: grassy bank by roadside, Asta, near Scalloway.

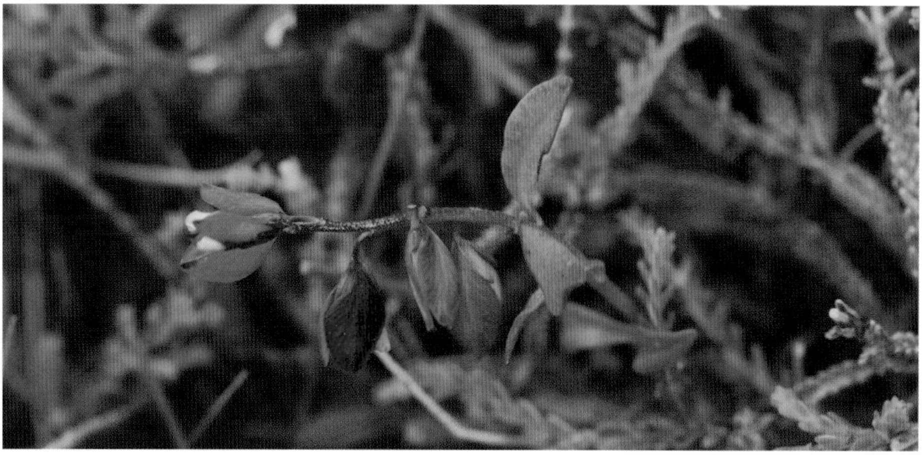

Plate 164 (s) **Heath Milkwort** (*Polygala serpyllifolia*)
Flowers usually dark blue or dark pink but often paler or nearly white, of an unusual shape owing to the two large wing-like coloured sepals; stems usually trailing; leaves small, narrow, the lower (and often the upper) opposite. Native. Damp heathy pastures, moorland. Photograph: heather moorland, Burwick, by Scalloway.

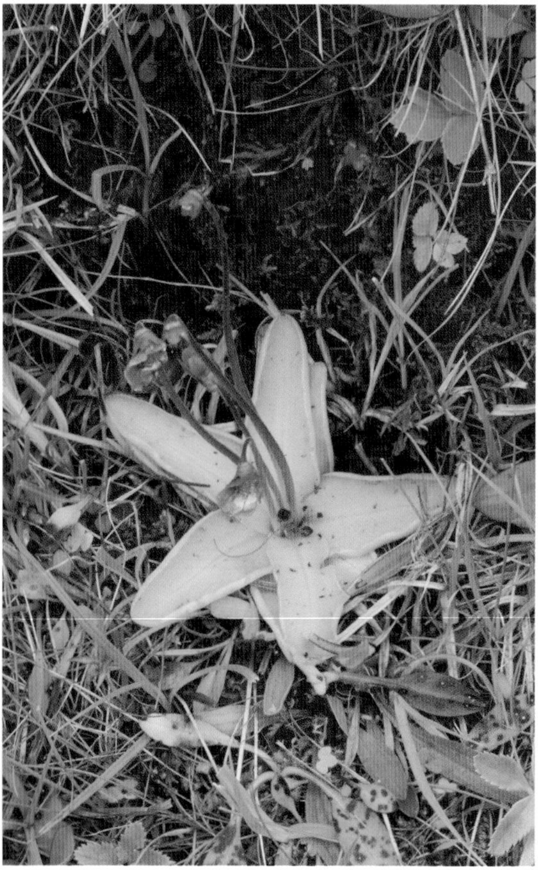

Plate 165 (s)
Common Butterwort
(*Pinguicula vulgaris*)
Flowers deep bluish-violet, solitary, 2-lipped with white patch in the throat, spur pointed; leaves yellowish-green and sticky, forming a basal rosette. An insect-catching plant. Native. Wet heaths and moors, dripping rocky streamsides. Flowering late May–July. Photograph: ditch, Utnabrake, near Scalloway.

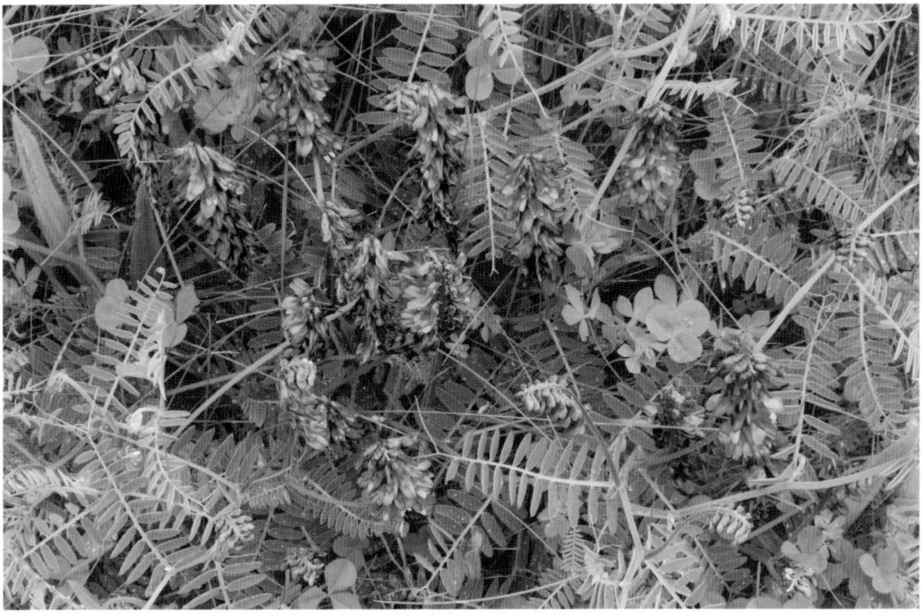

Plate 166 (m) **Tufted Vetch** (*Vicia cracca*)
Flowers bluish-violet, in one-sides spikes of 12–36 flowers; stems hairy; leaves pinnate, leaflets narrow, pointed, stipules small. Native. Arable land, pastures, grassy sea-banks, sand-dunes, roadside verges. Flowering June–August. Photograph: roadside verge, Sumburgh Airport.

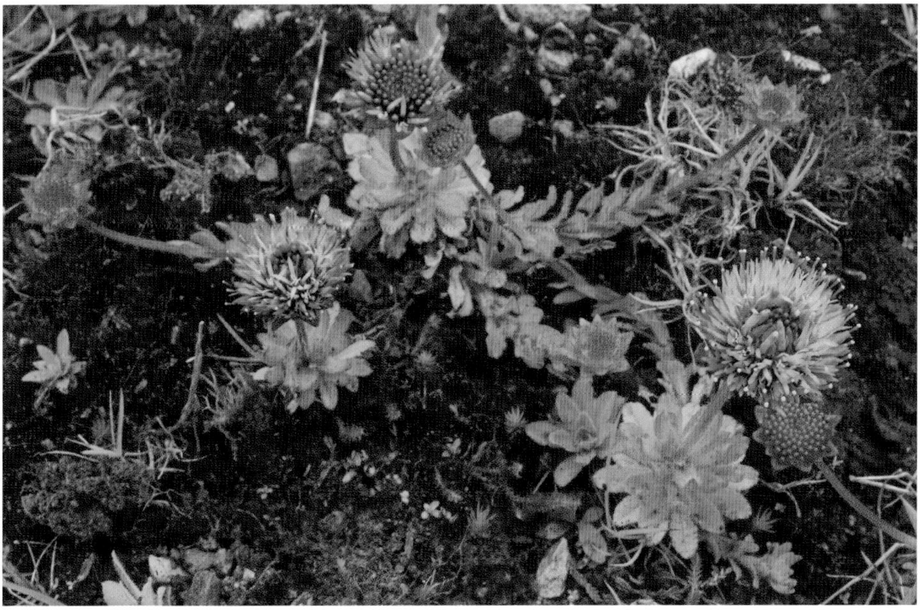

Plate 167 (s–m) **Sheep's-bit** (*Jasione montana*)
Flowers soft blue, occasionally white or lilac, tiny, in a globular flowerhead; involucre hairy; stems slightly hairy; basal leaves wavy, untoothed, hairy, upper leaves unstalked. Native. Dry grassland, grassy sea-cliffs, coastal banks, rocky streamsides. Flowering late June–August. Photograph: roadside verge near Green Head, north of Lerwick.

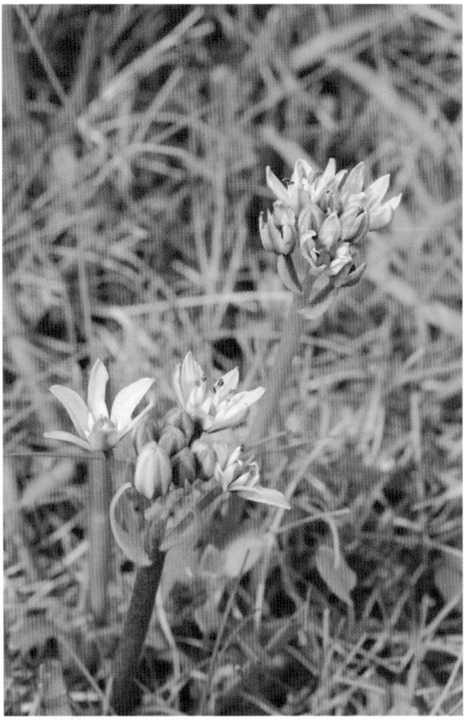

Plate 168 (s) **Spring Squill** (*Scilla verna*)
Flowers violet-blue, star-like, petals 6; stems smooth; leaves narrow, all from the base of the plant. Native. Dry pastures, coastal grassland, sea-banks, serpentine gravel. Flowering late May–June. Photograph: coastal grassland, West Burra.

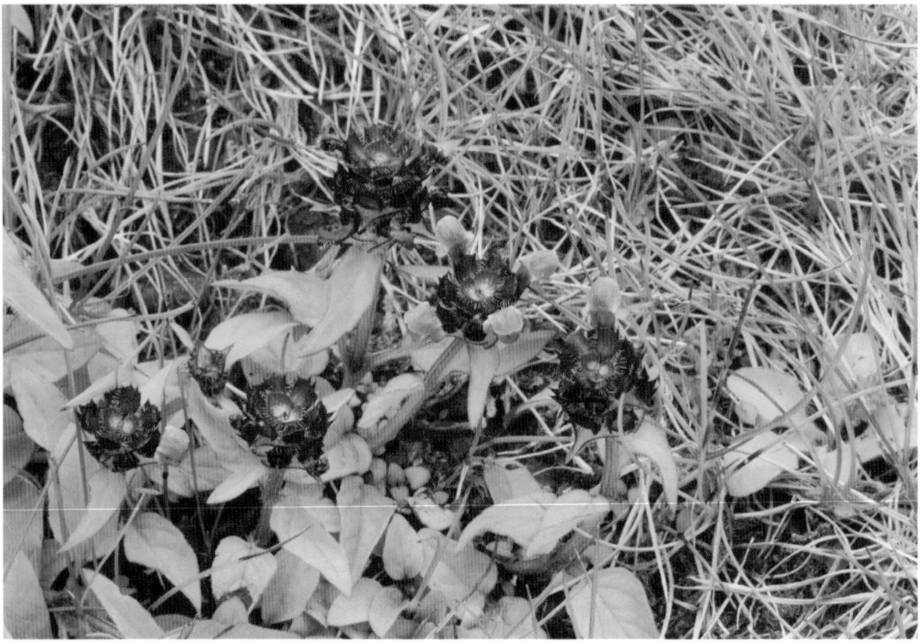

Plate 169 (s–m) **Selfheal** (*Prunella vulgaris*)
Flowers purplish-violet, 2-lipped in a squarish spike; stems slightly hairy; leaves oval, opposite, scarcely toothed. Native. Meadows, pastures, dry heathy ground, dry coastal turf, roadside verges. Flowering July–August. Photograph: roadside verge, Tingwall.

Plate 170 (m) **Bugloss**
(*Anchusa arvensis*)
Flowers blue, petals 5, joined; stems prickly; leaves lanceolate, wavy, prickly. Well-established alien. Sandy arable ground. Flowering June–October. Photograph: roadside verge by the beach at Boddam.

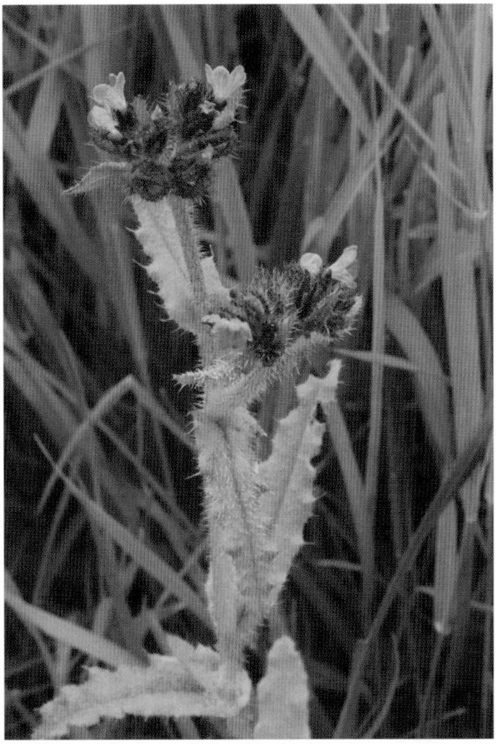

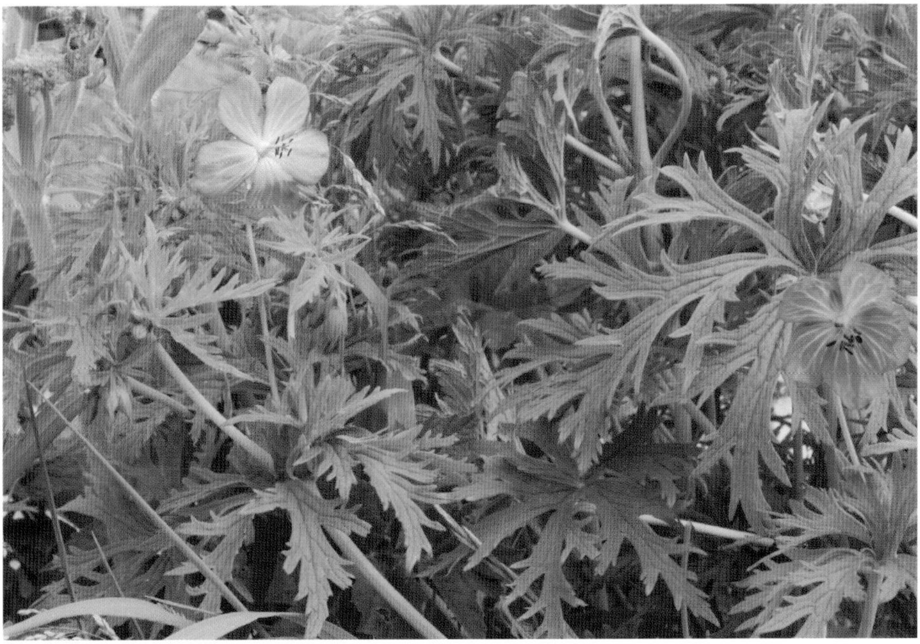

Plate 171 (m–l) **Meadow Crane's-bill** (*Geranium pratense*)
Flowers bluish-violet, large, petals 5; sepals hairy; leaves deeply palmately lobed. Casual. A garden outcast often seen near houses. Flowering July–August. Photograph: by ruined dwelling, Levenwick.

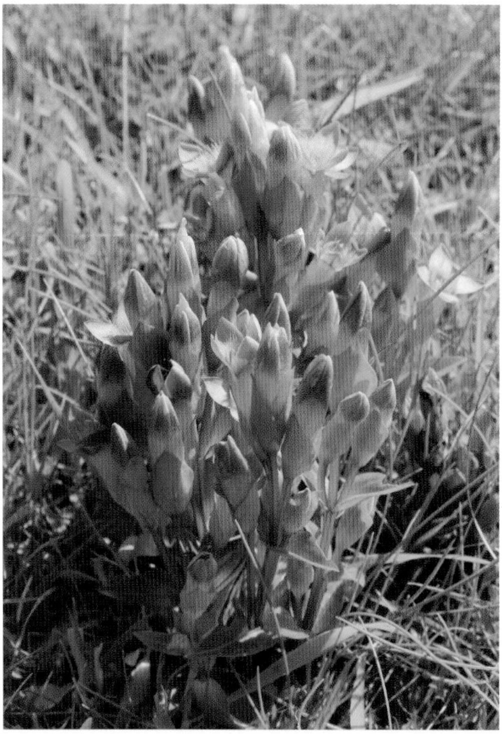

Plate 172 (s–m) **Field Gentian**
(*Gentianella campestris*)
Flowers bluish-lilac, petals 4; sepals, 2 large overlapping 2 small; stems erect, smooth, branching; leaves opposite, unstalked, untoothed. Native. Chiefly in dry stony pastures. Flowering late July–August. Photograph: heathy grassland, Meal, West Burra.

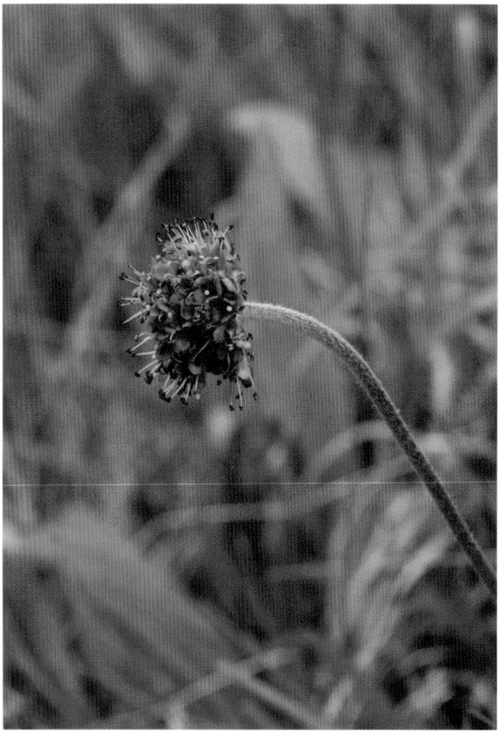

Plate 173 (s–m) **Devil's-bit Scabious**
(*Succisa pratensis*)
Flowers dark bluish-purple, tightly packed in a rounded flowerhead; involucre hairy; stems downy; leaves elliptical (the upper narrower), opposite, often blotched. Native. Pastures, marshes, streamsides, ditches. Flowering late July–early October. Photograph: damp meadow, Tingwall.

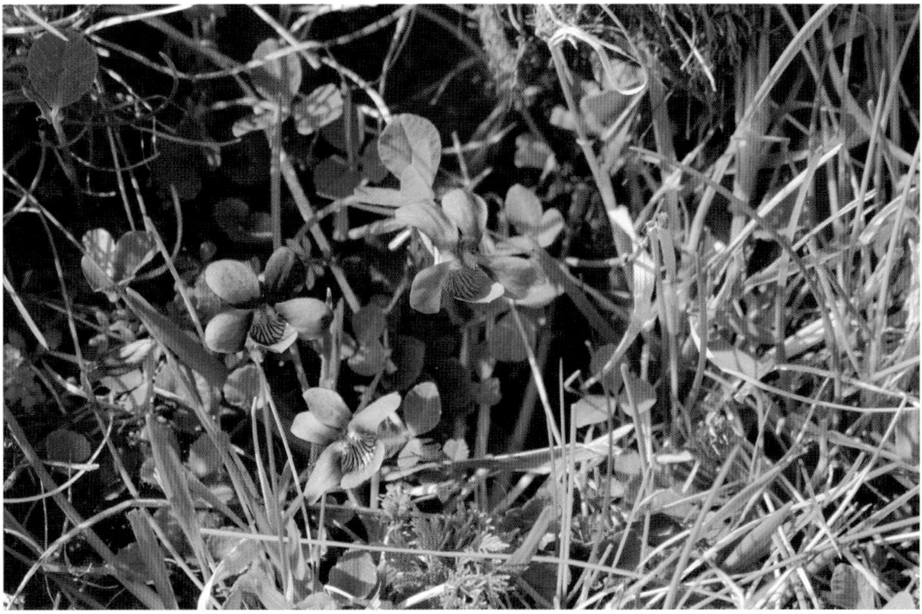

Plate 174 (s) **Common Dog-violet** (*Viola riviniana*)
Flowers bluish-violet, solitary, petals 5, unequal, spur pale, curved, notched at tip; leaves heart-shaped, alternate, finely toothed, stipules usually fringed. Native. Dry pastures, rocky streamsides, grassy heathery sea-banks. Flowering late April–June. Photograph: dry grassy banks near Berry Farm, Scalloway.

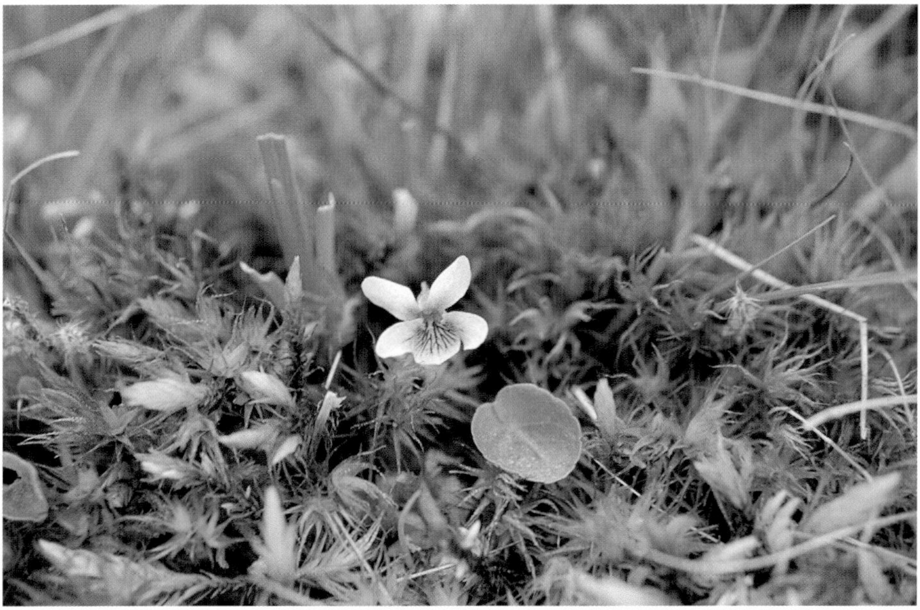

Plate 175 (s) **Marsh Violet** (*Viola palustris* subsp. *palustris*)
Flowers pale lilac, veined purple, 10–15 mm wide; leaves kidney-shaped. Native. Damp rough heaths, bogs, marshes. Flowering April–early June. Photograph: damp heathy pasture, Utnabrake, near Scalloway.

Glossary of Botanical Terms

Alien – an introduced species which has been brought to these islands by human intervention, deliberately or accidentally, and is regarded as a well-established alien or a casual. A **well-established alien** will appear year after year, often in the same place. A **casual**, on the other hand, is generally an annual of unpredictable occurrence and which may not be seen again in the same place.

Bract – a modified leaf, usually small, either at the base of a branch or the base of a flowerhead.

Calyx – the collective name for sepals whether separate or joined.

Corolla – the collective name for petals whether separate or joined.

Elliptical – a leaf about three times as long as wide.

Flowerhead – a collection of tiny flowers arranged in a tightly packed head, as in dandelions, daisies, thistles and a few others.

Involucre – a calyx-like structure immediately below a flowerhead, e.g. dandelions.

Lanceolate – a long narrow leaf, slightly wider below, gradually tapering to its tip as in a lance.

Leaf-axil – the junction of the stem and the upper side of the leaf.

Linear – a long, narrow leaf.

Native – a species which occurs naturally in Shetland, without any suspicion of its having been introduced by human intervention. An **endemic** native is one which occurs in Shetland, and on all available evidence, is not known anywhere else in the world.

Oblong – a leaf about two or three times as long as broad, and parallel-sided at least in the central part of the leaf blade.

Ovate – a leaf which is egg-shaped in outline, broadest at the base.

Palmate - where the leaf is divided into leaflet lobes radiating from a common point, e.g. meadow crane's-bill (Plate 171).

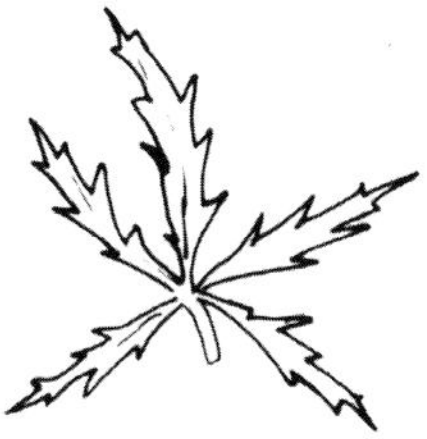

Palmate

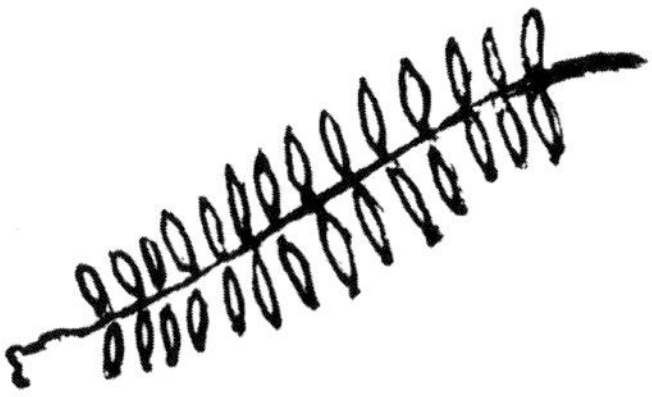

Pinnate

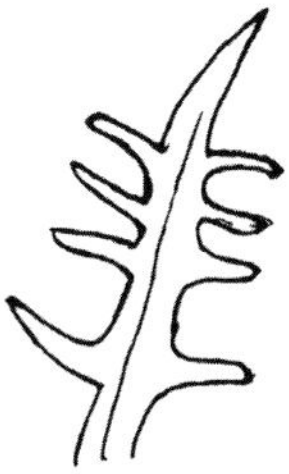

Pinnately lobed

Pinnate - where the leaf is divided into leaflets borne symmetrically on either side of a common stalk. The division may be complete, e.g. tufted vetch (Plate 166) or incomplete, e.g. autumn hawkbit (Plate 6) when the leaf is then described as being pinnately lobed.

Rosette - a circle of leaves, usually at the base of the plant, and often lying flat on the ground.

Spur - a usually slender projection arising from the base of a petal or corolla.

Stipules - paired, leaf-like appendages arising from the base of the leaf-stalk.

Tendril - an outgrowth, usually from the end of a leaf, often twisted or coiled, which enables a plant to grow upwards among surrounding vegetation by twisting itself around neighbouring plants, e.g. bush vetch (Plate 81).

Trifoliate - describes a leaf divided into three leaflets.

Umbel - a group of flowers with stalks all radiating from a common point on the stem, e.g. hogweed (Plate 134).

Whorl - a ring of two or more leaves or other organs, all arising from a common point on the stem.

References

Scott, W. & Palmer, R.[C.] (1987). *The flowering plants and ferns of the Shetland Islands*. The Shetland Times Ltd. Lerwick.

Scott, W. (2011). *Some aspects of the botany of the Shetland Islands*. Walter Scott. Scalloway.

Further Reading

Scott, W., Harvey, P., Riddington, R. & Fisher, M. (2002). *Rare plants of Shetland*. Shetland Amenity Trust. Lerwick.

Clapham, A.R., Tutin, T.G. & Moore, D.M. (1987). *Flora of the British Isles*, ed. 3. Cambridge University Press. Paperback versions 1989 and 2010.

Gear, S. (2008). *Flora of Foula*. Foula Heritage. Foula, Shetland.

Rose, F. (2006). *The Wild Flower Key. How to identify wild flowers, trees and shrubs in Britain and Ireland*. Frederick Warne.

Index of English Names

Plate numbers

Index of Latin Names

Plate numbers

PLANT IDENTIFICATION CHART

FLOWER	LOCALITY	DATE

PLANT IDENTIFICATION CHART

FLOWER	LOCALITY	DATE

PLANT IDENTIFICATION CHART

FLOWER	LOCALITY	DATE

PLANT IDENTIFICATION CHART

FLOWER	LOCALITY	DATE

PLANT IDENTIFICATION CHART

FLOWER	LOCALITY	DATE

PLANT IDENTIFICATION CHART

FLOWER	LOCALITY	DATE

PLANT IDENTIFICATION CHART

FLOWER	LOCALITY	DATE

PLANT IDENTIFICATION CHART

FLOWER	LOCALITY	DATE